Social Movements and Protest

This lively textbook integrates theory and methodology into the study of social movements, and includes contemporary case studies to engage students and encourage them to apply theories critically. A wide range of protest cases are explored, from American, European, and global arenas, including contemporary examples of political violence and terrorism, alter-globalization, social networking, and global activism. Key chapter features encourage students to engage critically with the material: method points uncover the methodology behind the theories, helping students to understand the larger study of social movements; debate points highlight classic arguments in social movement studies, encouraging students to critically assess theoretical approaches; and case studies connect theories to cases, allowing students to relate key principles to real-world examples. A companion website offers additional student and instructor resources, including lecture slides and worksheets.

Gemma Edwards is a lecturer in sociology at the University of Manchester, UK, and a member of movements@manchester, the Morgan Centre, and the Mitchell Centre for Social Network Analysis.

Consulting Editor John Scott, Plymouth University

Key Topics in Sociology

Consulting Editor **John Scott,** Plymouth University

This series of textbooks surveys key topics in the study of sociology.
Books cover the main theoretical and empirical aspects of each topic in a
clear, concise but sophisticated style, and relate the topic to wider sociological debates. Titles are useful to undergraduates studying a first course
on the topic, as well as graduates approaching the subject for the first time.
Designed for ease of use, instructors may teach from individual books,
or select a collection from the series for a broader sociology course.

Forthcoming Titles

Suki Ali, The Sociology of Race and Ethnicity
Kate Nash, The Sociology of Human Rights

Social Movements and Protest

Gemma Edwards

CAMBRIDGE
UNIVERSITY PRESS

University Printing House, Cambridge CB2 8BS, United Kingdom

Published in the United States of America by Cambridge University Press, New York

Cambridge University Press is part of the University of Cambridge.

It furthers the University's mission by disseminating knowledge in the pursuit of education, learning and research at the highest international levels of excellence.

www.cambridge.org
Information on this title: www.cambridge.org/9780521145817

First published 2014

Printed in the United Kingdom by T. J. International Ltd, Padstow

A catalogue record for this publication is available from the British Library

Library of Congress Cataloguing in Publication data
Edwards, Gemma.
Social movements and protest / Gemma Edwards.
    pages   cm. – (Key topics in sociology)
Includes bibliographical references and index.
ISBN 978-0-521-19636-9 (hardback)
1. Social movements.   2. Social networks.   3. Globalization – Social aspects.   I. Title.
HM881.E3293   2013
303.48′4 – dc23   2013032646

ISBN 978-0-521-19636-9 Hardback
ISBN 978-0-521-14581-7 Paperback

Additional resources for this publication at www.cambridge.org/gedwards

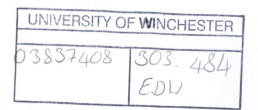

For Jason

Contents

Figures

Preface

Social Movements and Protest introduces social science students to the shifting terrain of 'social movement studies', providing them with a chronology of the field and bringing them up to date with conceptual developments. The book is first and foremost *for* students studying at the undergraduate level. It aims to encourage them to critically engage with the different ways in which social movements have been conceptualized and researched, and to evaluate the strengths and weaknesses of different approaches. The book argues that critical developments in the field have moved in the direction of a 'relational approach' to social movements, which it draws out and supports across the various chapters. It also argues that by engaging with 'new cases and new contexts' – ranging from lifestyle movements and terrorism, to globalization, new media, and protest in authoritarian regimes – we can stretch and problematize existing conceptualizations of social movements in ways that force us to rethink 'what social movements are'. In this respect, the book raises four main issues: the necessity of strains, resources, and organization; the centrality of the state; the desirability of collective identity; and the distinction between 'unorganized, individual action' and 'organized, collective action'.

Unlike other introductory accounts of social movement studies, the book takes an integrative approach to the discussion of theoretical approaches, research methodologies, and case studies. By including methodological discussions alongside theoretical ones, the aim is to prepare students to study social movements themselves. The distinctive features of the book are as follows:

- It traces and critically engages with different ways of conceptualizing 'social movements' and 'protest'.
- It introduces students to methodological debates alongside theoretical ones.
- It draws upon 'new cases and new contexts' to problematize existing conceptualizations of social movements ('new' not just in terms of contemporary developments – like new media – but 'newly considered topics' in social movement studies – like terrorism).

- It offers conceptual developments by exploring unorganized, individual protest that takes place *outside* social movement organizations (SMOs) (the concept of 'misbehaviour').

Looking at protest activity outside SMOs and embedded in people's everyday lives is an important corrective in a field that widely recognizes a bias towards 'organized' forms of action and 'public' protest events. The book aims to rework conceptualizations of social movements and protest to enable these different forms to come into view by shifting our sights from 'collective behaviour to misbehaviour'. The desire is not to leave 'collective' action behind in preference for individualized 'life politics', but to better understand the forms and strategies of *collective* efforts to change things that lie outside the normal vision of mobilization theories and contentious politics. The book does this by drawing upon the work of theorists like James Scott and John Holloway, and committing the social movement theorists' old trick of borrowing concepts from organizational studies, in this case the concept of 'misbehaviour' (Ackroyd and Thompson, 1999).

As it is written expressly for students, there are a variety of features to aid learning. Each chapter contains four reflection 'points', which include: *case points*, presenting interesting case studies; *debate points*, engaging with famous controversies; *methods points*, exploring the methodological challenges of different approaches; and *discussion points*, posing questions for wider reflection. These features are aimed at fostering critical engagement with the material presented. There are also suggestions for where to begin further reading. For the teacher of social movements, the chapters provide a useful starting point for a course of lectures, and offer concise summaries of existing literature and theoretical perspectives. Online material further supports the book for teaching purposes.

There are a number of people to acknowledge, first among them, the students on my course 'Power and Protest' at the University of Manchester, UK from 2008 to 2013, whose lively debates in class have allowed me to experiment with different ways of explaining theories, and have forced me to be as clear as possible in explication and, as much as possible, to leave the jargon behind. Hopefully, the style in which I present theoretical approaches in this book reflects their demands for clarity, although I suspect some jargon has inevitably crept in. I must also acknowledge the Manchester Social Movements Group – especially long-term members like Colin Barker, Kevin Gillan, Nick Crossley, Luke Yates, Susan O'Shea, Sarah Webster, Tessa Liburd, Ulrike Flader, Raphael Schlembach and Rachel Stevenson, and old members like Joseph Ibrahim and Ellen Harries – who provide a continual source of inspiration. Indeed, Kevin Gillan and Nick Crossley deserve a special mention for their supportive input when it comes to this book, as do the two anonymous reviewers for their helpful suggestions.

Abbreviations

AGM	alternative globalization movement
CB	collective behaviour
CBDM	consensus-based decision-making
CP	contentious politics
MNC	multinational corporation
MTT	McAdam, Tilly, and Tarrow (2001), *Dynamics of Contention*
NSM	new social movement
POS	political opportunity structure
PPM	political process model
PPT	political process theory
RAT	rational action theory
RMT	resource mobilization theory
SMI	social movement industry
SMO	social movement organization
SMS	social movement sector
SNA	social network analysis
WTO	World Trade Organization

1 Introduction: conceptualizing social movements

> Indeed, I've heard it said that we should be glad to
> trade what we've so far produced for a few really good
> conceptual distinctions and a cold beer.
>
> (American Sociologist, Erving Goffman, 1963, 261)

Erving Goffman's opening statement is his assessment of the field of sociological theory in the 1960s. This book is concerned with a subfield of sociology called 'social movement studies', which is multi-disciplinary, involving political scientists, economists, social psychologists, and human geographers. Modern social movement studies – which supplies the predominant conceptual framework for studying social movements and protest today – can be dated back to the early 1970s with theoretical developments in the US and Europe. Modern social movement studies however has an important predecessor in the shape of the field of collective behaviour (CB), a subfield of US sociology which claimed social movements and protest as its subject matter in the first part of the twentieth century, alongside the study of crowds, mobs, crazes, panics, fads, and fashions. CB reflected upon non-democratic movements, like fascism, and as such formed an understanding of social movements as the irrational expression of shared grievances, arising from deprivation or the alienating conditions of 'mass society'.

CB theorists, like the sociologist Herbert Blumer (1951 [1946]), made it clear that while much of the time social science concentrates upon questions of social order and reproduction, questions of social change are equally as important to study. Indeed, social movements have fascinated sociologists for decades because they open up the possibility of exploring the relationship between human action and social structures. Social movements are those collective efforts orientated towards social change that point to circumstances in which creative human action actually shapes and alters social structures, rather than being shaped by them. The study of social movements therefore brings to our attention those moments when, as Karl Marx put it, 'people make history'.

Critical engagement with the way in which CB 'conceptualized' social movements laid the foundations for social movement studies as we know it today. By 'conceptualized', I refer to attempts to produce a 'general idea' of what 'social movements are' beyond the specificities of individual cases. This is important work to undertake for two reasons. First, cases of social movements are extremely varied. They vary historically and cross-culturally, and include movements campaigning for various 'rights' (civil, labour, women's, gay, disability, children, and so on); movements campaigning on behalf of the environment, peace, or animals; movements seeking specific political reforms or diffuse cultural and personal change; and movements contesting globalization, corporations, and capitalist social relations. This variation means that remaining at the level of empirical study can make it very difficult to see the general features and dynamics that social movements have in common. Secondly, constructing a general idea of what social movements are as a category is essential if we are to know that what we observe and study is a 'social movement' and does not belong instead to another category, like the 'political party', 'pressure group', or 'voluntary organization', for example, which have particular dynamics of their own.

Social movement studies

The rejection of early CB notions of social movements as 'irrational group behaviour' did not, however, lead to an alternative conceptualization that everyone could agree upon. Indeed, social movement studies has gone through several phases of conceptual development since its inception in the 1970s, which have largely come about through disagreement and debate. We can identify a number of rival perspectives arising throughout the history of the field, presented in figure 1.1.

Conceptual development in social movement studies has taken a 'dialectical' form, meaning that approaches have evolved through a conversation between opposing ideas. We will draw out and engage with these debates in the course of the book. Randall Collins (2001, 36) argues for example that developments have often come about when new generations of scholars focus upon points of contention in existing

Figure 1.1
The chronological development of social movement studies.

theories, magnify their status, and embrace their opposite in order to create a 'new' perspective (Tarrow, 2004). This is why you will find that social movement studies is a field littered with conceptual 'dualisms' (binary oppositions). Where one approach stresses rationality, another 'rediscovers' emotion (Collins, 2001, 36). Where one approach stresses structural and political factors, another finds culture and social construction. Where one approach stresses strategies, another stresses identities, and so on and so forth. These dualisms are then written in to the 'story' of the social movements field, such that they achieve the status of 'real' distinctions in our conceptual thinking. In this book, the various chapters take these dualisms as a starting point for discussion, showing how thinking on social movements has shifted from one understanding to another. The point in doing so, however, is not to reinforce dualisms, but to deconstruct them in order to show *how* they create general ideas about 'what social movements are', which have their merits, but which are also problematic. This is the critical work that we will be doing in the chapters.

Focusing upon the disagreements and debates in social movement studies makes for a good story. The field, however, actually contains more agreement on conceptual questions than the story suggests (Collins, 2001, 37; Tarrow, 2004). Often, Collins (2001, 37) argues, it is the same people who are involved in prior perspectives and the rival perspectives that replace them. We will see this is the case for 'political process' theory and its critical development into the 'contentious politics' approach (see Chapter 4). Even when this is not the case, perspectives are often compatible at some level, or intended to be 'partial' (like 'resource mobilization' theory, Chapter 3). We will see in Chapter 4, for example, that when we set up the debate between the 'structuralists' and the 'constructionists' in social movement theory, we soon find out that no one who gets called a 'structuralist' really embraces the label themselves (Goodwin and Jasper, 2004a; Kurzman, 2004). In contemporary social movement studies, therefore, we can find some common ground, and some shared assumptions.

I suggest, in fact, that we can identify four 'conceptual distinctions' that have been drawn around the category of social movements through previous debates and are largely accepted in the field today. These conceptual distinctions shape our current understanding of 'what social movements are', and therefore, the kind of cases we study, and the kind of methodologies we use to study them. They are as follows:

(a) *Social movements are collective, organized efforts at social change, rather than individual efforts at social change.*

The first conceptual distinction tells us that a social movement is a form of *collective and organized* (rather than 'individual') action. This collective action has a particular orientation: it has the aim of producing *social change* (either for better or worse, depending on your viewpoint). This change can be directed at different aspects of society, for example political, ideological, social, economic, and cultural spheres. It can be a big change (like a revolution which transforms the whole of society's structures), or (what appear like) small changes (e.g. reform of a policy or law, or a change in cultural meanings). The key point is that the efforts to bring about this change must be *collective and organized* for a case to qualify as a social movement. Herbert Blumer therefore states that 'social movements can be viewed as collective enterprises seeking to establish a new order of life' (Blumer, 1951 [1946], 199). The way in which collective efforts are actually organized, however, has been a source of debate (which we will look at throughout the book). While some theorists point to the role of 'formal organizations' in pursuing social change (referring to 'social movement organizations' (SMOs), for example), others point to much more informal connections among social movement activists, often rooted in their pre-existing interpersonal relationships. Donatella Della Porta and Mario Diani therefore describe a social movement as 'informal networks' (Della Porta and Diani, 1999, 16).

(b) *Social movements exist over a 'period of time' by engaging in a 'conflictual issue' with a 'powerful opponent', rather than being 'one-off' events.*

The second important distinction is between collective actions orientated towards social change that are momentary in nature (and that we might more accurately call 'protest events'), and collective actions orientated towards social change that last over a period of time. Social movements are the latter (Blumer, 1951 [1946]; Tarrow, 1998). They are *durable* efforts at social change, not one-off protest events. Importantly, scholars in the 'political process' approach (that we look at in Chapter 4) suggest that what social movements are doing over a period of time is to episodically engage with a 'powerful opponent' over an issue of conflict. The nation state and political institutions have been seen as the central opponents for social movements. Sidney Tarrow therefore describes a social movement as 'sustained interactions' between 'ordinary people, often in league with more influential citizens ... in confrontation with elites, authorities and opponents' (Tarrow, 1998, 2).

(c) *The members of a social movement are not just working together,
     but share a 'collective identity'.*

The third distinctive feature of a social movement is that the people who work together to achieve social change are not just cooperating, communicating, interacting, and so forth; they also share a sense of themselves as a group who have a common understanding of the problem and the solution. New social movement (NSM) theory (which we look at in Chapter 5) therefore defines a social movement on the basis of a shared 'collective identity'. A collective identity involves a sense of 'we', against 'them' in a conflict over 'this', and has been seen as an essential characteristic of a social movement (Melucci, 1980). Mario Diani (1992, 13) therefore suggests that what makes informal networks of people who mobilize around issues of conflict into a 'social movement' is a 'shared collective identity', or 'shared beliefs and solidarity' (Della Porta and Diani, 1999, 16).

(d) *Social movements actively pursue change by employing protest.*

The employment of protest (acts of disruption or declarations of disapproval) in pursuit of their aim is the fourth distinctive feature of a social movement (Della Porta and Diani, 1999, 16). Social movements, for example, stage public 'protest events' like street demonstrations, strikes, sit-ins, walkouts, occupations, vigils, and so on. Della Porta and Diani (2006, 171–8) suggest that protest can be divided into three categories: *numbers* (e.g. a show of strength by the movement to express the size of its support, like a mass demonstration, which also creates an effective form of disruption); *damage* (e.g. causing damage by committing acts of violence against property or persons, or inflicting economic damage on an employer through a strike, creating a material and symbolic effect); and *bearing witness* (e.g. carrying out acts that show a moral commitment to a cause, like civil disobedience, or ethical consumerism). Protest events are often what the public at large associate with social movements because they are the 'visible' signs that tell us that a collective effort at social change is underway.

Challenging conceptual distinctions

In this book, we will critically engage with these four conceptual distinctions. The main argument is that each of these distinctions is already the result of previous debate and challenge, and that they are now facing a fresh round of debate and challenge. The previous debates that have shaped conceptual thinking, and which we will explore in the course of the book, are:

- Can social movements be understood in psychological terms? For example, do social movements rely upon the existence of strains in society and the grievances that they cause people?
- Can social movements be understood in 'rational' terms? For example, do social movements rely upon strategy and rational calculations of success?
- Can social movements be understood as 'organizations'? For example, do they rely upon formal organization and the mobilization of tangible resources?
- Can social movements be understood in political terms? For example, do they target the nation state and political institutions and rely upon the 'political opportunities' they provide?

In Chapters 2–5, we will consider these debates and how they have shaped the ways in which social movements have been understood by different perspectives in the field. I also argue however that the conceptualizations which have resulted from these previous debates are now facing challenges of their own.

In Chapters 6–8, we will consider these challenges, which, I suggest, come from two main sources: first, new cases; and secondly, new contexts. By 'new', I do not always mean historically new (i.e. a product of contemporary society), but also 'new' in the sense that social movement studies is starting to look at certain cases and contexts for the first time and which it traditionally ignored. The 'new' cases that will be considered in this book are:

- 'lifestyle movements', which involve individual lifestyle change as a mode of pursuing social change
- global social movements
- terrorism, and movements involving political violence.

The new contexts that will be considered are:

- globalization (specifically capitalist globalization as it has evolved since 1989)
- the rise of 'new media' (meaning 'information and communication technologies', hereafter ICTs, which include mobile communications and social media)
- non-conventional contexts of study, like repressive, authoritarian regimes in which collective action orientated towards change is not tolerated.

These new cases and contexts problematize, stretch, and challenge the four conceptual distinctions drawn around social movements, and will provide us with ways to critically engage with them. We will, for example, question the first distinction between individual and collective efforts at change (by looking at lifestyle movements in Chapter 5, and protest in non-conventional contexts in Chapter 8). We will question the second distinction, by exploring whether the 'powerful opponents' that social movements engage with over a 'conflictual issue' are any longer best thought of as nation states and political institutions (by looking at globalization in Chapter 6). We will question the third distinction by asking whether globalization and the altered context of mobilization it presents (which includes a technological context dominated by new media), raises doubts about whether a shared 'collective identity' is a necessary, or even desirable, feature of social movements. Finally, we will question the fourth distinction by challenging the idea that social movements are characterized by the use of protest events, which have largely been thought of as public in nature (see Chapters 5, 7, and 8). Lifestyle movements involve people in forms of protest that are individualized and submerged in their everyday practices (see Chapter 5);

terrorist movements bring home the covert and hidden nature of social movements before explosive moments of protest occur (see Chapter 7); and looking at different forms of protest in non-conventional contexts suggests that protest in repressive regimes sometimes has to be hidden and silent (or even takes a 'virtual' form online) rather than noisy and public, and might in certain circumstances be all the more effective for it (see Chapter 8). While we challenge conceptualizations of social movements in the chapters to come, we will also, therefore, necessarily challenge conceptualizations of 'protest' as well.

Main arguments

What, then, will be the critical assessment of the field of social movement studies that is forwarded here? The main arguments of the book are twofold. First, it will be suggested that conceptualizations of social movements have – through critical reflection – been moving in a similar direction, referred to as a 'relational' understanding of what social movements are and how they operate. I will tease out the development of this relational understanding of social movements and defend the advantages it brings on a conceptual and methodological level. Secondly, it will be suggested that some of the most important conceptual work to be done in social movement studies involves deconstructing the distinction that is drawn between collective, organized efforts at social change, and individual, unorganized efforts at social change. I engage in this work later in the book by exploring the relationship between social movements and unorganized forms of protest which I call 'misbehaviour' (Ackroyd and Thompson, 1999).

  I will show therefore that the four conceptual distinctions that provide a common basis for understanding social movements today result from debate, and that debate is far from done. While we do not necessarily need to 'trade what we have so far produced for a few really good conceptual distinctions' as Goffman (1963, 261) puts it, we do, however, need to continue the work of critically engaging with the conceptual distinctions that we have already got. It is through complicating and challenging these distinctions that our understanding of 'what social movements are' and the dynamics that animate them will be generated. In the chapters that follow, therefore, I'll take care of the conceptual distinctions; you enjoy the cold beer.

Useful features

There are number of features in the book to assist your critical engagement with the perspectives covered. You will find in each chapter a 'case point', a 'methods point', and a 'debate point', which offer a chance to stop and reflect on the approach by engaging with an interesting case study, a famous controversy, or the methodological implications of different conceptualizations. At the end of each chapter you will find a summary of the key points about the approach we have discussed, and the critical issues it raised. There are also questions posed in a 'discussion point' at the end of each chapter, which can be used as a way to think about the wider questions raised by the approach. Finally, there are 'further reading' suggestions at the end of each chapter, which provide you with guidance on where to begin your wider reading.

2

From the mad to the sane:
collective behaviour and its critics

> 'But I don't want to go among mad people', Alice remarked.
> 'Oh, you can't help that', said the Cat. 'We're all mad here.
> I'm mad. You're mad.'
> 'How do you know I'm mad?' said Alice.
> 'You must be,' said the Cat, 'or you wouldn't have come here.'
>
> (Lewis Carroll, *Alice's Adventures in Wonderland*)

This chapter is concerned with 'collective behaviour' (CB), a subfield of American Sociology which claimed social movements and protest as its subject matter in the first half of the twentieth century and reflected, in particular, on the rise of anti-democratic movements like fascism. CB should not be thought of as one united approach, but instead a field of research interest that attracted sociologists of very different theoretical persuasions. The two sociologists that we will look at here are Herbert Blumer (a symbolic interactionist) and Neil Smelser (a structural functionalist). We will delve into what these theoretical labels mean in the course of the chapter, but only cursory sociological knowledge is needed to know that symbolic interactionism is heavily critical of structural functionalism (and vice versa), meaning that the leading figures of CB in no way propose *the same* approach to social movements and protest. Blumer and Smelser are united in their desire to understand 'collective behaviour', not in their perspective on it.

Having said this, the tendency of critics has been to lump together the different strands of CB in order to highlight the common thread in their thinking. CB theorists of whatever persuasion, argues Doug McAdam (1982), share the assumption that *social problems* are the root-cause of protest, that social problems ignite psychological grievances and strong emotions, and that these emotions push individuals over the edge and out on to the streets. This common thread leads to a conceptualization of CB as 'irrational group behaviour' caused by 'strains' in society, and the 'grievances' they create for people. Like a bottle of pop once shaken, society is just waiting for those 'moments of madness' when frustrated individuals duly explode.

This conceptualization is a good one for us to start with, and not only because it comes first chronologically (spanning the 1930s–1960s). It also resonates well with our 'common sense' understanding of why protest happens. CB reinforces the impression that we get from the mass media, which portrays protesters as if they are motivated almost entirely by feelings of anger and frustration. Whether a demonstration, strike, or riot, we are told that the people involved are furious and fed up. They are no longer able to contain the dissatisfaction that they have with life, and, when the recurring debate about whether these people are simply 'wild' or 'criminal' has run its usual course, what we are left with is the distinct impression that this or that 'problem' in society has driven these people 'mad'.

How accurate is this understanding of the origins of protest? What role *do* social problems, grievances, and emotions play in the conditions that lead to social movements? In order to answer these questions we will critically explore the claims of CB's leading figures. By the close of the chapter, you should have knowledge of the merits of CB (which are often glossed over in accounts of social movement theory), as well as understanding why this conceptualization of social movements quickly became unpopular by the early 1970s.

Herbert Blumer's approach to understanding collective behaviour

Let us start our discussion of CB by considering the ideas of Herbert Blumer, a sociologist who is associated with the 'Chicago School' of symbolic interactionists working at the University of Chicago in the US in the 1930s and 1940s. Blumer's work (1951 [1946]), along with that of his teacher, Robert E. Park, helped to establish the idea of 'collective behaviour' and cement its place as a subfield of social-scientific study.

The term 'collective behaviour' might seem to you like an odd label for the study of protest and social movements. Park and Blumer argue that all of social life can be thought of in one sense as 'collective behaviour' because social life consists of people interacting with one another in families, groups, and communities. As 'symbolic interactionists', Park and Blumer are particularly interested in these group interactions and argue that, through them, communities establish and reinforce 'social norms' which regulate the behaviour of their members and make joint activities possible. Some of these norms are informal (like customs, conventions, and traditions), and some are formal and institutional- ized (like laws, rules, and regulations). The content of informal and formal norms shapes a group's culture, and structures and organizes its activities. The result of people behaving collectively, therefore, is the establishment of a 'social order', or what Blumer calls the 'cultural pattern' of society.

Blumer argues that whilst most sociologists study the social order once it has been established for some time, CB theorists open up the question of how the social order becomes established *in the first place*. This is important to consider because society's institutions, laws, and values did not always have the character that they do now: democracy has not always existed, private property is not naturally 'inviolable', and in the past it was an accepted custom that women serve men. So how does the social order of a society *change* if the individuals within it are behaving in accordance with the established 'cultural pattern'? If all forms of CB conform to society's rules and norms then nothing *could* ever change, but, quite clearly, it does.

Park and Blumer's answer was that *new* forms of CB can emerge within societies: behaviour which does not conform to the established norms. People can, for example, develop new and 'unconventional' ways of acting within social groups. Whilst most of the time group behaviour is rule-*conforming*, sometimes it can be rule-*breaking*. Counted among the topics of 'collective behaviour' therefore are protests and social movements because they tend to challenge society's established norms and act in unconventional ways. There are other categories of 'collec- tive behaviour' in addition to protest and social movements, however – including mobs and riots, crazes and panics, and fashions and fads. As with social movements, these categories of behaviour involve people acting as a group, but in ways that contravene society's prevailing norms rather than reinforcing them.

Alongside studies of political protest and social movements there- fore, CB also includes other topics, reflected in the B. E. Aguirre et al. (1988) study of the 'fad' for streaking naked across university campuses that took the US by storm during the Spring of 1974. Blumer argues that the essence of this behaviour is the same as protest behaviour:

it is *non*-cultural (it does not conform to existing cultural traditions or customs), *non*-moral (it does not conform to established notions of right and wrong), and *non*-institutional (it does not take place within routine patterns and procedures). We should also add to this that it is '*non*-rational' in the sense that it does not adhere to *established* notions of self-interest, cost, or reward in society. For Blumer it is no wonder therefore that those who engage in CB are often deemed 'mad' and 'irrational' – their behaviour goes against everything that everybody else in society has agreed is acceptable, normal, and sane.

At least most of us would find ourselves sharing society's judgement in the case of streaking naked across the university campus, but other cases highlight just how contextual and socially constructed our ideas of what is 'mad' and what is 'sane' really are. Women who refused to conform to society's expectations of them as 'feminine, docile, home-makers' (both as campaigners for the vote in the early 1900s and as feminists in the 1970s) were often described as 'wild' and 'mad'. After the struggles waged by these 'mad women' however, most of us believe in gender equality, and we (hopefully) think that women who want to be politicians, wear trousers, or mend cars are perfectly sane. Madness in some contexts, then, can be the first step to social change. Blumer echoed this in suggesting that the groups engaged in unconventional forms of CB are 'freed' from social restraints and able to think and act differently from the rest of society. The essence of CB, then, is cultural innovation.

Rule-*breakers*, however, can eventually become rule-*makers*, when, for example, CB establishes new norms, new customs, new laws, and new institutions – in other words, a new social order. What CB as a field of study is therefore essentially interested in is that process by which one social order succeeds another, or, put more simply, the age-old question of 'how does social change happen?'

> One may say that sociology in general is interested in studying the social order and its constituents (customs, rules, institutions etc.) as they are; collective behaviour is concerned in studying the ways by which the social order comes into existence, in the sense of the emergence and solidification of new forms of collective behaviour.
>
> (Blumer, 1951 [1946], 169)

Blumer therefore presents us with an intriguing puzzle: where does CB that goes against society's established norms come from?

The role of social problems

Blumer's first argument was that adverse social conditions (like poverty or enslavement) do not automatically produce rebellious CB. 'Social problems', in fact, only come into existence when there is a prior process of interpretation which construes certain events or conditions as 'unjust'. This argument arises from Blumer's symbolic interactionist perspective, which suggests that people do not unconsciously respond to social circumstances (like a knee-jerk reaction), but instead negotiate with others a 'definition of the situation' in which they find themselves, and respond in a reflective and deliberative manner to what they think is going on (G. H. Mead, 1934). As W. I. Thomas famously put it, 'if men define situations as real, they are real in their consequences' (Thomas and Thomas, 1928, 572). The social conditions that people experience therefore have to be first defined as 'problematic' in interaction with others if anyone is to feel aggrieved or have the urge to respond. Blumer states that:

> It is a gross mistake to assume that any kind of malignant or harmful
> social condition or arrangement in a society becomes automatically a
> social problem for that society. The pages of history are replete with
> instances of dire social conditions unnoticed and unattended in the
> societies in which they occurred.
>
> (Blumer 1971, 302)

In saying this, Blumer suggests that our focus should not be on social conditions themselves, but on how people come to define social conditions as problematic, in other words how they construct 'social problems' and come to feel aggrieved about life. He suggests that grievances form when people's normal routines are disrupted and they become unable to carry on in accordance with the existing laws, rules, or norms of society. This can happen for example in situations of war or rapid social change, like that connected with migration, urbanization, and industrialization. As a result, people develop 'wishes, needs and dispositions' which are unfulfilled and begin to construct a sense of grievance (Blumer, 1951 [1946], 171).

Academics have traditionally highlighted two key causes of grievance in modern societies: deprivation (e.g. poverty or the denial of political rights) and social marginalization (being isolated from others and social institutions). In *Why Men Rebel*, Ted Gurr (1970) argues that *relative* deprivation largely explains why people become aggrieved

enough to protest. Gurr claims that 'the more severe is relative deprivation, the more likely and severe is strife' (Gurr, 1968, 1104). By 'relative'
Gurr means that perceptions of deprivation are subjective, and often
depend upon the expectations that people have of life. The poorest,
or those who are enslaved, in fact, are seldom the ones who protest.
Instead, discontent is created when people's expectations are dashed.
We feel frustrated when we think that we deserve more in relation to
others, or to the past, or to the future that beckons. Suffering economic
hardship, unemployment, or political exclusion can therefore create a
sense of grievance.

The second factor associated with grievances in modern society is
social marginalization. People become marginalized when they become
disconnected from meaningful relationships, both with other people,
and with social and political institutions. Individuals may become
socially isolated if their family breaks up, if they live in a place with
little sense of community, if they are not in work or education, or if
they do not belong to any groups or organizations. Marginalization can
be a source of frustration in itself, making life feel pretty empty and
meaningless, but it is also important as a factor that 'pushes' people
away from society's norms and values.

Marginalization theories were especially popular as explanations
for why Western Europe veered towards political extremism in the
1930s. Political sociologists like Hannah Arendt, Eric Fromm, and Karl
Mannheim related Nazi and Fascist movements to what they termed
'mass society' (Gusfield, 1962). 'Mass society' refers to the conditions of
modern society in which social disconnection is widespread. Families,
communities, and social groups (like those based on class identity and
ethnic identity) are replaced by large-scale bureaucratic organizations
(states, markets, workplaces) in which social relationships are formal
and impersonal. People's lives therefore lack meaningful bonds – and
the kinds of bonds through which individuals are socialized into society's values. As a result, people can become detached from both the
democratic values of the political system, and society's goals.

Once disconnected from society, these individuals become attracted
to alternative forms of group belonging and community, which they
find in anti-democratic social movements, like fascism. This argument
was made by William Kornhauser in *The Politics of Mass Society* (1959),
where he suggested that social movements provide the meaningful
bonds that people in mass society are lacking. Marginalized individuals

want to join seemingly irrational mass movements, like fascism, so that they can believe in something, belong somewhere, and be someone – in stark contrast to their everyday lives in modern society. Participation in social movements is thus understood as a search for community, meaning, and belonging (Scott, 1990).

Debate point: do grievances cause protest?

Research conducted since the 1970s into the reasons why people protest and join social movements has not generated a great amount of support for the idea that social problems, and the grievances they create, should be at the centre of explanation. In an influential study which analysed longitudinal data about collective disturbances in France between 1830 and 1960, David Snyder and Charles Tilly (1972) claimed that the theory of relative deprivation was unable to explain fluctuations in disturbances. By using indicators of economic deprivation, they concluded that short-term hardships could not explain the variations in the number of people who participated in disturbances. Doug McAdam (1982) found a weak correlation between civil rights demonstrations 1955–65 and levels of socioeconomic deprivation amongst black people. This evidence (and much more since), has placed a question mark over the assumption that social problems and grievances explain protest. Social problems and grievances are, in fact, far more widespread than instances of protest. If grievances do not always lead to protest, then it is only logical to conclude that grievances (alone at least) cannot be the cause. Researchers in the 1970s also found that the experience of deprivation, levels of anger and frustration, and people's beliefs and attitudes, could not account for why they participated in protest events, like riots, civil rights marches, and student demonstrations (McPhail, 1991). Why? Because they found that many of those who *did not* participate shared the same characteristics – they were equally as deprived, equally as upset about it, and often shared attitudes and beliefs in common with those who did participate. Without also researching a control group of people who did not participate, we cannot sufficiently isolate the factors that are particular to the protesters. This was something that Doug McAdam was able to address in his study of student participation in American civil rights' 'Freedom Schools' by researching both the students who did participate, and those who did not (McAdam, 1988; McAdam and Paulsen, 1993). He found that the factors that accounted for participation did not relate to grievances, beliefs, and emotional commitment to the cause, but to the presence of supportive friends and relatives and personal connections to others who were participating.

Research also found something else that ran contrary to CB accounts: the people who did participate in protest were not socially disconnected at all; on the contrary, they were *the most connected* (Tilly, 1978). Social ties to others 'pulled people in' to protest rather than pushed them away. This was a radically different argument compared with 'mass society' theory. According to that theory, connections to social groups and institutions, like family and friendship groups, workplaces, communities, and so forth, socialize people into society's democratic values and goals and therefore make it less likely that they will join protests and mass movements. Critics, like Maurice Pinard (1968), however argued the opposite: it is just these kinds of connections that people *can* use to communicate grievances and mobilize protest and social movements.

- Can we adequately explain protest and social movements by referring to the grievances held by those who participate? If not, why not?
- Do you think that a person is more likely to protest if they are marginalized in society or if they are well connected to others? What are the reasons for your view?
- Select a recent story in the news which linked a protest event to relative deprivation or marginalization. How might you critically challenge this link?

Blumer argues that there is also a second way in which grievances can form. Over time, societies experience gradual shifts in moral values, termed 'cultural drifts' (Blumer, 1951 [1946], 200). People develop new 'interests', 'identities', 'expectations', and 'emotional states' (Blumer, 1951 [1946], 171). As such, they can find that social conditions drag behind their new moral sensibilities. To return to our previous example, feminism reflected a cultural drift in modern, Western values concerning the status of women. We have come to expect that women are treated as equals in all areas of life. Instances where women get paid less at work, or do a disproportionate amount of the household chores, subsequently create grievances – even though women in the past suffered the same conditions without complaint.

Again, according to symbolic interactionism, people do not come to perceive social conditions as problematic on their own, and nor do they develop new aspirations in isolation. In fact, the process of interpreting life in such a way as to feel aggrieved depends upon interaction with individuals whom Blumer (1951 [1946], 204) calls 'agitators'. Agitators work to change people's perception of their lives so that taken-for-granted aspects are brought into question. They are especially important to social movements because they not only stir up dissatisfaction, but they try to convince people that some form of collective action is the solution. Without this impetus, there is nothing to stop people putting their problems down to their own failings, or deciding that injustice is inevitable and there is nothing they can do about it. Movement activists often report that these are frequent human responses to grievances, and invest a lot of energy in trying to overcome them. We will pick up the idea that aggrieved people often feel as if they are unable to bring about change in Chapter 3.

When he wrote of agitation, Blumer really had *individuals* in mind; those people who help you see things in a 'new light' by offering alternative ways to understand society. Individuals agitate through public speaking and by producing literature – even fiction can be a source of agitation, like the nineteenth-century novels of Charles Dickens who raised awareness about the 'hard times' suffered by the poor in the midst of the industrial revolution. Today, we might think about musicians or artists in a similar way – Rage Against the Machine, Public Enemy, or Banksy perhaps – whose lyrics and images stir up ideas about social and political injustice. The important point, then, is that grievances do not automatically flow from adverse social conditions. Instead, people only feel frustrated and angry about life once grievances have been actively constructed in social interaction with others. The process of grievance construction is therefore an active one, which involves people in ongoing interpretative work to produce collective definitions of the situation. We will revisit this argument in much more detail in Chapter 4.

Social unrest

Blumer's second argument was that once constructed as such, grievances do not automatically lead to protest but contribute instead to a general condition of 'social unrest'. Through disruptive events or

agitation, people are 'jarred loose from their customary ways of thinking and believing and...have aroused within them new impulses and
wishes' (Blumer, 1951 [1946], 204). When these impulses and wishes
remain unfulfilled they experience 'inner tension' marked by strong
feelings of apprehension, frustration and insecurity (Blumer, 1951
[1946], 171). As a consequence they become psychologically disturbed,
emotionally unstable and volatile – even bordering on 'neurotic' as
Blumer himself puts it (1951, 171). He calls individuals who are experiencing these feelings 'restless' in that they begin to behave in erratic
and unpredictable ways. Their random behaviour and displays of emotion easily attract the attention of others and stir up feelings of restlessness in them too. Through a process that Blumer calls 'social contagion'
– where you literally 'catch' the disturbed emotional states of those
around you – restlessness infects the whole social group and results in
'social unrest':

> in a state of social unrest, people are psychologically unstable, suffering
> from disturbed impulses and feelings. Their attention is likely to be
> variable and shifting, and lacking in usual continuity.
> (Blumer, 1951 [1946], 173)

We should think of social unrest not as the direct cause of CB, but as its
backdrop. It is the 'crucible', argues Blumer, out of which new forms of
social activity can arise (Blumer, 1951 [1946], 173). With the usual har-
mony of everyday life broken, people feel insecure and unstable. It is
just this kind of situation – marked by 'psychological breakdown' – in
which a new 'psychological *make-up*' can appear (Blumer, 1951 [1946],
185). Social unrest does not automatically lead people to participate in
CB, but it does make them ripe for the picking: they become ready and
eager to jump on board with action that flies in the face of established
ways of doing things.

The crowd

Blumer highlights 'the crowd' as one of the first responses to social unrest
(Blumer, 1951 [1946], 179). Restless individuals are easily captured by
events that excite and stimulate their already heightened emotions, and
their first response is to 'mill' around the event in an aimless fash-
ion (Blumer 1951 [1946], 174). It is important to note that Blumer
thinks that the milling process involves people in a very different

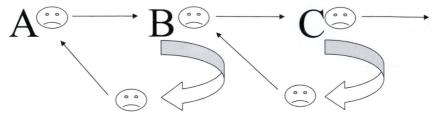

Figure 2.1
Circular reaction (the interstimulation of emotions).

kind of interaction compared with normal symbolic interaction. In this interaction, the usual deliberative and interpretative processes are suspended and instead emotions take over and determine people's responses. Blumer (1951 [1946], 170) calls this type of interaction 'circular reaction' (see figure 2.1).

Circular reaction involves responding to another person by reflecting back to them the emotions that they have displayed to you, as shown in figure 2.1. The feelings expressed by person A spark the same feelings in person B and person B displays those feelings too (they imitate A's emotions in other words). When they do so, they not only spread the feelings to person C, but reinforce them for person A, making them feel more intense for person A. Circular reaction is therefore a type of interaction which is based upon what Blumer (1951 [1946], 170) calls the 'interstimulation' of emotions rather than deliberation and interpretation. In figure 2.1, A stimulates B's emotions (who then stimulates C's emotions), but importantly, B's imitation of A stimulates A's emotions in return. A's emotions therefore become intensified because they appear all the more real in the light of B's confirmation.

For Blumer (1951 [1946], 174), circular reaction generates feelings of 'collective excitement'. Emotions have become contagious and all-consuming, meaning that people are no longer able to control themselves and fall victim instead to a kind of group 'hypnosis'. With their capacities for critical thinking suspended, people tend to follow the herd and become easily swayed. For Blumer, circular reaction explains how crazes and panics emerge, and how crowds in general form. Once in a crowd, argued Blumer, individuals are pretty much guaranteed to lose their senses altogether.

Blumer's ideas about crowd mentality have their roots in the nineteenth century 'crowd psychology' of Gustave Le Bon. Le Bon's book *The Crowd* (2009 [1896]) was a key reference point for Park and Blumer.

In it, Le Bon reflects upon the 'era of crowds' spanning the French Revolution of 1789 to a century later. Le Bon is interested in explaining how otherwise law-abiding people could suddenly rise up and commit sensational acts – whether violent and barbaric (like chopping off the heads of monarchs), or heroic and inspiring (like self-sacrifice). Le Bon's answer was that the crowd transforms the way in which individuals think and behave.

The transformation that individuals experience within the crowd leads them to behave in a far from civilized manner. They change from rational individuals who are able to judge situations and control themselves, to little more than animals acting on their instincts and following the herd (Le Bon, 2009 [1896]; Blumer, 1951 [1946]). This change is the result of an individual's ideas, feelings and personality being replaced by the 'collective mind' of the crowd. Overwhelmed by the contagious emotions of the group, everybody acts in the same way and without thinking. Due to the lack of thought and general excitability, the crowd is easily swayed by any suggestion that chimes with its common mood. This explains why crowds can be dangerous, unpredictable, violent, and immoral. Le Bon states:

> Isolated, he may be a cultivated individual; in a crowd, he is a barbarian – that is, a creature acting by instinct. He possesses the spontaneity, the violence, the ferocity, and also the enthusiasm and heroism of primitive beings, whom he further tends to resemble by the facility with which he allows himself to be impressed by words and images … and to be induced to commit acts contrary to his most obvious interests and his best-known habits. An individual in a crowd is a grain of sand amid other grains of sand, which the wind stirs up at will.
>
> (Le Bon, 2009 [1896], 37–8)

This description of the 'madness of the mob' – despite being over a century old – continues to resonate with the way in which crowd behaviour is popularly depicted in the press. You are no doubt familiar with the argument that people temporarily 'take leave of their senses' in a crowd; they 'lose their heads' so to speak. When an undergraduate student was arrested for swinging from the flag of the Cenotaph war memorial during student tuition fees protests in London, he argued that it was 'a moment of idiocy' that led him to act in a way which he never had before, or since.

Empirical studies of crowds, however, undermined a large part of Blumer's argument by suggesting that his version of crowd psychology was inaccurate and misleading. Clark McPhail and his colleagues directly observed political, sports, and religious gatherings between 1967 and 1987, recording in detail what they saw and heard people doing. Their fieldwork highlighted what they called 'the myth of the madding crowd' (McPhail, 1991). McPhail's primary observation was that much of the behaviour and conversation taking place within the crowd is rational (or at least no less rational than outside the crowd), challenging Blumer's assumption that people switch from normal symbolic interaction to emotionally driven circular reaction. Furthermore, the crowds involved in political demonstrations are usually the result of a prior process of planning and coordination, rather than a spontaneous outburst of emotional individuals. Neither therefore can it be said that individuals within the crowd necessarily lose their *self*-control, even in situations like riots. Anthony Oberschall argues that what is experienced during a riot instead is the loss of *social control*, meaning that people decide to act in ways that the authorities would usually clamp down on (e.g. looting) because they calculate that they can get away with it (Oberschall, 1995, 16).

Critics from within symbolic interactionism have also taken issue with the idea that crowd behaviour (and CB more generally according to Blumer) is not regulated by social norms or values (and hence can involve immoral actions). Ralph Turner and Lewis Killian (1987) argue that within crowds people still adhere to group norms and expectations – but these are 'emergent' rather than pre-established. By 'emergent' they mean that new expectations about how people should behave arise from the immediate situation and are negotiated and defined in crowd interaction. Emergent norms appear out of the new definition of the situation that is constructed by the crowd and people act on the basis of it. Whilst this definition continues to constrain people who are part of the group, it is also permissive with respect to society's established norms.

McPhail's research also revealed that crowds are, in fact, very rarely violent (especially the crowds involved in political demonstrations). When crowds do turn violent, it is often the product of their interaction with police rather than any 'collective psychology' that drives people to be irresponsible. Le Bon's picture of the barbaric crowd therefore seems a somewhat rare and sensationalized example. Carl Couch (1968, 313) added to this the point that crowds involved in social and political protest have, by and large, been far less destructive and violent than the state authorities who deal with them. Finally, McPhail observed that people in crowds are not like a herd of cattle. They do not copy one another's behaviour without thinking – and we know this because the crowd is not unanimous. Kurt and Gladys Lang's (1970) study of the crowds involved in the 1960s race riots in the US showed that different people were there for different reasons, ranging from gangsters wanting a slice of the action, to the beginnings of the civil rights movement. Neither can it be said that crowds are anonymous. Like other forms of CB (as we will see in Chapter 3), the people involved are most likely there with their friends in tow. Adrian Aveni (1977) therefore talked of 'the not-so-lonely crowd' in which members are personally known to at least one, and in many cases, several, others.

McPhail's observational research has serious ramifications for Blumer's theory. Blumer suggests that within crowds people do not interact in normal, rational ways. Instead of the usual 'symbolic interaction' he gives an explanation based on emotionally driven 'circular reaction'. If the critics are right, however, this is a mistake. CB – behaviour that is rule-*breaking* – may not be routine or conventional, but it is nevertheless misplaced to suggest that it operates on a completely *different basis* compared to normal social behaviour (in other words, on the basis of the circular reaction of emotions rather than symbolic interaction in which people consciously deliberate their actions with others and themselves). Instead, critics argue for the continuing value of symbolic interactionist (rather than psychological) accounts of the crowd for aiding an understanding of how and why people behave as they do – without having to suggest that they become transformed into irrational and immoral people (Turner and Killian, 1987; McPhail, 2006). There is some irony here therefore that should not be lost: the one bit of Blumer's theory that he did not think would help to explain crowd behaviour – symbolic interaction – might well be the only bit of his theory that does.

Methods point: the value of social experiments

Clark McPhail (1991) suggests that Herbert Blumer came to the wrong conclusions about the crowd because he did not put into practice the methodological strategy that he had made famous alongside Robert E. Park and other symbolic interactionists at the University of Chicago in the 1930s and 1940s. This method involved using fieldwork to closely observe and describe the phenomena to be explained. McPhail mounted a fierce attack on Blumer for ignoring this method in his work on the crowd and conducting 'armchair theorizing' instead. When it comes to explaining CB, McPhail thought that it was absolutely vital to get familiar with the subject matter before making claims about it. He argued that alongside participant observation, social experiments can be a useful way to generate detailed descriptions about what actually goes on in the social world. McPhail engaged in various social experiments at the colleges where he lectured. On occasions he was known to walk out during a lecture in order to disrupt routine social behaviour and see what happened next! In 1965, his students turned the tables on him by staging a walkout ten minutes before the end of his lecture. Later that day, McPhail collected written accounts of the walkout from the students involved. McPhail found that, first, the walkout was not spontaneous. The students needed time on their own at the start of the class to plan the walkout – deciding who will do what, and when. This time was cut short by the arrival of the lecturer and this created confusion for the students about when and whether the walkout would take place. Without some prior planning and coordination it would be very difficult for new lines of CB to emerge. Secondly, in contrast to the image of the crowd as unthinking and unanimous, two students out of the twenty-five decided not to take part in the walkout because they were not convinced about the reasons for it. Thirdly, students were more likely to commit to and carry out the walkout when a number of other students signalled they were willing to do the same and when no one in the group dissented. Public declarations of intent and the absence of challenge were very important and made students feel like there was 'safety in numbers'. This gives support to Turner and Killian's idea that crowds develop new understandings of what is right and wrong (i.e. emergent norms) and the majority act in accordance with these.

- Do social experiments help us to understand what people really do in crowd situations that have not been manufactured?
- If you wanted to find out how being part of a crowd on a protest event affected people's behaviour, what methods could you employ?
- Weigh up the merits and drawbacks of: 1. interviews with participants after the event; 2. participant observation during the event; 3. surveys completed by participants during the event. Which would you employ?

Social movements

Blumer (1951 [1946]), does not stop his discussion of CB with the crowd. He also talks about social movements and the processes by which they form. Blumer admits that 'social movements' are much more organized and strategic compared to momentary crowd events. Indeed, social movements (as opposed to crowds on protest events) are characterized by their durability. Blumer defines 'social movements' as:

> Collective enterprises seeking to establish a new order of life. They have their inception in a condition of social unrest, and derive their motive power on one hand from dissatisfaction with the current form of life, and on the other hand, from wishes and hopes for a new system of living.
>
> (Blumer, 1951 [1946], 199)

Blumer argues that social movements do not appear 'ready formed'. Instead, they arise over a period of time out of prior interactive processes. In Blumer's (1951 [1946], 199) terms, they have a 'career'. In the earliest phase, social movements are nothing more than individual responses to 'cultural drift', reflected in 'voices in the wilderness' calling for social change and beginning the process of agitation (Blumer, 1951 [1946], 201). Blumer calls this phase the 'general social movement', and there is no guarantee that it will ever amount to anything more than individual efforts at change. In some cases, however, individual efforts can become collective and organized, leading to the formation of 'specific social movements' (Blumer 1951 [1946], 202). Specific social movements involve coordinated strategies to pursue concrete goals and they take an organizational form. As an example, individual calls for people to live in more environmentally friendly ways would constitute a general social movement, whereas an organized group with concrete goals and strategies, like Greenpeace, would constitute a specific social movement. This distinction is important because it will arise again in Chapter 3, when a difference is drawn between 'social movements' as preferences for change and 'social movement organizations' (SMOs) as the groups that pursue these preferences (McCarthy and Zald, 1977).

So what is the process by which specific social movements form? Blumer argues that there are four key stages in the development of a social movement (see figure 2.2).

What is really key in each of these stages is the ability of agitators to create emotional attachments between participants and the cause. This

Stages in the career of a social movement	Mechanisms by which the development occurs
1. Social Unrest	Agitation
2. Popular Excitement	Development of Esprit de Corps
3. Formalization	Development of Group Morale
4. Institutionalization	Development of Ideology and Tactics

Figure 2.2
Emotions and the career of a social movement.
Source: adapted from Herbert Blumer, 1951 [1946], p. 203.

is because emotional attachments to the cause provide participants with the motivation to get involved (and continue to be involved) in activism which actually carries a fairly high cost and relatively little reward (as we will see in Chapter 3). Involvement with a cause can come at great personal cost, for example, whether in time, energy, money, freedom, or even life. Thinking about it rationally, we might wonder why anyone would bother to commit so much to a cause, especially when there often appears little chance of success. Social movements really are a 'struggle' too. They face all kinds of setbacks and obstacles that can easily demoralize and harm participants. Those who participate – and especially those who carry on – need to have a strong emotional investment in the cause, therefore, in order to propel them to act, at times, against their own interests.

Blumer suggests that the role that emotions play in different stages of a social movement's 'career' vary. In each of the four stages shown in figure 2.2, however, emotions act to weave passion, commitment, and loyalty between people and the cause and, in doing so, knit the individuals involved together as a group that is capable of persisting over time and formulating goals.

In the first stage of 'social unrest', agitators play the important role of getting 'under the skin' of people and trying to inspire emotional reactions to social problems (Blumer, 1951 [1946], 205). James Jasper (1997) refers to this emotional reaction as the 'moral shock' that first gets people interested in a cause. In the second stage of 'popular excitement' – such as instances of crowd behaviour – emotions are the glue that holds the acting group together by generating what Blumer calls 'esprit de corps'. Esprit de corps is defined by Blumer as 'the organizing of feelings on behalf of the movement' and it creates a sense of belonging to the group and sharing in its mission (Blumer, 1951 [1946], 205). Three sets of interactive practices help to generate esprit de corps: first, the identification of common enemies (people whom you blame) which cements the existence of the group and loyalty to it ('you are with us or you are against us'); secondly, the formation of personal relationships within the group (participants become friends); and thirdly, the development of group rituals ('ceremonial behaviour'), like meetings, rallies, parades, and demonstrations that reconfirm commitment to the group. When members participate in these rituals their sense of belonging to the group is reinforced because they feel like they are a part of something bigger than themselves. The result of esprit de corps, then, is 'solidarity': members recognize themselves as belonging to the same group and sharing the same aims, and they are willing to help and support each other in doing so.

Case point: 'esprit de corps' in the suffragettes

How does esprit de corps develop within social movements? Blumer describes esprit de corps as 'the sense people have of belonging together and of being identified with one another in a common undertaking' (Blumer, 1951 [1946], 206). Ceremonial behaviour – like rallies, parades, and rituals – plays a key role in creating a sense of belonging and shared purpose. Often, movement rituals include what Blumer (1951 [1946], 208) calls 'sentimental symbols' like slogans, songs, poems, hymns, and uniforms through which the feelings people have for one another, and the cause, are expressed and reinforced. Rituals played an important role in establishing solidarity amongst suffragettes in the UK (the militant women who campaigned for the vote 1903–14). At Eagle House, Bath (in south-west England), which was owned by the wealthy Blathwayt family, suffragettes from all over the country would gather for social visits (Edwards, 2014). An interesting ritual began at the house in the 1907 – every suffragette who visited would plant a tree in the garden. The type of tree was symbolic of their level of participation: conifers for those who had been to prison for the cause, and hollies for those who had not. They were planted

in concentric circles, with the trees of the most acclaimed suffragettes, like Emmeline Pankhurst, at the centre. Each tree also
displayed a sign showing the name of the suffragette and the date
it was planted. Suffragettes would visit the trees in 'the suffragette field' to rest and reflect. Randall Collins (2001) calls rituals
like this one a 'focus of emotional attention' for the participants
of a social movement. As Blumer argued, they also give members
'the sense of being somebody distinctly important' (Blumer, 1951
[1946], 207) and help them to feel positively about their participation. Not only did visits to Eagle House help suffragettes build
strong bonds of friendship, but the tree planting ritual helped to
reinforce the feeling that they belonged to a special group who
would do anything for one another, or for the cause.

- Can you think of other examples of the ways in which members of social movements create a shared sense of identity
  (dress, symbols, events, and so forth)?
- Are there parallels between being a member of a social movement and being a member of a religious group?
- Do people participate in social movements purely out of emotional commitments?

In its third and fourth stages of development shown in figure 2.2, a social
movement starts to become more formal and established. It becomes an
organization with its own rules, policies, beliefs, and tactics. In order
for the movement to sustain itself in the long-term it needs to develop
members' feelings of attachment and loyalty beyond 'esprit de corps'.
Esprit de corps lives off popular excitement and it is strong when a
movement is enjoying good times, but to ensure members' commitment when the chips are down, a more long-lasting 'group morale' has
to emerge. Blumer describes this as an 'enduring collective purpose'
(Blumer, 1951 [1946], 208). In order to establish this sense of purpose,
movements must develop political ideologies which – like religious ideologies – inspire adherents with a sense of blind faith. According to
Blumer (1951 [1946], 208–9), movement ideologies contain beliefs like:

- the inevitability of the change which is sought
- the invincibility of the movement

- the divine, righteous, or sacred nature of the cause
- the absolute necessity of pursuing the cause.

These beliefs help members to develop an unwavering attachment to the goal of the movement. They become adamant that the goal will be realized, no matter how much they have to sacrifice for it. In social movements, argues Blumer, 'the goal is always over-valued' (Blumer, 1951 [1946], 208).

Blumer assessed

The merits of Blumer's approach to understanding CB largely come from his symbolic interactionist perspective. This perspective is particularly helpful in aiding our understanding of how social problems relate to protest and social movements. Rather than assuming any automatic relationship between people's experience of adverse social circumstances and their participation in protest, Blumer reminds us that something important intervenes in between. That 'something important' is the active process of interpretation and definition of the situation that people engage in with others. They act on the basis of collectively produced definitions about their social circumstances, and do not have a knee-jerk reaction to those circumstances themselves. Social problems – like poverty and social marginalization – must therefore be constructed as 'problems' and as 'unjust' before they affect people's actions. Equally, agitators must, through interaction with potential participants, help people to interpret their lives and situations as ones which are subject to change. Grievances are important in Blumer's account because they lead to the general condition of social unrest out of which CB can form, but grievances themselves, he reminds us, are socially constructed rather than naturally occurring. We should therefore not be surprised that research which tests for correlations between economic deprivation and the occurrence of protest fails to provide evidence for a direct link.

If this is the value of Blumer's approach to CB then it should also give us a clue about the drawbacks. In his assessment of CB, particularly the crowd, Blumer quite consciously leaves the symbolic interactionist perspective behind. To understand a large part of CB, he suggests – somewhat oddly – that we should not employ the idea of symbolic interaction, but that of circular reaction. In proposing this, Blumer argues that much CB operates on a very different basis from normal social interaction. In short, he tells us that CB is emotionally driven rather than deliberative and interpretive. This viewpoint is not reserved for crowd behaviour: even the development of social movements depends upon creating emotional attachments and beliefs that weld participants to the cause, come hell or high water.

While Blumer is right to acknowledge the importance of emotion in social movements and protest – a factor that we will soon see disappear and then get 'rediscovered' again in other approaches – he nevertheless gives us a problematic notion of what emotions are and how they relate to action. Blumer sees emotions as taking over from normal rational deliberative action. People are rational and deliberative and then they *switch* to being emotional in the context of CB. This view of emotions – as an opposite and alternative to rationality as a basis of human behaviour – is problematic because it means that Blumer ends up suggesting that CB is essentially 'irrational' in nature. The evidence we have for this is Blumer's argument that the participants of CB are restless and neurotic, driven by their emotions rather than critical thought, and motivated by investments in a cause that they 'over-value'. In this way, Blumer offers us a conceptualization of CB as 'irrational group behaviour'.

Although the other leading figure in the CB field – Neil Smelser (1962) – is theoretically opposed to Blumer, and writing some seventeen years after Blumer's work on crowds and social movements was originally published in 1946, I will suggest that he too offers a similar conceptualization of CB as 'irrational group behaviour', although, as we will see in the next section, for quite different reasons.

Neil Smelser's approach to understanding collective behaviour

Unlike Blumer, Neil Smelser is not a symbolic interactionist, but is instead attached to Talcott Parsons' (1970) 'structural functionalism' (Rule, 1988). Rather than viewing society in terms of group interactions, structural functionalists view society as if it is a 'living system', composed of interrelated parts which each function together to meet the needs of the system as a whole and thus enable it to operate in a well-ordered manner. Sub-systems like the economy, polity, cultural system, and personality system, for example, fulfil society's needs for material survival, mobilizing and utilizing resources, reproducing norms and values, and socializing its members into them (Parsons, 1970). Functionalists also take a different approach to social theorizing compared to symbolic interactionism: they argue that social science should adopt explanations akin to the natural sciences and seek to uncover general laws about society. Smelser (1962, 18) therefore sets himself two tasks: first, to uncover the general conditions under which CB emerges in society and, secondly, to uncover the factors that determine the *form* that CB takes – in other words, to explain under what conditions CB will take the shape of a riot, or craze, or panic, or mob, or social movement. The first condition that Smelser relates to CB takes us back to the idea of social problems and grievances.

Structural strains

Functionalism is known for its focus upon social order and system maintenance, rather than rebellion and social change. Indeed, the functionalist approach to social problems is to see them as 'dysfunctions' or 'pathologies' within a normally smooth-running and well-integrated social system (Merton,1961). In his book, *Theory of Collective Behavior*, Smelser (1962) makes a similar assumption by suggesting that CB results not from the tensions and pathologies that people experience inside themselves (Blumer's 'neurosis' idea, which Smelser rejects), but from the tensions and pathologies that arise in the *social structure* of society. He calls these 'structural strains' and argues that they arise in circumstances where the existing social structure stops being able to meet people's needs and expectations. Under normal conditions, the social system runs smoothly without creating strains because it is able to evolve and adapt to new needs in the environment. In times of rapid social change, however, like the industrial revolution in the nineteenth century by way of example, the ability of the social system to meet people's needs and expectations can break down. As a result, strains appear in various parts of the social system. Strains can arise in the economy, for example, when people's motivation and achievement are not appropriately rewarded (perhaps because an economic downturn reduces their pay). They can arise in social roles, when individuals experience competing demands (like working to provide for your family but staying home to look after them as well), and they can arise in the cultural and normative fabric of society when people start to question society's goals, or when the relationships that normally integrate them into society's values become broken (leading to a condition that Emile Durkheim calls 'anomie'). In a statement reminiscent of Ted Gurr's comments about relative deprivation, Smelser contends that 'some form of structural strain must be present if an episode of collective behaviour is to occur. The more severe the strain, moreover, the more likely is such an episode to appear' (Smelser, 1962, 48).

Generalized beliefs

Social problems – as 'strains' – are therefore related in Smelser's account to structural breakdown, not psychological breakdown. Nevertheless, he still suggests that 'structural strains' have a negative impact on people's state of mind (Smelser, 1962, 11). In creating social situations that are 'undefined' and 'unstructured', strains are responsible for producing feelings of uncertainty for those experiencing them (Smelser, 1962, 9). It is this uncertainty, argues Smelser, that is actually most damaging to people. If an economic crisis hits on the eve of graduation from university, for example, then students will experience a great deal of uncertainty about their job prospects. In fact, individual feelings of uncertainty play an essential role in Smelser's account of CB. They motivate people to look for answers to their grievances – ideas about why it is happening to them and what they can do about it. Since society has no answers for them, they start to develop their own beliefs, or they become attracted to political or religious ideologies. These provide them with some comfort and a way to resolve feelings of anxiety and uncertainty. When social groups establish and share a certain diagnosis of the situation Smelser calls their beliefs 'generalized beliefs'.

CB is based upon a particular subset of 'generalized beliefs' according to Smelser, those that 'redefine social action' (Smelser, 1962, 8). What this means is that they are beliefs that point to some aspect of society that needs to change. In order to comfort myself before graduation, I could believe that a hard-working graduate will do well whatever the economic climate. This type of belief would hardly inspire CB on my part (just a great deal of reading and revision). I could, however, believe that greedy bankers had ruined the economy, robbing me unfairly of my chance for success, and that greedy bankers are a symptom of

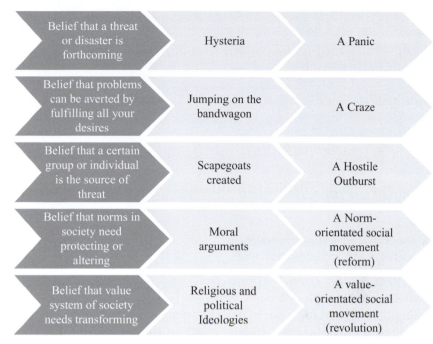

Figure 2.3
The relationship between beliefs and collective behaviour.
Source: adapted from Neil Smelser (1962).

capitalist corruption. With these thoughts I would be far more likely
to see the need for some kind of action to bring about social change.

By highlighting the need for generalized beliefs to develop out of
strains, Smelser is already starting to suggest that the situation is more
complex than a simple cause–effect relationship between social problems and CB. People engage in CB not directly because of strains, but
because they hold beliefs that society needs to change. These beliefs
lead people to think that some type of action – as opposed to doing
nothing – is necessary and desirable. Furthermore, the form of CB that
they engage in – whether they riot, rebel, demonstrate, or join social
movements – is shaped by the specific content of the beliefs they hold
(see figure 2.3). It is the nature of generalized beliefs therefore that
determines the form of CB.

A general model of collective behaviour

Smelser added to his theory a proviso: even when structural strains
do lead to the development of generalized beliefs orientated towards

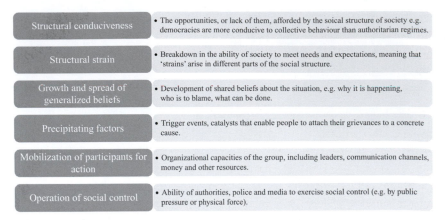

Figure 2.4
Smelser's value-added six-point model.
Source: adapted from Neil Smelser (1962).

change, CB is not an inevitable outcome. In fact, Smelser argues that
rather than CB emerging out of one condition, it emerges out of a combination of conditions. Whether generalized beliefs develop and take
hold, and whether their existence will lead to a collective response,
depends upon the existence of multiple factors, expressed by Smelser
in a 'value-added' six-point model of CB (see figure 2.4). This model
outlines the multiple causal conditions out of which any episode of
CB arises. Smelser calls it a 'value-added model' because each factor
adds something else that is *necessary* to the conditions in which CB
could emerge. The nature, order, and combination of these six factors
together determine if and what kind of CB will result from strain.

Anthony Oberschall (1968) provides a helpful illustration of how
Smelser's model can be used to understand the emergence of protest
in his analysis of the 1965 Watts–Los Angeles race riots in the United
States. A number of grievances surrounding economic deprivation,
unemployment, and policing were present in the Watts community and
had been for some time ('structural strains'). The community widely
believed that the police and the authorities were racist and brutal and
to blame for a large part of the suffering ('generalized belief'). They had
thought this for some time, but a 'trigger' event was needed in order
for them to act ('precipitating factor'). A trigger is an event that enables
people to attach their feelings of anger and frustration to a concrete
cause; something that they can rally around. In Watts, the arrest of
a 21-year-old black man for running a red light while driving drunk

became the catalyst for the riots. All sorts of rumours spread through the community about this event, with people saying that the police had been heavy-handed, and even that they had beaten up a pregnant woman who tried to intervene ('generalized belief').

The rumour was, in fact, false, but in many ways, Oberschall argues, the truth does not matter. As long as the event can be interpreted in line with people's existing beliefs then it acts as a kind of 'symbol' for their shared discontent. Once the riot – which involved widespread arson and looting – was underway, it allowed people with long-standing grievances against the police and authorities to seize an opportunity to get their own back whilst the chances of being reprimanded were low. The resources that rioters had at their disposal helped them to coordinate their actions, with existing gangs providing leadership, and television coverage (unwittingly) enabling rioters to both identify where they should go to get a slice of the action, and helping them to evade the police ('mobilization of participants for action').

The magnitude and duration of the riot was largely the result of the police effort to control it ('social control'). It was not a simple case of the police using force to quell the disturbance. When the police waded in and confronted rioters they became the focus for the crowd's attention and anger, and they actually reinforced the 'us versus them' mentality which escalated the violence. But whilst people rioted over a few days – setting fire to buildings and looting shops – they did not form longer-lasting movements, they did not produce political leaders, and they did not arm themselves for rebellion. The reasons for this were threefold: they lacked the resources necessary for an insurrection ('mobilization of participants for action'); they lacked the kind of beliefs that would lead them to such action (they wanted to lash out against police, not bring down the system) ('generalized beliefs'); and should they have tried to mount an insurrection, they would surely have been subjected to an even more brutal repression by the authorities ('social control').

Smelser assessed

Smelser's model is useful to the extent that it shows that CB is the result of multiple causal factors (Rule, 1988, 163). It shows that grievances and beliefs are important, but not enough, and that some factors are more important in the beginning of an episode, whilst others come to the fore later on. In doing so, it provides a useful reminder that an explanation of CB needs to include an awareness of factors other than individual *dispositions* (like emotions and beliefs). If people are to act then more needs to be in place than simply their inclination to do so: they need to have a 'structurally conducive' environment, and the capacity to 'mobilize' action as well. We will pursue these suggestions in Chapters 3 and 4, where the capacity for mobilization and the structural environment become of central importance. Nick Crossley (2002) argues that few critics have acknowledged the place that Smelser gives to these other factors in his explanation of CB, preferring to reduce him to a 'straw man' who represents a simplistic strain theory of social movements. Any detailed engagement with Smelser's actual work, however, shows that this is not the case (and we will revisit his work in a new context in Chapter 7 on terrorism, which again posits a *multi*-causal explanation). In fact, Crossley (2002) argues that the range of factors that Smelser includes in his model correlate well with the factors that social movement theorists have seen as important (and that we will cover in subsequent chapters). To that extent, the model provides a useful starting point for social movement research (Crossley, 2002).

Nevertheless, there are significant methodological difficulties associated with using Smelser's model which challenge this assertion. Anthony Oberschall (1968) argues that its main limitation is that you have to 'work back' from an episode of CB and take for granted that all of the six factors in the model must have been present (otherwise, presumably, it would not have occurred in the first place and you would not be studying it). The episode of CB is therefore taken as evidence for the existence of the factors that are also used to explain it (Rule, 1988, 163). That does not sound like a great theory. In fact, the model is in danger of becoming self-confirming: if you look hard enough you will find all of the six factors that you were supposed to find in order to explain your case of CB (Currie and Skolnick, 1970). In his definition of CB for example, Smelser states that 'people under strain mobilize to reconstruct social order in the name of a generalized belief' (Smelser 1962, 385), thereby working his 'conditions for emergence' into the very definition of CB itself (strain, mobilization, generalized belief). In this sense, Smelser's method means that his model cannot actually be disproved (Rule, 1988, 164). Alan Scott (1990, 42) therefore criticizes the model for being 'tautological' (i.e. it is self-reinforcing): CB cannot actually be identified outside the list of conditions that Smelser tells us produce it in the first place. James Rule (1988) subsequently suggests that we need to demand more from Smelser than a list of conditions that you would be hard pressed *not* to find related to CB; instead:

> we need Smelser to provide a rule specifying how much strain and other predisposing conditions are necessary to count as fulfilling the conditions of his theory and how we are to recognize such things independently of the effects they are supposed to produce.
>
> (Rule, 1988, 164)

We can find merit, however, in the way in which Smelser highlights the importance of people's *beliefs and ideas* about their situation. As Brinton puts it: 'no ideas, no revolution' (Brinton, quoted in Smelser, 1962, 79). This reminds us again that people do not have knee-jerk reactions to social problems. Instead, as a group they interpret their lives, creating shared ideas about injustice and unfairness; about threats, enemies, and conspiracies; about who is to blame; and what can be done. Smelser makes it clear that it is the nature of the beliefs that people develop in the face of social problems that motivates their action, not the problems themselves. The way in which Smelser relates social problems to beliefs and beliefs to actions, is, however, problematic. Alan Scott (1990, 43) contends that Smelser assumes that beliefs automatically arise from given social circumstances and then cause our action. Specifically, under conditions of structural strain, people will develop generalized beliefs that 'redefine social action'. Scott suggests otherwise:

> Strain does not cause my beliefs, as Smelser assumes; rather the beliefs I have will influence whether or not I see my situation as strained. Similarly, beliefs do not come into being in order that I can act in a certain way ... my acting in a certain way will be dependent on the beliefs I hold.
>
> (Scott, 1990, 43)

While Smelser makes it clear that CB is not to be thought of a knee-jerk reaction to social problems, our beliefs, however, seemingly are. Lacking the kind of symbolic interactionist perspective offered by Blumer, Smelser is unable to capture the complex process of interpretation and definition that takes place within interaction and which shapes the way in which people make sense of their social circumstances and decide how to act within them. Beliefs shape circumstances (they define what is 'real' for us), as much as they are shaped by them.

Smelser makes some further claims about the nature of generalized beliefs which are also problematic. He argues that they are rooted in 'exaggerated' and 'distorted' views of reality, saying that they have more to do with 'rumour, ideology and superstition' than with rational reflection (Smelser, 1962, 80). 'Rumours', for example, are the initial result of people's 'flounderings around' for meaning, and they are rarely concerned with the facts of the situation (Smelser, 1962, 85). Smelser therefore seems to suggest that people cling on to 'distortions' of reality in an attempt to resolve the uncertainty that structural strains have caused them, becoming hysterical or hostile in the process. For these reasons, they are also prime targets for 'indoctrination' by political leaders and may become attracted to the 'fantasies' contained within political ideologies. This mixture of rumour, ideology, and superstition leads Smelser to describe generalized beliefs as 'magical beliefs' which point to 'the existence of extraordinary forces – threats, conspiracies, etc – which are at work in the universe' (Smelser, 1962, 8). The participants of CB are subsequently portrayed on the one hand, as people who are hostile and, on the other hand, as people who worship political leaders. This leads Smelser into some murky Freudian territory, where he suggests that participation in movements can be viewed as an outlet for what he calls 'oedipal conflicts' (simultaneous emotions of love and hate).

For Smelser, what marks out CB from other forms of behaviour orientated towards social change, then, is not that it is rooted in beliefs as such, but that it is rooted in *irrational* beliefs (Currie and Skolnick, 1970, 39). Currie and Skolnick (1970) suggest that Smelser based his assumption about the distorted nature of generalized beliefs on his own bias against protesters, rather than convincing empirical evidence suggesting that they are, in fact, deluded, hostile, or superstitious. Indeed, Carl Couch (1968, 315) argues that the participants of protest and social movements are no more attached to 'mad ideas' than the people we find in the 'official' political arena – they just happen to express ideas that challenge the rest of society and are therefore deemed 'irrational'. Indeed, protest and social movements can be seen as highly 'rational' responses to social problems when there is no 'normal' way left for expressing and resolving grievances. Smelser's 'short-circuiting' could, then, be a rational rather than an irrational response.

Smelser's description of generalized beliefs is somewhat surprising because he explicitly states that he wants to get away from Blumer's crowd psychology and the notion that the people who participate in CB are irrational or psychologically disturbed (Smelser, 1962, 11).

Consequently, his critics were quick to point out that he failed (Currie and Skolnick, 1970). He ended up inferring instead that the generalized beliefs of participants are irrational and implied that, as people, they are a bit on the mad side too. If they were rational then they would address their grievances through the normal channels society has set up (e.g. contacting your local political representatives, or joining a pressure group). Instead, the participants of CB 'short-circuit' the normal channels by attaching themselves to beliefs which 'by-pass many logical and empirical contingencies' (Smelser, 1962, 94) – in other words, fly in the face of reason and fact!

Alan Scott (1990, 45) suggests that Smelser's functionalist perspective is ultimately responsible for the way in which he views CB as an 'abnormal' response to social circumstances. Functionalism, as previously stated, focuses on how social order is achieved. The answer for functionalists is that social order is achieved through integrating members of society into a system of shared norms and values. Their behaviour thus becomes patterned by social norms and 'institutionalized'. But as we know from Blumer, what is distinctive about CB is that it does not adhere to society's established norms. It is therefore defined from a functionalist perspective as 'non-institutionalized' behaviour; in other words, a form of 'deviance' (Scott, 1990, 45). Smelser therefore conceptualizes CB as abnormal and irrational group behaviour, which arises as a response to the uncertainty and ambiguity created by structural strains.

Summary

Although Herbert Blumer and Neil Smelser's very different approaches to CB have been heavily criticized, they nevertheless impart important lessons which help to challenge some common-sense assumptions. Our common-sense understanding of social movements and protest, for example, suggests that they arise as responses to social problems in society and the grievances these create for people. Such an understanding is often confirmed in media accounts of protest, which cite problems like poverty and social marginalization as the cause. Whilst Blumer and Smelser do accord social problems and grievances a central role in the emergence of CB, they also correct two common misunderstandings:

- Social problems and grievances are not naturally occurring aspects of social reality, but have to be socially constructed in interaction. People act on the basis of collectively produced definitions of the situation.
- While social problems and grievances have an important relationship to CB, they are not the sole cause. Instead, we need a multi-causal explanation that identifies a range of conditions.

Furthermore, Blumer and Smelser's emphasis on factors ranging from social psychology to beliefs, grievance construction, and emotion, find substantial common ground with contemporary debates in social movement studies – debates that are returning to these issues after decades of rationalist dominance (and which we will come on to in subsequent chapters). Blumer in particular is adept at speaking to these concerns with his work on ritual, ceremony, and solidarity, even if contemporary scholars are reluctant, and rightly so, to readopt the theoretical approach to emotions that he offers.

Despite these merits, our defence of CB should not be full-scale. Whether they mean to or not, both Blumer and Smelser, albeit from very different theoretical perspectives, portray the participants of CB as psychologically disturbed and emotionally unstable. They have been driven mad by strain and unrest, reduced to unthinking members of the mob, motivated by emotional investments and irrational beliefs. In short, they are 'mad people with mad ideas'. CB is therefore conceptualized by both theorists as 'irrational group behaviour'.

This chapter has challenged this conceptualization by exploding three myths in Blumer and Smelser's accounts of CB:

- The myth of 'the madness within': grievances and the psychological anguish and emotions they produce in individuals are not enough to explain participation in CB.
- The myth of 'the madding crowd': interaction in the crowd does not take place on the basis of emotionally driven 'circular reaction'. Instead, symbolic interaction, which involves critical–rational reflection, continues to be important to how we understand crowd behaviour.
- The myth of 'mad people with mad ideas': the beliefs that motivate CB are not necessarily any more irrational or 'magical' than the beliefs that motivate routine political behaviour.

The major mistake of CB, in fact, is to claim that because participants are emotional, CB must therefore be *different* from normal rational behaviour. This logic is flawed, and we will see exactly why in the next chapter, when critics will suggest that the only people with 'mad ideas' might well be the CB theorists themselves. Protesters do not fall out of wonderland and onto the streets. Neither does an understanding of their behaviour require a psychological assessment of 'mad hatters'. Instead, it requires us to engage with the question of how normal, sane people come to decide that protest is their best option. It is to this 'rationalist' alternative that we now turn.

DISCUSSION POINT

Choose an example of a protest that has taken place recently (you might want to start with one in your local area). Collect together material about this protest, like newspaper accounts, online discussions, and campaign material. Think about whether the following theories help you to understand why the protest happened:

- relative deprivation and social marginalization
- Smelser's value-added six-point model
- Blumer's theory of crowd behaviour.

Which of the three theories fares the best in terms of explaining your case? What are the relative strengths and weaknesses? Can they be used in combination?

FURTHER READING

Blumer's ideas on social movements and crowds can be found in A. McClung Lee's *Principles of Sociology* (1951 [1946]). Smelser's *Theory of Collective Behavior* (1962) contains a clear introduction to his structural-functionalist approach. For a critical evaluation of crowd theories you cannot beat Clark McPhail's highly accessible *The Myth of the Madding Crowd* (1991) which also covers deprivation theories of protest. Doug McAdam presents a very clear critique of classical approaches to social movements in Chapter 1 'The classical model of social movements examined' in *Political Process and the Development of Black Insurgency* (1982).

3

From the rational to the relational: resource mobilization, organization, and social movement networks

> Individuals are not magically mobilized for participation
> in some group enterprise, regardless of how angry, sullen,
> hostile or frustrated they may feel. Their aggression
> may be channelled to collective ends only through the
> coordinating, directing functions of an organization.
>
> (Shorter and Tilly 1974, 338)

If social movements cannot be thought of as the irrational expression of shared grievances, then how can they be conceptualized? In this chapter, we consider the answer given by resource mobilization theory (RMT), which emerged in the 1970s in the US in response to widespread dissatisfaction with collective behaviour (CB) theory. RMT remains a dominant and diverse approach to social movements. Here, we focus on one version first offered by J. D. McCarthy and Mayer Zald (1977), whilst in the next chapter we pursue the more structural and political version of mobilization theory known as the 'political process'/'contentious politics' approach. It is fair to say, however, that they both grow out of the same set of core assumptions offered by 'rational action theory' (RAT), and both share the same set of problems because of it.

First, we will engage with RMT's alternative to CB, including tracing their main concerns to RAT and Mancur Olson's (1965) 'collective action problem'. We will look at the conceptual tools offered by McCarthy and Zald for understanding the process of resource mobilization, and consider what kind of resources are important to social movements. We will see that the idea of movements as 'multi-organizational fields' has led to a contemporary conceptualization of social movements as 'networks' rather than discrete 'organizations'. We end by considering the implications of this shift, which, I suggest, requires us to adopt a 'relational' rather than 'rational' logic of collective action.

By the close of the chapter you should understand the nature of the alternative conceptualization of social movements offered by CB's critics. You should be able to critically engage with RMT by compre-hending the limits of their rationalist perspective. You should also be-come aware of the advantages of conceptualizing social movements in 'network' terms, as well as the methodological tools available for researching social movement networks.

Resource mobilization theory (RMT)

In this first section of the chapter, we consider the alternative theory of protest and social movements that was offered by RMT in the 1970s, before looking in detail at the way in which RMT drew upon RAT and applied it – through the work of Mancur Olson (1965) – to the study of collective action.

Anger, frustration, and passion do not make for a protest or social movement on their own. Aggrieved groups need more than their feel-ings, dispositions, and inclinations if they are going to act collectively to change things: they need the *means* to act as well. Resource mobiliza-tion stresses this point by pushing social movement analysis beyond the 'hearts and minds' approach of CB (Leites and Wolf, 1970; McCarthy and Zald, 1973). No matter how upset and angry people are, they vary in their ability to launch collective action in response to their grievances. RMT therefore argues that an explanation of social movements should concen-trate on *how* resources are successfully mobilized, rather than *why* people are aggrieved (McCarthy and Zald, 1977; Jenkins, 1983). Grievances, it is argued, are 'necessary but insufficient' explanations for collective action (Jenkins and Perrow, 1977; Jenkins, 1983). Grievances do not automati-cally lead to collective action because there has to be an intervening pro-cess that can have varying degrees of success: *resource mobilization*.

In fact, grievances are 'secondary' factors when explaining collec-tive action for another important reason according to RMT: they are a relatively constant aspect of life (Jenkins and Perrow, 1977). While structural functionalists, like Neil Smelser (1962), saw strain and con-flict as rare occurrences of crisis in an otherwise smooth-running social system, RMT adopts a conflict approach, pointing to the inequalities and diverging interests *built in* to the social system that are constant sources of conflict (McAdam, 1982). There does not need to be a 'breakdown' or crisis, then, in order for social conflicts to arise, because they are normal and frequent occurrences (Wilson, 1973). The question of why people are

aggrieved in the first place does not therefore hold much analytic interest: we do not need an analysis of some 'special occasion' but, instead,
an implicit acknowledgement that most of the time society is ridden
with enough conflicts to supply people with the grievances and motivation to protest. That much does not change. What does change, however,
is the availability of the resources required for collective action. The
emergence of protest and social movements are thus better explained
by changes in the availability of resources (on the personal and societal
level) and not in terms of strains, social problems, and grievances.

Resources

Groups require a variety of resources for collective action, which can
be divided between 'tangible' and 'intangible' resources (see Freeman,
1979, 172–5):

- 'tangible resources': *money* (to purchase campaign materials, pay
  staff, hire facilities, travel); *participants* (who offer their labour);
  organization and *communications infrastructure* (to coordinate
  action); *leaders* (who can both administer the tasks of the movement
  and articulate its cause to the wider public)
- 'intangible resources': *skills and know-how* (to set up campaigns
  and make them successful, and interact with the public and media);
  public support (to provide the group and its cause with legitimacy
  and status).

The availability of resources varies for different groups. Some groups
are closely knit and able to communicate easily about their grievances,
others are not. Some groups are fairly rich, and able to invest lots of
money in campaigning, others are not. Some groups have established
ways of coordinating collective activities, others do not. Some groups
are experienced in using political skills, organizational know-how, and
public communication, others are not. The important point is that the
uneven spread of resources among the aggrieved population means
that organizing a protest or social movement is more *costly* for some
compared to others. The more resources you have to start with, or are
able to mobilize along the way, the less costly it will be to establish and
sustain a social movement, and the more likely it will be that people
will do something about their grievances. In order to understand the
nature of this argument – which relates people's decisions and actions

to considerations of 'costs' and 'benefits' – we need to look in detail at the theory of 'rational action' on which RMT is premised.

Rational action theory (RAT)

In turning to RAT, RMT does not adopt a *completely* different perspective on human behaviour compared to CB. Instead, it inverts the view of protesters that is presented by CB in order to cast the participants of protest in a 'rational' (rather than 'irrational') light. CB theorists thought that *in normal circumstances* (i.e. in situations free of strain or unrest) people behave rationally. Indeed, CB arguments are premised on the idea that when it comes to protest and social movements, people 'switch' from normal rational action to emotional (and hence) irrational action. Resource mobilization theorists, on the other hand, argue that the participants of protest and social movements do not make any such 'switch'. Instead, they remain 'rational actors' throughout. Individuals decide to join a protest or a social movement (or not) because of a rational process of decision-making, and, furthermore, their resulting collective action is rational in nature too.

RAT was partly attractive to RM theorists because of its ability from the outset to cast protesters as rational human beings rather than 'mad people with mad ideas'. This was important to the new generation of social movement theorists in the 1970s, not only because CB imported notions about the social psychology of protest that were problematic, but because the new scholars were politically attracted to, and sometimes active in, social movements themselves (like the student movement and anti-Vietnam war protests). They were insiders, not outsiders, when it came to protest, and they wanted a positive image of protesters that could break away from the negative stereotypes of emotional, irrational, deviants generated by media accounts, and seemingly reinforced by CB. Explaining the dissatisfaction experienced by new scholars in the 1970s, Doug McAdam writes that:

> My first exposure to the academic study of social movements came in 1971 when, much to my surprise, the professor in my Abnormal Psychology Class devoted several weeks to a discussion of the topic. I say 'surprise' because, as an active participant in the anti-war movement, it certainly came as news to me that my involvement in the struggle owed to a mix of personal pathology and social disorganization.
>
> (McAdam, 2003, 282)

We saw in the previous chapter, however, that decoding what is 'rational' and what is 'mad' is not a straightforward exercise. Blumer (1951
[1946]) highlights, for example, that the difference between the two is
socially constructed (i.e. the criteria for what counts as 'rational action'
and what does not is established by group norms), and that these change
over time (recall the 'mad women' of the feminist movement who later
turned out to be more sane than the rest of society). For these reasons,
it is necessary to be clear about what 'rationality' is supposed to mean
according to rational action theorists; especially as they claim that it
is *universal* rather than in flux. To do this, let us consider the passage
below which outlines the key elements of the theory of rational action:

> Consider yourself an individual who knows what you want before you
> enter into any situation of decision-making. When in such a situation,
> aim at establishing cognitive control over it; that is, provide yourself with
> as complete information as is available (or as much as you can afford).
> Systematically relate the information gathered to your preferences.
> Design strategies to see which preferences you can satisfy and to what
> degree. Weigh up your preferences, that is, make them comparable, so
> that you can establish a hierarchy of strategies. Decide.
>
> (Wagner, 2001, 24)

From the statement above, we can see that, first, it is assumed that
human beings are *individual* decision-makers ('consider yourself an
individual...'). Secondly, they are pretty knowledgeable about the
world in which they make decisions ('provide yourself with as complete
information as is available'). Thirdly, they have *preferences* (desires or
goals), and these are *pre-given* ('knows what you want before entering any situation'). Fourthly, individuals *strategize* in order to pursue
their preferences ('design strategies to see which preferences you can
satisfy... establish a hierarchy of strategies'). Fifthly, by weighing up
which strategies best satisfy their preferences, they are able to *make a
decision* about how to act in any given situation ('Decide').

What kind of rationality is implied by this picture of human action?
Rationality appears to be exercised by individuals in relative *isolation*
from others (they make decisions on their own) and in a consciously
calculative way (they weigh up all the options). The rational individual
is *self-orientated* (they act to satisfy their own preferences), and *strategic*
(they consciously design the best way to get what they want). This kind
of rationality is best described as 'instrumental rationality', which can

be defined as finding the most 'effective' means to an end. In order to determine what an 'effective' means to an end is, rational actors must weight up the *costs* and *benefits* associated with the different options. They are concerned with choosing strategies that bring the most benefits while incurring the least costs. It is 'rational', for example, only to incur costs if it helps you to get what you want. Subsequently, the decisions of a rational individual will always lead to actions that are personally worth their while, in other words, they are 'self-interested'.

This model of human action has been very popular in the social sciences, especially within economics, and is referred to as 'rational man' (Elster, 1989; Hollis, 1994). It has also gained currency in society at large, where assumptions of rational action operate in all sorts of everyday contexts. When it comes to elections, for example, politicians in democratic societies approach citizens *as if* they are rational actors who weigh up the costs and benefits of the different policy packages on offer and choose the party that will satisfy them the most. Rational action theorists claim that assuming people act *as if* they are rational actors, and knowing their preferences (what they want out of a situation), helps to predict what they will do.

There is also a further factor to consider, however, which brings us back to the opening point about the importance of *resources*. In order to predict accurately we also need to know the *resources* that a person starts out with. Without this information, we cannot properly assess the costs for them – costs of time are not so important if you have all the time in the world, and financial costs are not so important if you are loaded. Once we know preferences and costs we can pretty much *predict* what choices people will make and how changing the incentives or costs of action will affect their decision. RAT therefore tells us two things: first, that individual action is self-interested in the sense that people pursue their preferences in ways that maximize their benefits and minimize their costs; and, secondly, that their decisions about how to act will be affected by the changing costs and benefits in the wider environment.

Protest and social movements as 'rational action'

Both of these assumptions were incorporated into resource mobilization theories of protest and social movements. Writers like Oberschall (1973), Tilly (1978), and McAdam (1982) argue that an individual's preferences arise from their 'interests' (whether these be material, political, or moral in nature) and that they act instrumentally in order to further them (i.e. they choose the most effective means to their ends). Individuals who share a similar position in the social structure of a society (like a class position) come to share interests in common and therefore share preferences which can give rise to concrete political goals. Participating in protest and social movements is the most effective means of pursuing these goals when it is not possible to gain success by conventional political means (e.g. voting for a different leader, petitioning your MP). Social movements are therefore conceptualized and defined as the organized, rational pursuit of shared interests (Oberschall, 1973). In this conceptualization, we have come some way from the irrational, emotional image of CB.

Within this framework, both individual participants and social movements are viewed as 'rational actors'. Marwell and Oliver (1993) argue that whilst the assumption of rational action does not help to explain all types of action, it works particularly well when thinking about social movements. Both protesters and social movements are *forced* to be instrumental in their action because they have scarce resources (i.e. limited amounts of money, time, energy, and so forth) (Marwell and Oliver, 1993, 11). As social movements operate outside the conventional political system, resources can be especially scarce, and costs (like repression) especially high (Oberschall, 1973). Social movements must strategize in order to maximize the benefits they can achieve using their very limited resources. They want to spend as little of their precious resources as possible for the greatest return. Mobilizing resources and utilizing them effectively (through organization, tactics, and strategy) therefore becomes central to social movement success.

The 'collective action problem'

Social movements, then, can be thought of as a form of 'collective action' which is defined as the pursuit of shared interests. This much is fairly uncontroversial. What is controversial, however, is how to understand the process by which individuals who share interests in common come to act collectively to pursue them. One assumption that we might be tempted to make using RAT is that collective action will happen when individual *self-interests* become recognized as the '*shared interests*' of a wider group, and so those individuals in that group act together to pursue them. This understanding of how collective action comes about is adopted by economic theorists of organizations. Indeed, an organization is defined as the pursuit of shared interests on the part of a group (Olson, 1965).

This understanding of how collective action comes about is fundamentally challenged, however, by a rational action theorist called Mancur Olson. Olson's book *The Logic of Collective Action* (1965) gives a very different reading of the situation, and throws a proverbial 'spanner in the works' with regards to the assumption that is made by other rational action theorists (and, Olson argues, by Karl Marx): that people who share interests in common will necessarily join together in collective action to pursue them. On the contrary, in a statement that was to yield a great deal of influence over social movement studies for decades to come, Olson said that:

> unless the number of individuals in a group is quite small, or unless there is coercion or some other special device to make individuals act in their common interest, *rational, self-interested individuals will not act to achieve their common or group interests.*
>
> (Olson, 1965, 2, my emphasis)

This creates a real quandary. Whilst we may have been unconvinced by CB theorists who cited *emotions* as the driving force of collective action, it seems that if we switch back to *reason* then no collective action should happen at all. Rational self-interest, suggested Olson, does *not* account for collective action. There needs to be some additional 'special device', as he puts it in the quote above, in order to compel rational individuals to act. This sounds somewhat counterintuitive with regards to RAT. If people pursue self-interests on their own, then why not adopt the same logic to argue that they pursue shared interests with others?

To answer this question we first need to consider the nature of collective action as opposed to individual action – or its peculiar 'logic' according to Olson. 'Collective action' is defined as action that is undertaken by two or more individuals in pursuit of 'collective goods' (Marwell and Oliver, 1993, 4). 'Goods' are a type of benefit gained through action. For individuals, their action can lead to the achievement of private goods – like money gained through paid work for example, which they are able to use for their own benefit (to pay their mortgage, buy food, go on holiday). Collective action however strives for different kind of goods, which are 'public' rather than 'private' in nature. To consider this difference between private and public goods let us consider a 'hypothetical scenario' involving a keen gardener.

In her own back garden, our gardener incurs the costs of planting, mowing, and weeding which are necessary to make the garden look good. These costs include giving up many weekends to work in the garden, paying for plants, and undertaking hard labour. In return, she gains a 'private' good – a beautiful garden that only she can see from her back window, and only she can sit in during sunny weather (unless she decides to invite you around). Now imagine that our gardener is doing exactly the same tasks, but not in her own back garden but in a park in the middle of our town. She invests the same resources, incurs the same costs, but now she has produced a 'public' good rather than a private one. The beautiful garden is shared with everyone in the town – they can look at it and sit in it even though they did not do any planting, weeding, or mowing themselves. This reflects the essential character of public goods: unlike a private good, a public good 'cannot feasibly be withheld from... others' who would find them beneficial (Olson, 1965, 14).

The question, then, is why our gardener – or anyone else for that matter – would volunteer to give up their time, energy, and money to produce a 'public good' for others' benefit when they could be at home producing 'private goods' for their own benefit? Surely any self-interested person would do the latter. Furthermore, doing the latter is even more attractive when people like our gardener exist, who will make the park look nice for me whilst I set up my deckchair and relax. This scenario, where rational self-interested individuals will not contribute towards the attainment of 'public goods' but will 'free ride' and let others do it instead, is known as the 'collective action problem'.

The collective action problem is a significant dilemma for social movements who pursue public goods as a matter of course. The example that Olson (1965) gives is the labour union. Labour unions are organizations established with the express purpose of pursuing the shared interests of workers in particular occupations. They engage in collective action around issues like pay, holidays, pensions, and working hours. However, because unions pursue 'public goods', workers will benefit from their actions whether or not they personally participate in campaigns. In the case of a strike for example, a worker who crossed the picket line and received their day's pay rather than going on strike, could not be prevented from benefitting from any advantages won through the strike.

Furthermore, it is hardly in the spirit of collective action to prevent benefits from being widely shared. British suffragette Emily Wilding Davidson threw herself in front of the King's horse in 1913 in the hope that *all women* would be given the right to vote, not just herself, or her fellow campaigners. Green activists campaigning for the protection of the environment and a reduction in pollutants strive for public goods which are to be enjoyed by everyone (give or take a few speculative builders and keen motorists). It is necessarily so – they would be hard pushed to keep a breathtaking countryside view, or cleaner air, just for themselves, and to do so, of course, would counter the *public* rather than private nature of their goals in the first place.

What this means is that a minority of people are putting all the effort in to achieving public goods for a great deal of others who are not contributing at all. In the case of social movements, the activists are always a minority of the overall population who will potentially benefit from their action, and they incur the financial, emotional, and personal costs for everyone else (including arrest, jail, loss of reputation, and even death). Collective action, it seems, necessarily involves a few people incurring the costs of participation, while a great deal more reap the benefits without breaking a sweat.

It is easy to understand the relevance of costs here. Joining the activists means incurring the costs on behalf of everyone else. Why would any sane person do this? You would have to be mad, surely, to simply volunteer to take on the costs (like a gardener who would *choose*, without some form of payment, to expend their time, energy and money making the town's park look good rather than their own back garden). What, however, if you thought that the *benefits* of contributing to collective action yourself would outweigh the costs? It could be said, for example, that I am prepared to incur the costs because I know that my contribution will help to secure a public good that I, and others, would not otherwise have. If I do not act then the public good is less likely to be achieved. I spend my weekends doing gardening in the park so that the community, and myself, can enjoy a beautiful park rather than a wasteland. This would certainly be a rational logic that could explain participation (Oliver, 1984).

However, Olson points out that most of the time it is very difficult for people to foresee that their small individual contribution will make any difference to the effort to secure a public good. I could spend an hour a day weeding in the park, but it would be very unlikely that anyone would even notice my efforts. The benefits, then, are minimal compared to the costs I incur. Marwell and Oliver (1993) argue that this comes down to individual feelings of 'efficacy' – namely the capacity people feel they have for affecting outcomes through their actions. Like an individual gardener faced with a big plot, it is difficult for an individual worker in a large union to see that their own small contribution would make any *extra* difference to the outcome of the strike. There would certainly be no immediate or measurable impact of their own individual contribution, unlike when you text in a vote for an act on the X-Factor and within hours see them kicked off, or retained. With no such obvious 'added' benefit of your own action, a person can only conclude that their participation would not make much overall difference, in other words it would be futile.

If we take the assumption of rationality to its simple conclusion, argued Olson, then rational, self-interested individuals will not participate in collective action to pursue their shared interests. They will put down their spade and sit back in the deckchair; pack up the placard and have an extra hour in bed. Even when a group shares interests in common, then, it is rational for them *not* to participate in collective action. This claim offers up quite a challenge for theorists of social movements, who have to abandon the idea that collective action *necessarily* arises from the existence of shared interests alone. It also creates a problem because the empirical evidence relating to the existence of social movements and other voluntary organizations attests to the fact that *some* people at least do participate in collective action to pursue their shared interests and provide 'collective goods'. Some people *do* incur the costs for everyone else. Why?

Participation in collective action

One way to answer this question would be to invoke factors like emotion and ideology – both of which Olson (1965) argues are 'irrational' sources of motivation. This is the route that we saw Blumer (1951 [1946]) pursue in Chapter 2, when he argued that emotional commitment was the key to explaining why people participate in social movements. The free-rider problem can be resolved by the feelings of solidarity that emotionally connect participants to one another and the group, making them willing to incur the costs on behalf of others. Olson disagreed with this, however. Not because he thinks that these factors are irrelevant, but because he thinks that they only explain a minority of cases (the ideologically driven 'fanatics' who are intent on self-sacrifice). For most people, and in most cases, however, emotional and ideological commitment is not enough to secure participation. Even governments, he argues, have to coerce us into contributing taxes to provide for public goods that we all value, like education and healthcare, and look at the vast ideological resources they have at their disposal. It is unlikely that social movements, with their comparatively miniscule resource base, would succeed where governments have failed. Instead, social movements have to appeal to people's rational side (not their emotional one). They have to find ways to make participation the outcome of a rational choice. Indeed, RMT scholars have written extensively about how social movements overcome the collective action problem by drawing upon, or creating, the conditions under which participation in a movement becomes attractive for rational actors. Three examples are discussed below.

(a) *Social sanctions*

One way to ensure participation in collective action would be to coerce rational individuals by removing free-riding as a possibility (Olson, 1965). Individuals can be coerced to participate through something like the union 'closed shop' that requires everyone in an occupation to join the union. Alternatively, interpersonal forms of coercion can be used, whereby non-contributors are subjected to social pressures and sanctions from others in the group (Oberschall, 1973). They may 'get a bad name' if they attempt to free-ride, or others may threaten to withdraw their friendship and favours. These social sanctions can only really work, however (argues Olson) in small groups where interpersonal, face-to-face contact is frequent, thus ensuring that pressures are exerted and sanctions enforced.

(b) *Selective incentives*

Many social movements are too large to employ social sanctions, however. Instead, they have to find ways to *coax* rational individuals into contributing, by offering added benefits which are 'private'. Olson calls these added private benefits 'selective incentives' (Olson, 1965, 133) which act as 'positive inducements' to participation because they are only gained through participation, and are not available to free-riders. The main incentive that participation in social movements offers is 'purposive' in nature: it promises people the opportunity to pursue and achieve their preferences for social change (Clark and Wilson, 1961). However, Zald and Ash (1966, 333) suggest that because this promise is often difficult to fulfil, social movements rely heavily upon 'secondary' incentives. These include 'material incentives', like getting paid to participate in collective action or receiving some insurance discount or membership rewards. Olson also argues, however, that 'people are sometimes also motivated by a desire to win prestige, respect, friendship, and other social and psychological objectives' (Olson, 1965, 60). These kinds of incentives arise from social interaction and are referred to as 'solidary incentives' (Wilson, 1973). They point to the personal pleasures gained from the social interactions involved in participation, like socializing, having fun, making friends, and feeling important. Rather than social sanctions then, they are social rewards. We can also add to these 'moral incentives' that come from engaging in action that an individual believes is the right and just thing to do (Wilson 1973; Jasper 1997).

(c) *The critical mass*

Unlike Olson, Marwell, and Oliver (1993) argue that coaxing rational actors to participate in collective action in large groups is not such a problem. Paradoxically, large groups are not an issue because they have more resources, and an increased likelihood that some people within the group will be committed enough to contribute to the provision of public goods (Marwell and Oliver, 1988). Essentially, this is all that collective action really requires – it does not need *everyone* who is affected to be involved, but a 'critical mass' of 'highly interested and resourceful actors' who are up for the challenge and can find and communicate with one another (Marwell and Oliver 1988, 1). Critical mass theory assumes that rational actors are *interdependent* rather than isolated decision-makers (Marwell and Oliver 1993, 9). A critical mass is formed when enough of the people in some pre-existing group (e.g. a workplace or friendship group) decide to participate in collective action. The more people who decide to take part, the stronger and more able the group looks to others, and they start to think that collective action could actually work. In this way, argue Marwell and Oliver, feelings of futility can be overcome. In other words, the sense of 'efficacy' that people experience increases as the number of contributors increases.

The three proposed solutions to the collective action problem (a–c) appear reasonable enough (although we will have much to challenge later in the chapter). One outstanding issue, however, as Roger Gould (2003) highlights, is abundantly clear: the solutions depend upon some form of collective action *already being in existence*. Some organization, or individual, who is already committed to the cause has got to exist because it is they who then 'coax' others into participation by providing sanctions, rewards, and incentives (Gould, 2003). Marwell and

Oliver's critical mass theory demonstrated, however, that once a 'social movement organization' (SMO) has reached a certain size, recruiting further rational actors should not be the problem. Instead, the problem that remains is the 'start up' costs of collective action in the first place, namely finding some well-resourced people who will invest in establishing an organization that others can join (Marwell and Oliver, 1988). This is perhaps essential when it comes to aggrieved populations who are poor and do not have the resources to launch their own struggle – they need an 'angel' to help them as Suzanne Staggenborg puts it (1988, 160). Who are these 'angels', and why do they choose to incur the start up costs of collective action?

External elites and movement entrepreneurs

One answer given by RMT is that the individuals who establish collective action in the first place are well-resourced and skilled 'movement entrepreneurs', powerful external elites, or wealthy sympathizers. The reason why they decide to soak up the start up costs is, first, because they have an abundance of resources so collective action is not so costly for them and, secondly, because they think that they can profit in the long run from collective action (personally, financially, or politically).

According to McCarthy and Zald (1977), 'movement entrepreneurs' act a lot like entrepreneurs in the business world – they spot a 'gap' in the market in terms of grievances that remain unresolved. Remaining in the language of business economics, they recast 'grievances' as 'preferences for change' or 'demand' in the population. Rather than springing up spontaneously from some societal crisis, protest is a business, and it 'ebbs and flows' as societal preferences change (Zald and Ash, 1966, 329). The emergence of a social movement is explained, then, as a response to a fluctuating market in preferences for social change. The term 'social movement' is used by RMT to refer to these preferences (McCarthy and Zald 1977, 1217). However, they draw an important distinction between 'social movements' (SMs) as preferences, and the SMOs which entrepreneurs establish in order to address them. This distinction (not unlike the one that Blumer made between general and specific social movements) is easy enough to grasp. Entrepreneurs have, for example, spotted a gap in the movements market over the last few decades for collective action around environmental issues. They have set up a number of SMOs like Greenpeace, Friends of the Earth, WWF, Earth First!, and so on in order to meet this demand.

Professional SMOs

The existence of movement entrepreneurs has given rise to an interesting trend in the nature of social movements according to McCarthy and Zald (1973; 1977). They suggest that American society in the 1970s was witnessing a growing trend in what they called 'professional' SMOs established by well-resourced movement entrepreneurs who were motivated to give up their present resources in order to profit later on from collective action. Professional social movements have particular characteristics. They are bureaucratic, have centralized decision-making structures, and are staffed by paid employees. They do not depend upon participation by the aggrieved population in order to campaign; in fact, their membership base is either non-existent or exists purely on paper. An example of a professional SMO is Greenpeace. You can sign up to be a member of Greenpeace, make a donation, and in return receive a newsletter, pen, T-Shirt, and the like, but they do not depend upon your active participation. Protest itself is also 'professionalized' as money is pumped into sophisticated advertising campaigns and the production of glossy pamphlets, and even celebrity endorsements (McCarthy and Zald, 1977, 1231).

Protest events as angry outbursts of frustration may not actually occur at all. Indeed, the passivity of members is expected rather than problematic. The people who are activists are following a professional career path and being paid a salary to fundraise and campaign *on behalf* of someone or something else. This could be a disadvantaged/vulnerable group in society (disability rights movements, domestic violence groups, children), groups who cannot protect themselves (pro-life, animal rights), or issues of public concern (environment, peace, drunk-driving). Increasingly therefore, social movements are bureaucratic organizations led by paid staff who engage in mobilizing resources so that they can pursue collective action on behalf of particular 'interest cleavages' in society.

Whilst it is important for SMOs to mobilize all types of supporters – from 'adherents' (believers in the cause who are important to public opinion), to 'constituents' (those who invest their resources), to 'cadre' (the hard core of activists who are highly committed and involved in decision-making), McCarthy and Zald argued that one group in particular – the 'conscience constituents' – were becoming increasingly important for collective action in America in the 1960s and 1970s (McCarthy and Zald 1973; 1977). 'Conscience constituents' are people who will not personally benefit from collective action, but who invest their disposable resources in the SMO anyway because they sympathize with the cause. In McCarthy and Zald's eyes, conscience constituents were becoming even more important than the aggrieved population for initial mobilization. It was the affluent middle classes they argued who supplied essential resources for the wave of heightened SMO activity in the 1960s. Together with a buoyant student movement that had time and energy at its disposal, these 'conscience constituents' provided the injection of resources to launch, lead, and maintain an array of 1960s SMOs (McCarthy and Zald, 1977, 1224). They were the 'angels' that aggrieved groups had been waiting for.

Debate point: is outside help essential for successful mobilization?

J. Craig Jenkins and Charles Perrow (1977) suggest that alliances with external elites are crucial for social movement mobilization and success. Their research wanted to find out why the 1960s became such a 'stormy period', as they put it, for political insurgency. In a study of farmworkers' protests, they show that before the 1960s, farmworkers' attempts to further their interests through campaigns of the National Farm Labor Union had largely failed. However, in the 1960s, through the group the United Farm Workers, they enjoyed relative success. What accounted for the upturn in their fortunes? First, they suggest that social problems and grievances are an insufficient explanation. Farmworkers experienced significant grievances in the decades before the 1960s. Grievances remained 'relatively constant' in fact. Secondly, tactics also remained the same. In both time periods the farmworkers used strikes and boycotts. Subsequently, they suggest that the farmworkers' success can be put down to an increase in resources in the 1960s, which came from middle-class liberal support organizations. In the 1960s, the government were divided over policies relating to farmworkers, and liberal groups became prepared to 'sponsor' farmworker protests because it was in their political interests at the time to forge an alliance and support their demands. They gave the farmworkers financial donations, and also supported their boycotts, thus enabling this tactic to become a successful one. Jenkins and Perrow concluded from their study that 'for several of the movements of the 1960s, it was the interjection of resources from outside, not sharp increases in discontent, that led to insurgent efforts' (Jenkins and Perrow, 1977, 226).

This argument about the need for external help in the mobilization process has, however, been heavily criticized by others within RMT, who have a different interpretation of how collective action is initially established. Doug McAdam (1982) argues that aggrieved groups do not have to rely upon an external injection of resources – either from external elites or movement entrepreneurs – because they possess a rich array of resources in indigenous social networks. Within communities, workplaces, associations, and friendship groups, for example, people have access to communications infrastructure, decision-making structures, leaders, and networks of trust and reciprocity (which are now popularly called 'social capital'). They also share a 'collective identity' which, together with dense networks between people, has been found to facilitate collective action (Tilly, 1978). What Aldon Morris (2000) calls 'agency-laden institutions' can therefore be a rich source of resources and 'ready-made' organization. Both Morris (1984) and McAdam (1982) point, for example, to the important role played by black churches in the civil rights movement in the US in the 1960s. The churches provided leaders and mobilized congregations. Oberschall (1973) therefore suggests that social movements are highly likely to form out of indigenous social networks. In short, groups that already exist are mobilized 'en mass' and transformed into a social movement – a process that Oberschall (1973) calls 'bloc recruitment'.

- Do groups who are resource-poor (e.g. lack money and political influence), rely upon outside help to mobilize? What about to achieve success?
- How might outside help be beneficial to an aggrieved population? How might it be counter-productive?
- In what ways can local communities provide resources for political mobilization?

The dynamics of social movement organizations (SMOs)

By whatever means SMOs get their initial injection of resources, they must continue to find ways to generate and increase them. RMT offers several concepts for thinking about the process of resource mobilization and the factors that shape its success, in particular the influence of cooperation and conflict between SMOs (Zald and Ash, 1966; McCarthy

Figure 3.1
Levels of social movement activity in a multi-organizational field.
Source: adapted from McCarthy and Zald (1977).

and Zald, 1977). In Chapter 4 we will consider how interactions with the government and authorities affect the mobilization process. In this section, however, we concentrate upon interactions between SMOs, countermovements, and the media. In doing so, we must not forget that SMOs also experience conflict within their own organizations too, and that factions and splits can have important outcomes for their success (Zald and Ash, 1966, 332).

One of the strengths of RMT's differentiation between 'social movements' as preferences for change, and 'SMOs' as the vehicles that engage in collective action, is that it acknowledges from the outset that more than one SMO can exist on the same issue (Zald and Ash, 1966). More often than not this is the case. Take the environment for example: there are several big organizations that campaign around environmental issues, and hundreds of smaller 'Green' groups at a local level. They have their differences when it comes to ideological outlook and tactics, but essentially the same issues – carbon emissions, deforestation, road and airport building, recycling, and so on – will be common fodder for their campaigns. McCarthy and Zald argue that all of the SMOs that exist on an issue form a 'social movement industry' (SMI). For example, all of the SMOs that campaign on environmental issues form an 'environmental SMI'. SMOs therefore operate in 'multi-organizational fields' (Curtis and Zurcher, 1973). Figure 3.1 above maps out the levels of social movement activity within this field.

If all the SMOs in an industry are able to work together on campaigns, then mobilization will be a less costly process. They can share the costs of planning, advertising, and conducting a campaign, they can pull together their various supporters to make donations and to turn out to events, and they can make bigger waves by producing one loud unified public voice. Such alliances are especially important for SMOs who, by necessity, operate outside formal politics, offering an 'alternative system of resources' that can compensate somewhat for a lack of institutional assistance (Rosenthal, 1985, 1052).

In many cases, however, SMOs within the same industry *compete* over resources rather than cooperate. Ideological divisions and tactical differences may be too much to overcome. Joseph Ibrahim's (2013) study of the British anti-capitalist movement points to such divisions between anarchist and socialist groups, which lead them to produce separate mobilizations around the same issues. This was evident in the 2005 protests against the meeting of the powerful 'Group of 8' nations (the 'G8') in Gleneagles, Scotland, where anarchist and socialist groups organized their own events. Both groups also argued that key resources had been diverted away from the 'real' campaign by what they saw as the co-opted, government sanctioned 'Make Poverty History' initiative, which included the Live8 music concerts organized by Bob Geldof and U2's Bono (Ibrahim, 2013).

Countermovements play a similar role in this respect. Countermovements are not rival groups within the same SMI, but movements that establish themselves in direct opposition to the goals of the SMO. Many SMOs give rise to a countermovement. Think of collective action around abortion for example. We have a 'Pro-Choice' movement that campaigns for legal access to abortion for all women as a matter of the mother's human rights, and a 'Pro-Life' movement that campaigns in direct opposition by arguing that abortion should be illegal and contravenes the human rights of the unborn child (Meyer and Staggenborg, 1996). It is likely as well that SMOs and countermovements have regular debates and stand-offs with one another and the result of this public war of words and deeds has a major impact on their mobilization potential. The case point illustrates this with an example of the 'resource deprivation' battle between Scientology and Anonymous. This case is important to engage with because it also raises questions about what kind of 'resources' are important to social movements in the age of the internet.

Case point: Scientology versus Anonymous

Michael Peckham (1998) studies the interaction between movements and countermovements, and the consequences for mobilization by looking at the battle between the Church of Scientology and the internet-based anti-censorship group, Anonymous. Peckham shows how the interaction between the two movements largely takes place on the internet, a space that Anonymous is keen to defend from Scientology's attempts at censoring adverse publicity. Peckham (1998, 320) argues that the interaction between the two movements is best cast as one of 'resource deprivation' – or 'damaging actions' – as each movement tries to discredit the other in order to diminish its resource base and increase the costs of mobilization. The key resource that the movements attempt to deprive one another of is the 'intangible' resource of 'public reputation'. Both Anonymous and Scientology try to discredit the reputation of the other in an attempt to deprive it of public legitimacy. Anonymous flooded the internet with highly critical stories about Scientology's treatment of ex-members, while Scientology used its huge PR machine to smear Anonymous in return. Each sought to create a negative environment in which the other lost participants, financial donations, and public support.

By looking at movement and countermovement interactions that take place on the internet, Peckham also raises important questions about what kind of 'resources' are necessary for mobilization in an 'information age'. He suggests that the internet changes the resource environment for social movements significantly. The internet has 'a levelling effect on resources' (Peckham, 1998, 321). It provides a low-cost way of communicating and coordinating activism that means that social movements do not require a big, formal organization behind them in order to mobilize effectively. In fact, the internet raises questions about whether SMOs need to exist 'offline' at all. Peckham (1998, 320) states that 'since access to the Internet is worldwide, an individual with free access through a community freenet can potentially compete with large, well-funded organizations'. The implications of Peckham's argument create a challenge to RMT's understanding of resources. RMT, Peckham suggests, should rework its traditional idea of resources (which include the tangible and intangible resources listed earlier in the chapter), to include 'virtual resources' (Peckham 1998, 320).Virtual resources cannot however just be 'added to the list' of potential resources because they also have the effect of making traditional resources, like money, staff, facilities, leadership, and so on, less important. Hara and Estrada (2005) support this by arguing that the internet provides resources like knowledge, credibility, interpersonal interaction, and identity support, which can improve or replace more traditional resources.

- Think of further examples of movements and countermovements. How do they go about depriving each other of resources?
- What kinds of resources do you think are most important to social movements today, and therefore most important for countermovements to attack?
- How does the internet change our understanding of resources and their importance for movement mobilization? Could a social movement mobilize entirely online and still be successful?

SMOs do not only have to compete over resources within their own industry, or with countermovements. They must also compete with other SMIs. The labour protest industry for example must compete with the peace industry, the feminist industry, the global protest industry, and so forth. Taken together, all of the SMIs in society make up a 'social movement sector' (SMS) (see figure 3.1), which again competes with other sectors – like the public, private, and charitable sectors – for people's disposal resources (McCarthy and Zald, 1977, 1224). This is an important point because it acknowledges that, in most cases, people have limited amounts of personal resources to invest in protest activities, and that participation in an SMO can be a great drain on finances, emotions, and time (Hirschman, 1982). This is the same with any activity we choose we do. If I am a serious member of the university hockey team, then a large amount of my time, money, and energy is invested in this one activity. There is not much left over for the volleyball team, or for going to gigs, or, presumably, for participation in any kind of SMO. Such is life. What it means is that people have to make decisions about where to spend their finite resources. One of the greatest challenges for the SMS as a whole is to find ways to compete with people's other public and private activities in order to mobilize their money, time, and energy for collective action. Once that battle has been won, it is still up to SMIs and SMOs to persuade people that they should devote their resources to one particular issue over another.

Public opinion and the media

To recruit support, SMOs need to positively influence people's perceptions of them and of the protest sector in general. This is especially important because the mass media tend to give protest and social movements short shrift – unless sensationalizing the more violent and confrontational aspects. How SMOs interact with the mass media can therefore have a significant impact on their ability to create a public voice, build alliances, save face, damage the reputation of a countermovement, or persuade people to participate. McCarthy and Zald (1973) consider the role of the media to have power even beyond this. If they are clever about it, the entrepreneurial leaders of SMOs can use the media to manipulate potential supporters and opponents. They can, for example, 'manufacture' grievances where they did not exist, or make grievances that do exist appear more widespread, intense, and urgent (McCarthy and Zald, 1973). They can manipulate the image that opponents have of the SMO, making the group and its support base seem stronger, more vocal, more active, than it actually is (thus putting pressure on opponents to concede demands). In this respect RMT seems to come close to suggesting that SMOs do not really need the aggrieved group at all – just a clever media strategy and PR campaign that can conjure up the perception of one.

Since McCarthy and Zald first wrote about resource mobilization in the 1970s, there have been advances in communications technology that fundamentally affect the role of the media and public communication within SMOs. New media have changed the nature of mobilization processes, the tactics available, and the costs involved. They have given rise to a growing sector of 'indymedia' (independent media) for example, enabling activists to film events as they happen on their mobile phone and upload them to YouTube, or narrate them on twitter (Juris, 2005a; Pickerill, 2007). The advent of mobile communications in particular has meant that activists rely less upon the mass media because they can create their own story (Castells et al., 2006). We will come back to the role of the mass media in Chapter 4, and new media in Chapter 6.

SMOs assessed

The idea of a social movement as an 'organization' much like a business organization that operates in a competitive environment with others, is a useful way to conceptualize certain kinds of social movements – especially those who adopt organizational structures that are much like other formal organizations. Viewing social movements as organizations does however throw up some challenges when thinking about what those organization look like.

First, social movement organizations certainly do not all fit with the picture of 'professional' SMOs forwarded by McCarthy and Zald. In fact, social movements are known to be extremely diverse in the organizational structures they adopt. Historically, they have ranged from highly centralized and bureaucratic, to decentralized, informal 'networks'. Some have had identifiable leaders who exert a great amount of control over the organization, and some have had many leaders, or even express a desire for no leaders (the anarchist ideal). The nature of social movement organization also seems to affect tactics, with fairly institutionalized and moderate activities like lobbying governments associated with formal organizational structures, and more radical direct action tactics associated with decentralized networks (Staggenborg, 1988, 599).

Secondly, there is little agreement in the literature about where SMOs fit into these extremes, or which would lead to the most success. On the one hand, William Gamson argued in the *Strategy of Social Protest* (1990 [1975]) that centralization and bureaucracy are positively correlated with SMO success, measured in terms of winning new advantages and enduring over time. Gerlach and Hine (1970), on the other hand, argue that movements with a decentralized, loose-knit 'network' structure are more successful because more adaptable to changing environments. Gerlach (1999) refers to environmental movements, for example, as having a 'polycentric' network structure in that they are 'many-headed' (they have no leaders). Gerlach (1999) argues that polycentric networks are more flexible and adaptable compared to bureaucratic structures and harder for authorities to repress (an argument that will arise again in Chapter 6 on the structure of global social movements). It is also the case that some movements shirk away from establishing formal organizations on purpose. The environmental group 'Critical Mass' for instance, uses spontaneity as a tactic for success. They create 'flash mobs' (instant crowds coordinated via mobile phones) (Rheingold, 2002) to organize protest events at the last minute – like mass cycle rides.

A further problem with the concept of a 'social movement organization' was raised in the case point, which looked at Scientology's online battle with the movement 'Anonymous'. This case raised questions about the continued importance of 'tangible' resources in particular (like facilities, offices, money, and so on) in the age of the internet. The internet has the effect of making protest a low-cost activity, providing individuals and small groups with the means to compete with large organizations. Jennifer Earl and Katrina Kimport (2011) therefore argue that the growth of internet based 'e-tactics' – which are low-cost and easily accessible – are making SMOs less relevant. Tactics, like online petitions, for example, are particularly quick and easy to employ, and are often used by individuals who have no connection to SMOs (Earl and Kimport, 2011). This has led to an explosion of online protest around a whole range of issues relating to consumption, entertainment, and sport, for example. Earl and Kimport's (2011) point is that this new landscape of protest challenges RMT, which tends to assume a priori that protest is a 'high cost' activity, requiring extensive resources and organization to provide appropriate incentives for participation. Instead, low-cost forms of online protest, like e-petitions, are opening up a form of activism that is not in need of an SMO. We will return to the issue of individual forms of protest outside SMOs in Chapter 8.

Whilst 'professional social movements', as formal organizations, may have been a particular mode of organizing protest at a certain time in history (America of the 1960s and 1970s), and by a particular group of people (the affluent middle classes), we should be careful therefore about identifying all social movements with this organizational form (Jenkins, 1983), or in some estimations, any organizational form (Earl and Kimport, 2011). Raising a similar objection from a different angle, Piven and Cloward (1977), for example, criticize RMT for putting too much emphasis on resources and organization in the emergence of protest because poor people often do not have the resources required to establish a formal organization. Instead, they adopt a different mode of protest which involves spontaneous, disruptive tactics, including civil disobedience and riots. This argument finds parallels with James Scott's (1985) claim that protests by poor and powerless groups employ spontaneity as the best strategy for success. For Piven and Cloward (1977), not only are formal organizations overemphasized by RMT, but they are overrated as well. Picking up on themes first raised in Robert Michels's (1915) work about the inevitable tendency towards authoritarianism in organizations, they suggest that formal organization could actually be counterproductive for success. Once formally organized, social movements tend to become more conservative in outlook, more moderate in tactics, and more easily co-opted by elites, essentially because they become more interested in their own survival rather than the cause.

There is a further conceptual problem with the idea of social movement organizations. We can get hung up on debating the characteristics of an SMO's organizational structure, but RMT has already told us that several SMOs can arise around the same 'social movement' (i.e. the same preferences for change in the population). To identify a social movement in terms of a single SMO is therefore misleading. The boundaries are more complex than that. RMT has offered us in the very least a 'multi-organizational field' definition of a social movement (Curtis and Zurcher, 1973). It is not worth our while therefore trying to decide whether social movements are highly organized groups, or more decentralized informal networks, because they could actually contain both (Saunders, 2007).

Jo Freeman (1973) offers a useful example of this from the Women's Liberation Movement in the 1970s. Freeman argues that there were two branches to the movement which had quite different structures and styles. The 'older branch' consisted of formal organizations with democratic structures and clear leaders, like the National Organization of Women (NOW) which was at the core of the movement, and various legal, human rights, and professional organizations like Women's Equity Action League and Human Rights for Women. On the other hand, the 'younger branch' of the movement avoided formal organization. They did so quite deliberately. They thought that formal organizations and elected leaders led to confinement and lack of inclusivity, something many of the women who had been active in left-labour groups had experienced already for themselves. They therefore established small, local groups, often around pre-existing friendships, which seemingly lacked organization and coordination and did not want to identify leaders. These groups were linked by common newsletters and personnel, but otherwise 'did their own thing'. Within the same social movement therefore we find both highly organized, institutionalized SMOs, and informal, decentralized groups.

Social movements as 'networks'

The multi-organizational nature of a social movement has led to a re-conceptualization of social movements in contemporary social movement studies as 'social networks'. These social networks consist of the relationships between organizations and other actors who are engaged in collective action around a specific issue. This idea is captured in Mario Diani's definition of a social movement as:

> a network of informal interactions, between a plurality of individuals, groups or associations, engaged in a political or cultural conflict, on the basis of a shared collective identity.
>
> (Diani, 1992, 13)

This re-conceptualization is valuable for highlighting that the boundaries of a social movement are much fuzzier and harder to draw than the idea of social movement organizations suggested. For Diani (1992), the boundaries of the movement are really drawn by the existence of a 'collective identity'. Organizations can be considered part of a social movement not only because they interact with one another, but because they share a sense of what the issues are and why they are important (even if they disagree over the exact diagnosis of the situation or tactics). This idea of a social movement suggests that SMOs are not the only players in the field. Even individuals could be considered part of a social movement if they share in the collective identity. Clare Saunders (2007), for example, argues that individuals who choose to buy organic products could be considered part of environmental movement networks, even though their action takes place outside environmental SMOs. If we want to think about the structure and dynamics of social movement networks then we must move beyond SMOs and consider the pattern of alliances, conflict, and exchange that shape what a movement network looks like and how successfully it is able to mobilize resources.

Interpersonal ties

It is clear that relationships of cooperation and exchange between SMOs in a social movement network are underpinned by a more informal, interpersonal, network of ties between activists. Social networks of friendship and other kinds of association (like joint participation in non-movement-related activities) affect the formal pattern of relationships between SMOs (Edwards, 2014). For example, interpersonal social networks (e.g. of friendship and kin) often underlie recruitment to SMOs. Studies have found that personally knowing someone already involved in an SMO is one of the best predictors of participation (Snow et al., 1980; McAdam and Paulsen, 1993).

This produces a complex overlap between personal and organizational social networks, which has led some to argue that the network of relations between SMOs tends to 'map onto' pre-existing interpersonal networks between activists. Roger Gould's (1991) study of the Paris Commune 1871, for example, found that networks between organizations 'overlay and interact with pre-existing informal networks' such as family, friendship, and neighbourhood (Gould, 1991, 717). Thus, we cannot fully understand the pattern of organizational ties – in other words, the structure of the movement network – without appreciating the pattern of interpersonal ties that underlies it.

The interpersonal connections between activists are also of prime importance to a social movement when SMOs themselves cease to exist. Interpersonal social networks provide what Verta Taylor (1989) calls an 'abeyance structure' which keeps activists connected and in possession of a minimal resource base during times when SMOs are not active or have disappeared. These times are called periods of 'latency' for social movements, in which they are much less visible and not engaged in protest events. The feminist movement has been a prime example of how interpersonal networks between activists have enabled a social movement to reappear in successive waves of activism whilst never entirely disappearing in between. Investigating the recent wave of feminist organizing around LadyFest, Susan O'Shea (2013) shows, for example, how the key activists involved had met in the 1990s while organizing RiotGrrl, and some of them had been active in the previous wave of women's liberation in the 1970s. Interpersonal networks are important then, not just for underpinning organizational networks and keeping social movements alive in quiet times, but for supplying those more intangible resources that seem also to be crucial for collective action like connections between different generations (Mueller, 1994; Whittier, 1995) which supply collective memories of past struggle, as well as significant campaigning skill and know-how.

Analysing social movement networks

What mechanisms or dynamics shape social movement networks? We have already considered the idea that interpersonal networks are important. There are more likely to be ties between groups if activists know one another, for example because they are friends or because their memberships overlap (Rosenthal et al. 1985). What else shapes the structure and pattern of interactions in a social movement network? Diani tackles this question in relation to the environmental movement in Italy. Diani's (1990, 1995) research covers twenty ecology groups in Milan during 1984 and 1985, including (amongst others) the WWF, Italia Nostra, Green List, animal rights groups, the Environmental League, and autonomous grassroots groups. He gathered data on the activities of these groups and their exchanges with one another by interviewing their core members. Contrary to other studies, he did not find that personal social networks had a significant effect; instead, exchanges and alliances between environmental SMOs in Milan were shaped partly by ideological proximity (sharing a similar ideology when it comes to environmental issues), but predominantly by instrumental opportunities (taking the chance to gain benefits from the resources of other SMOs while incurring few costs).

Methods point: social network analysis (SNA)

If social movements can be conceptualized as 'networks', then what methods should we use to research them? Social movement scholars have become increasingly interested in a methodological technique called 'social network analysis' (SNA) in the past two decades (McAdam and Diani, 2003). SNA provides computer software tools for creating visual maps of social networks and analysing them (Wasserman and Faust, 1994; Scott, 2000). These visual maps are called sociograms, and you can see an example of one in figure 3.2. The sociogram consists of 'nodes' (the circles), which can be SMOs, or individuals for example, and the 'ties' between them (the lines), which can denote relations of information exchange, the sharing of resources, collaboration on a campaign, or overlapping memberships for example.

SNA software like UCINET (Borgatti et al., 2002) can be used to create visualizations like the one shown. In the sociogram depicted, the nodes are sized by 'degree centrality', namely how many connections they have to other nodes in the network. Most networks of course contain hundreds, even thousands,

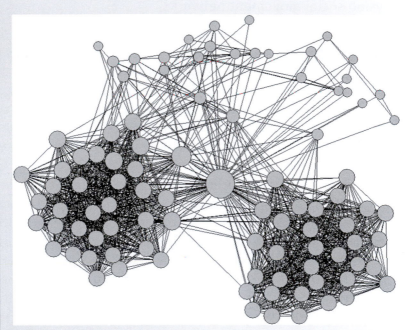

Figure 3.2
An example of a sociogram.

of nodes and their properties can only be analysed using network measures. Basic network measures include 'centrality measures' (Bonacich, 1987) to see who is most central to the network, either in terms of having the most ties to others, or acting as a 'bridge' that connects others. Network centralization measures also tell you whether a network is heavily centralized around particular nodes, which can be useful for determining if one SMO dominates a movement network. 'Density measures' can be used to measure how dense the network is in terms of the proportion of ties that exist in relation to the possible number that could exist. Procedures can be employed to identify subgroups or cliques within the network. These are dense patches where all the nodes are connected to one another. Marginal or isolated nodes can also be highlighted, as well as analysing which nodes are in the network's core and which in the periphery. These network measures (along with many more than you can pursue in UCINET) can provide an important insight into the structure of social movement networks. They can help in understanding the interactions that take place between SMOs and individuals, including alliances, coalitions, factions, splits, and overlapping memberships. They can help us to think about leadership roles in social movements, and identify key players in movement networks (Stevenson and Crossley, 2014).

SNA is not only useful for taking what Saunders (2007) calls a 'relational approach' to movement networks by mapping the actual relationships between SMOs. It can also be used to conduct a 'structural' analysis of movement networks, employing a technique called 'block modelling' to identify groups within the network who share a similar profile of ties and therefore occupy a similar structural position in the network. Diani (1990, 1995) used this technique in his study of environmental movement networks in Italy. The debate between relational versus structural approaches should not be overstated, however. The two are not mutually exclusive, as demonstrated by Edwards and Crossley (2009) in a study of the personal network of a suffragette in which they both map actual relationships and run a block model procedure to help identify structurally similar groups within the network. While SNA offers useful tools, it can be difficult to interpret network maps and measures without a more qualitative understanding of the meaning and content of ties. A mixed-method approach to network analysis (see Edwards, 2010) is therefore preferred by many social movement scholars (Diani and McAdam, 2003).

Networks assessed: the relational logic of collective action

It is clear that the idea of social movements as 'networks' necessitates a 'relational' understanding of social movements. 'Relational' means that our analysis of social movements does not concentrate on the individual (their emotions, grievances, psychological state, and dispositions), neither does it focus on the organization (its structure, strategy, and attributes), but instead it focuses upon the relations between them. It is the pattern and structure of the relations between individuals and organizations that helps us to understand the emergence, trajectory, and dynamics of social movements. This relational approach was really there in truncated form within RMT, with its emphasis upon movements as 'multi-organizational fields' ridden with conflict and cooperation. The network approach makes this image concrete, and supplies methodological tools for analysing it (Diani and McAdam, 2003). It is clear therefore that while thinking of social movements as networks does not have to signal a whole new conceptualization of social movements because it is compatible with the RMT approach, it does however have several attractions as a separate way of conceptualizing social movements which improves upon what we have been offered by RMT (an argument forwarded by Diani, 2003).

I would argue that the idea of movements as networks takes us significantly further away from RMT however because it challenges its rational assumptions in fundamental ways. Whilst ideas of cost, benefit, and strategy are still applicable to the interactions that take place between SMOs in movement networks (as Diani's study showed), the importance of interpersonal networks in the process of mobilization highlights the limitations of rationalist ideas. It shows that far from being isolated decision-makers, human beings are actually socially embedded in relationships with others – and these relationships fundamentally shape the decisions that they make and the perceptions that they have of costs and benefits (Jasper, 1997).

RMT theorists were largely on board with this from the start. They never really imported the idea of an isolated rational actor into their theories of social movements. Oberschall (1973) had argued for example that RAT provided an 'undersocialized' view of the human agent, a point that sociological critiques of RAT have shown to be extremely convincing (Ferree, 1992; Crossley, 2002). The interdependence of rational actors was also made clear in Marwell and Oliver's 'critical mass' theory (Marwell and Oliver, 1993, 10). The concept of 'collective rationality' rather than individual rationality has therefore been preferred in social movement theory (Finkel et al., 1989). The rational actor was compromised from the start.

The embedded nature of social action does not, however, merely create a kind of 'game theory' – as rational action theorists describe it when actors have to consider the moves of others before they make their own (Gould, 2003). As Roger Gould (2003) argues, potential participants of collective action are not enacting poker moves on their family and friends so that they can find their way out of some prisoner's dilemmas. Instead, they are influenced by them – they talk and debate and form their views about what is right and wrong, what injustices in this world make them furious, and what they should and could do about it together. Social networks are not just structural patterns of ties; they are formed by ongoing processes of social interaction and communication that are culturally constituted (White, 1992; Mische, 2003, 2008). As Morris puts it (2000, 447), 'their cultural materials are constitutive in that they produce and solidify the trust, contacts, solidarity, rituals, meaning systems, and options of members'. Interpersonal social networks are important then not only, or even primarily, because they allow recruiters to activism to put in place sanctions and rewards, or because they supply a ready-made way to coordinate collective action, or because they provide resources that lower the costs of activism, but because they are the mechanisms through which people come to care about causes in the first place (call it 'grievance construction', or 'preference formation'), communicate this with others with whom they share their lives, and coordinate collective action with others whom they already understand, trust, and support. As Goodwin et al. argue (2001, 8) it is the 'affective bonds' involved in social networks that make them valuable for mobilization. Taking a relational approach to social movements does not sit happily alongside RMT, it takes us way beyond it. In doing so, it takes us back to issues of emotion and culture that the rationalist framework was so intent on pushing aside.

Let us pause to remember why RMT was so intent on pushing emotion, in particular, aside. CB had equated emotion with irrationality (Blumer, 1951 [1946]; Smelser, 1962). RMT did not so much tackle this assumption as side-step it. It too thought that being emotional meant that you were irrational, and so opted for RAT which would drop emotion from the picture altogether. We need to break however from the idea that acting out of emotion cannot also be rational (something Oberschall, 1995, 10, seems to agree with). For Olson, rationality really came down to the idea that people would not choose to pursue their ends in a way that would not work. He argued that to be irrational would be to choose an ineffective means to your end: 'a man who tried to hold back a flood with a pail would probably be considered more of a crank than a saint, even by those he was trying to help' (Olson 1965, 64). It is clear that protesters, more often than not, do fit his criteria of rationality: they are incurring the costs of activism themselves because they think that what they do matters, either to fulfilling goals, affecting outcomes, or on moral grounds (Jasper, 1997). This is why Olson's point that the perceived futility of collective action is often the biggest obstacle to participation is an accurate and useful one (Marwell and Oliver, 1993). Nevertheless, activists are not confined to instrumental considerations. They employ different 'logics of action' that sit alongside rational choice in any given situation.

Helena Flam (1990) offers us a useful way to think about this by suggesting that there are actually three logics of action: 'rational man' (whom we encountered at the beginning of the chapter), 'normative man' (whom we encountered in Blumer and Smelser's theories), and 'emotional man'. Emotional man is unfree (because constrained by cultural and emotional expectations), inconsistent (because our emotions are), cost-indifferent, and other-oriented. Flam argues that emotional man is a very appropriate model for thinking about collective action. In fact, it is necessary because in a 'context of interdependency' the rational logic is not sufficient for people to achieve their goals (Flam, 1990, 41). Emotional man does not create a collective action problem, but is the solution. Emotional attachments to others make emotional man naturally cooperative, *and* optimistic about the chances of success. Flam's models are ideal types of course, and in any situation all three logics of action are actually intertwined – people employ emotional, rational, and normative considerations together when they are deciding what they should do.

Summary

In this chapter we have traced a shift from a 'rational' understanding of social movements to a 'relational' one. The rational approach adopted by RMT concentrates our attention on the resources available for collective action, and the costs and benefits of participation. The key points of the approach are as follows:

- RMT offers an alternative to CB because it concentrates not on *why* social movements and protest happen, but *how* people – who are normally aggrieved about something – are able to successfully mobilize the tangible and intangible resources needed for a struggle.
- This question of 'mobilization' is underpinned by RAT. Individuals (and social movements) decide to mobilize when the benefits they can achieve outweigh the costs they will incur.
- Selective incentives given by a movement are therefore vital in shifting the balance of costs and benefits in favour of individual participation.

Importantly, RMT gives us a conceptualization of social movements that emphasized SMOs, and did the groundwork for a relational approach by looking at the interactions of cooperation and conflict between SMOs. This pointed our attention to a range of important factors that had been completely ignored in CB, like the role played by external elites, indigenous social networks, countermovements, 'virtual' resources, and the media.

We found that it was very difficult therefore to think about social movements in terms of 'discrete' organizations. Not only is there some compelling evidence to suggest that not all forms of protest are – or strive to be – 'organized' in the sense used by RMT, but SMOs have also historically taken different forms. By focusing heavily upon formally organized 'professional SMOs' who tend to use more institutionalized tactics, RMT is in danger of 'normalizing protest', as Piven and Cloward (1992) put it, or in other words, making all protest and social movements seem as if they are highly institutionalized and routine organizations much like pressure groups. They subsequently ignore the more spontaneous, disruptive, and sometimes violent modes of protest adopted by groups, and in contexts that are not the affluent middle class in America of the 1960s (and which we will encounter later in the book). To be fair to RMT, McCarthy and Zald always called it a 'partial theory' for these very reasons (McCarthy and Zald, 1977; 2002).

I have suggested therefore that it is not worth our while trying to pin down the organizational forms of social movements to either centralized bureaucracies or decentralized networks, or institutionalized or non-institutionalized tactics. This is because social movements are better thought of as 'networks' of organizations and other actors who cooperate on collective action campaigns and share a collective identity (Diani, 1992, 13). This re-conceptualization of social movements as 'networks' has been beneficial in making concrete the idea that movements involve interactions of cooperation and conflict between different groups, and also that these patterns of interaction are often rooted in, and shaped by, interpersonal social networks amongst activists. It has also led to the development of new methodological tools for analysing social movements, and SNA offers both structural and relational ways to think about movement networks. More is still to be done however on developing these techniques, and on specifying the 'mechanisms' that produce the patterns that we observe in movement networks (McAdam, 2003). Otherwise, as James Kitts (2000) argues, despite all the importance we attach to networks, the explanations we have of exactly why they are important remain 'black boxes'.

Thinking about networks has brought home the embedded nature of social action. This has three critical consequences for a rationalist approach:

- Social networks are more than structures for the exchange of resources. They are also cultural, emotional, and communicative relationships between human beings.
- Social networks are beneficial to mobilization in a number of ways, but they also force us to reconsider what 'rationality' means in a context of interdependence.

- A relational approach to social movements requires us to adopt a different 'logic of collective action' – or at the very least to acknowledge that rational, normative, and emotional logics are combined in any action.

Activists do not think that they are 'trying to hold back a flood with a pail', even if some onlookers do. Nevertheless, human beings, whether engaged in activism or not, are 'much more than rational actors' (D. Gould, 2004, 173). In the next chapter we will unpack these cultural and emotional dynamics of collective action further, whilst also considering how the wider environment in which movement networks operate shapes their appearance and success.

DISCUSSION POINT

- What kind of resources do aggrieved groups need to have in order to launch a successful protest? Which ones are most important in your view? Does the internet mean that anyone can launch a protest today?
- What would it take to persuade you that participation in a protest event or social movement was worth your while? Do people make this decision with their heads or their hearts, do you think?
- Will the poor, or groups with few resources, ever protest without the help of others? Do you think that forging allies with external elites benefits or harms a group's chances of success?
- Does formal organization help or hinder protest?

FURTHER READING

Anthony Oberschall's *Social Conflict and Social Movements* (1973) is a good introduction to the rationalist approach, alongside McCarthy and Zald's classic paper 'Resource Mobilization and Social Movements' in the *American Journal of Sociology* 1977, 82(6): 1212–41. For a lively critique of RMT see Francis Fox Piven and Richard Cloward's *Poor People's Movements: Why they Succeed and How they Fail* (1977). The relational approach to social movements is comprehensively presented in Mario Diani and Doug McAdam's *Social Movements and Networks* (2003), while the emotions of protest are reconsidered in the edited collection by Jeff Goodwin et al., *Passionate Politics: Emotions and Social Movements* (2001).

4

From political processes to cultural processes: political opportunity, frames, and contentious politics

> Collective action is a dialectical process, a complex journey
> toward an imprecisely defined destination with side-trips
> and diversions, with opportunities seized or forgone,
> constraints avoided, surmounted or conceded in a series
> of more or less complex interactions with other actors
> encountered in its course.
>
> (Chris Rootes 1999, 12)

This chapter is concerned with the 'political process' approach to social movements which concentrates explicitly on the 'external environment' in which social movements operate, and gives this environment explanatory weight when it comes to accounting for why social movements emerge in certain places at certain times, and whether or not they have successful outcomes.

The approach is labelled 'political' process because the main writers have suggested that the most important aspects of the environment that movements face are *political* ones. In fact, the state and political institutions play a central role, it is argued, in the emergence and fortunes of social movements; a claim that we will critically evaluate in later chapters. In looking at how political process theory has studied the external environment of movements, we will encounter some central debates – not least the debate surrounding how to relate political structures and culture to social movement mobilization – that will require us to put our 'relational' thinking to work once again.

Like political processes themselves, political process theory has not stood still. Since its inception in the 1970s, it has gone through a number of important developments, often in response to the controversy it has generated. Two such developments will be examined here. First, in the mid 1990s, political process theory developed to embrace the 'cultural turn' that was brought to its door by social theory more generally and by scholars of social movements unhappy with what they saw as a 'structuralist' bias in the theory (McAdam et al., 1996; Goodwin and Jasper, 2004a). This will lead us into a heated debate between the so-called 'structuralists' and their counter-parts, the so-called 'cultural constructionists', that has placed an appropriate dose of ongoing contention at the core of contemporary debates. Secondly, since the turn of the twenty-first century, the main proponents of political process theory have offered an approach called 'contentious politics', which despite receiving a mixed reception, builds in important ways upon relational thinking (McAdam et al., 2001; Tilly and Tarrow, 2006).

By the end of the chapter you will understand why it is important to focus on the relationship between social movements and the world around them. You will be able to critically evaluate the concept of 'political opportunity structure' which is employed to understand this relationship. You should appreciate why the concept of cultural 'framing' is such an important complement to that of 'political opportunity', and be able to engage with the wider debates about culture that this has generated. You also will also be aware of the contentious politics agenda, and the status it has within social movement studies.

Political process theory (PPT)

In this chapter, we will be considering the work of three of the leading social movement theorists from the US: Charles Tilly (1929–2008), Doug McAdam, and Sidney Tarrow. At times, they have been referred to as 'structuralists' in their approach to social movements (although, as I will show, they are not unproblematically categorized as such). They have attracted this name because their extremely influential political process theory (PPT) places a great amount of explanatory power regarding the emergence and fate of social movements on the *external environment* and, moreover, its political components (like the state and political institutions). PPT suggests that political structures that exist prior to the ideas or actions of any one individual, and appear to them (revolutionary moments excepting) as relatively durable and unmovable, affect what social movements do and when and how they do it.

What is distinctive about PPT, compared to the other approaches we have looked at so far, is its claim – stated in strong terms by some, and much weaker terms by others – that social movements *rely* on the political environment being 'favourable' before they are able to mobilize or be successful. In the strong version of this claim, social movements *can only* arise and have successful outcomes if the political environment is favourable. In the weak version, social movements are *likely* to arise and have successful outcomes, *other factors depending*, if the political environment is favourable. I avoid placing names against these positions because it is true to say that whilst most people would associate PPT with some claim as to the centrality of the political environment in shaping movement fortunes, whenever the strong version of the case has been levelled at a PPT theorist they have denied that it is reflective of their position (Tarrow, 2004).

This denial is not without grounds – it is supported by the developments that have taken place in PPT in which its leading proponents have talked about factors other than the political environment that are crucial in addition to it. We will come to this work – and these other factors – in the next section. Let us for the moment remain with this strongly stated claim, even if it has 'straw man' tendencies (Goodwin and Jasper, 2004c, 76), in order to understand what is distinctive, and I would argue, particularly interesting about PPT as it was originally presented.

Critics of PPT have suggested that to claim that movements rely upon a favourable external context in order to thrive and succeed is, on the one hand, not 'big news' (Goodwin and Jasper, 2004c, 79) and, on the other, invites the kind of circular argument ('tautology') that was found in strain theory (Goodwin and Jasper, 2004b, 6; Opp, 2009, 169): if movements have mobilized or been successful, presumably we can link it back to some sort of favourable context, hence we look for one and find one. If they do not mobilize and they are not successful, presumably we can link it back to some sort of unfavourable context, hence we look for one and find one. The claim does not seem to offer much analytic purchase if that is what it is saying.

PPT is, however, more interesting in its claims than that. There is no necessary reason – again as critics have pointed out – to assume that social movements *do* rely upon a favourable context. In line with the arguments of the first two chapters, perhaps the psychological strains experienced by activists, or their organizational capacity and connections, compensate for and overcome an unfavourable context. In this case, the wider political environment would not crucially matter, or only have a tempering effect on movement fortunes.

This, however, is not the case according to PPT. Their main claim is that activists can be as angry and aggrieved, as well-organized, tactically astute, and brilliantly led as they like, but without a favourable political context they will get nowhere (Tarrow 1998; Koopmans, 1999, 100). This is, in fact, where PPT diverges from the resource mobilization theory (RMT) of the last chapter and with which it shares overlaps (like, for instance, some commitment to rational action theory (RAT)). PPT argues that RMT puts too much store by the internal factors of social movements and fails to properly probe what Tilly calls 'the world around' them (1978, 55). The debate point below presents the differing viewpoints of mobilization theory and PPT as expressed in a classic debate between William Gamson and Jack Goldstone.

Debate point: Gamson versus Goldstone

In the *Strategy of Social Protest* (1990 [1975]), William Gamson studied fifty-three protest groups in the US (between 1800 and 1945). Using quantitative methods, Gamson examined the factors that were correlated with social movement success. He measured success in two ways: winning new advantages and becoming a legitimate feature of the political landscape. On the basis of his findings, Gamson argued that movement organizations that were bureaucratic and centralized had the most success. The implications of the study were to suggest that if social movement organizations (SMOs) adopted the right strategy they had a better chance of achieving their goals. Gamson's data was contested by Jack Goldstone, leading to a well-known debate in social movement studies (Goldstone, 1980; Gamson 1980; Frey et al. 1992). Gamson had made his dataset available for re-analysis, and so Goldstone conducted his own statistical analyses and came to very different conclusions. Goldstone found that SMO success was correlated to national political or economic crises. New advantages were won not because of the organizational form of the SMO, but because crises created favourable external conditions. These favourable conditions for collective action were created because crises weakened the political system and provided new openings for demands to be heard. Goldstone suggested that if an SMO could hold out until a time of crisis – like a war or economic depression – then they had a good chance of winning new advantages. Bureaucratic structures only help to ensure success indirectly by enabling groups to keep going until a crisis hits. The implications of Goldstone's argument were to suggest that there is little that SMOs and their leaders can do strategically to make success more likely. This was the part of Goldstone's critique that

Gamson found particularly hard to swallow. In a response to Goldstone, he suggested that they had very different perspectives on social movements and that he preferred to concentrate upon the *internal* factors of SMOs and the things that leaders *could control*, like organization and tactics. He claimed that he had not dismissed the importance of external crises in his statistical analysis of the data, but that he had preferred to think of a crisis as an *opportunity* which had implications for the strategy of the protest group.

- In what ways can we measure social movement success?
- What is the difference between a 'crisis' and an 'opportunity'?
- Does social movement success depend upon internal factors (leadership, organization, skill), or external factors?

PPT, therefore, does make an interesting claim that it is worth considering: do social movements *rely* upon favourable conditions in the world around them in order to emerge and be successful? Do they rely, most importantly, upon the *political* world around them being favourable? Do political *structures* explain the 'ebbs and flows' of social movements the best? Let us begin to address these questions.

A world of political opportunity (and threat)

What does PPT mean by a 'favourable' context for collective action? By 'favourable context' they mean a context in which the environment provides potential challengers with what they label 'political opportunities' for action (Tarrow, 1998). In the Gamson versus Goldstone debate, Gamson (1980) argued that he did take into account the external environment of social movements, but unlike Goldstone (1980) who liked to talk of 'crisis' and 'breakdown' creating the favourable conditions for social movements, he preferred to talk of such things as creating 'opportunities' for action. The idea of an 'opportunity' therefore, implicitly at least, relates what is going on in the world around a social movement to the strategic response that activists themselves construct (Gamson, 1980). The language of opportunity, as Steven Buechler (2004) suggests, puts a positive spin on the more negative language of 'breakdown' that was found in strain theory, and turns things that happen in 'the world around' the movement into the very stuff of *chances* to be seized (Koopmans, 2004).

A political environment becomes favourable for collective action, then, when it presents cues to challengers that suggest that the 'time is right' (and ripe) for a challenge (McAdam, 1982). What is seemingly so crucial then about a political opportunity is that it affects the calculations that rational actors (as PPT primarily sees them) make of the costs and likely success of collective action, or – recast as Flam's emotional actors (that I preferred to talk about in the last chapter) – affect their levels of fear, anxiety, excitement, and anticipation about what is happening and what could happen. I should also mention here that alongside political opportunities, PPT has also talked about the political *threats* to a group's interests as important parts of the external environment (see van Dyke and Soule, 2002; Almeida, 2009). Although discussed much less often in the literature (McAdam, 2004), a conducive political context for collective action is also, ironically, one which threatens potential challengers' interests to the point that they adopt a 'do or die' attitude (Goldstone and Tilly, 2001). Tilly (1978, 55) therefore describes the 'world around' a social movement as one which 'sometimes threaten the group's interests...sometimes provide new chances to act on those interests'.

The centrality of the nation state

But why does PPT claim that the most important opportunities and threats for collective action are those related to the *political world* around the social movement? Tilly and Tarrow argue that social movements as we know them today emerged hand in hand with specifically *political processes*, namely the rise of the modern democratic nation state from the eighteenth century onwards (Tilly and Tarrow, 2006). They became the popular vehicles through which ordinary people engaged in various forms of political 'claim-making' in which the state was their direct target. Democratization goes hand in hand with social movements, which have become the accepted way in which citizens make claims on democratic governments. This kind of approach is particularly relevant for an important set of social movements termed 'citizenship movements' (Jasper, 1997; Goodwin and Jasper, 2004b).

Citizenship movements target the nation state explicitly with their demands for political rights and inclusion. Think, for example, of working class and female suffrage movements, the American civil rights movement, movements seeking legal reforms and changes to state policy (like pro and anti-abortion movements), movements campaigning for the extension or retraction of state intervention (like welfare movements), and movements demanding political forms of recognition (gender, sexuality, ethnicity, disability, and so on). In fact, the steadily growing number of social movements making claims upon democratic institutions means that in Western liberal societies at least, we live in a 'social movement society' (Meyer and Tarrow, 1998), and as democratization spreads across the globe, even perhaps, 'a social movement world' (Goldstone, 2004).

Political opportunity structure

We know now why PPT talks about the world around a social movement as a world of opportunity that is primarily political in nature. But where exactly do 'political opportunities' come from? PPT's answer is that political opportunities are embedded in the political structures of a regime. For example, routine elections in liberal democratic regimes may offer chances for collective action, and regimes in which the executive and the legislative functions of the state are distinct offer more opportunities for influence. Political opportunities can also arise from shifting alignments and divisions among political elites. For example, we came across Jenkins and Perrow's (1977) farmworkers study in Chapter 3, which showed how political divisions gave rise to a new alignment of interests between farmworkers and the middle-class liberal elite who backed their boycott and enabled a successful outcome for the Union. Chances for political influence are therefore structured in different ways according to the type of political regime that exists, and this regime provides activists with what PPT calls a 'political opportunity structure'. Tarrow and Tilly define the 'political opportunity structure' as a concept that points to:

> features of regimes and institutions that facilitate or inhibit a political actor's collective action and to changes in those features.
>
> (Tarrow and Tilly, 2009, 440)

Peter Eisinger (1973) is credited with the first use of the term. Political regimes offer what Eisinger calls an 'open' political opportunity structure when they are representative and responsive to citizen demands, and offer a 'closed' political opportunity structure when they exclude citizens, are unresponsive to their demands, and in extreme cases do not tolerate protest at all and use force to repress it.

To consider this point further, think about the political regimes that exist in different countries and the opportunities for political influence that they offer. Liberal democracies (under whose label we might include countries like the United States, UK, France, Spain, Italy, Germany, Sweden, Switzerland, Netherlands, and Australia) ensure that people have *at least* some opportunity to influence the political system through elections, where they choose between different political parties who compete for their vote. The party elected to government 'represents' the people – albeit sometimes only in theory – but in cases where they stray too far from what the electorate want there are accepted forms of redress that can be used to hold them to account. Street demonstrations are one such form, as we saw in 2003 when decisions to go to war with Iraq were met with mass protests in which people exclaimed 'not in my name'.

We might therefore describe the political opportunity structure of a liberal democratic country as in many ways 'open', although when compared to each other we might describe some countries as more 'open' or 'closed' than others. Kitschelt's (1986) cross-national study of anti-nuclear movements in Western democracies suggested that, comparatively speaking, the German and French systems were 'closed' because they denied the movement formal representation and were not responsive to its demands, whilst Sweden and the United States were 'open' because they allowed anti-nuclear activists political access and influence.

In contrast to liberal democracies, non-democratic, authoritarian and semi-authoritarian political regimes (under whose label we might include countries like Russia, China, Cuba, Syria, Vietnam, Somalia, Saudi Arabia, Iran, North Korea, and Jordan) could be described as offering more of a 'closed' structure of political opportunities. People do not have a chance to influence the political system through elections in which they choose between political parties. Instead, authoritarian regimes tend to have only one party (e.g. the Communist Party in China). The party may appoint itself to power or may rule on the basis of less-than-transparent elections (recall the election scandal in Iran in 2009). As a consequence, political power is centralized in the hands of few politicians, or a single leader (sometimes a dictator) who is not accountable to a constitution, a parliament, or an electorate (think of Libya under Gaddafı). They do not have to respond to people's demands, and may not tolerate demands even being aired. Power is maintained through using repressive force, like a state military and police force, which can crush collective action attempts (think of the bloodshed following the Syrian protests in 2012). Again, in comparison to each other, we might argue that some of these countries provide a more 'open' or 'closed' political opportunity structure.

Whilst the structures of the political regime in place provide differing opportunities for collective action, PPT also highlights the way in which the political interactions and choices taking place within the regime affect political opportunities. These opportunities are not so much stable features of political structures, but arise from contingent and quickly changing circumstances. Tarrow (1998) identifies four contingent circumstances in which political opportunities can arise:

- the opening up of access to the polity to new challengers
- elite realignments
- elite divisions
- changes in the capacity and propensity to use repression against challengers.

The work of Kriesi et al. (1992) highlights the second and fourth of these. They found that when in opposition, left parties like the Social Democrats were influential allies for many of the 'new social movements' of the 1980s because they wanted to bolster opposition and weaken the party in power. However, when in power, left parties paved the way for a decline in new social movement (NSM) activity as chances for reform improved anyway. Kriesi et al. (1992) also talk about the prevailing strategy of the state towards challengers. They found that France adopted an 'exclusive' strategy towards NSM challengers in the 1980s (in both formal and informal ways) and were highly repressive of protest. This led to rare but large-scale and violent outbursts of protest. Switzerland, on the other hand, adopted a 'facilitative' strategy, including NSM challengers through direct democracy. With the Swiss state not actually in a position to implement reforms however, moderate protest was a continuous feature in Switzerland.

Bringing the factors discussed so far together, Tarrow and Tilly (2009, 440) compile a list six 'properties' of political regimes that shape the political opportunity structure (see figure 4.1).

Figure 4.1
Elements of the political opportunity structure.
Source: Tarrow and Tilly (2009), p. 440; phrasing is theirs.

Before we move on to a critical assessment of PPT, it should also be noted that Tarrow (1998) argues social movements can themselves be central to altering the political opportunity structure. He suggests that the 'early risers' (the social movements that come first and take advantage of a political opportunity) alter the opportunity structure for those who come next (Tarrow, 1998, 87). They do this by weakening political authority and providing some 'generalized' resources for mobilization (like a model of collective action for others to copy, and attention from the public and media). They can highlight where the weak points are in the political system for others to take advantage of, or they may create them themselves, thereby opening the floodgates to other challengers. This leads to an intense period of contention in society, which Tarrow (1998, 87) calls a 'cycle' or 'wave' of contention. 'Cycles of contention' are heightened periods of social conflict with a start point and an end point (Jung, 2010, 27). We could think here of the cycle of contention in the 1960s, which saw a proliferation of social movements – from the American civil rights movement, to students, women and gay liberation movements, and anti-war movements. Tarrow's argument is that the political opportunities created by changes in the political system are really only of crucial importance to movements at the beginning of a cycle; after that, opportunities for protest in society become 'generalized' for a time, and others can take advantage of them. Jung (2010) supports this by claiming that political opportunities are only important during the initial phase of mobilization, while internal factors (like institutionalization and radicalization) explain movement decline.

It is clear from this discussion that the main tool used to mine the world around a social movement in PPT is that of 'political opportunity structure', made up of the structural and shifting components reflected in Tarrow and Tilly's (2009) list in figure 4.1. An important question regarding our approach to social movements is stirred by this concept: does it imply that we can read the emergence and fate of social movements from the political structures in the world around it? This would be a 'structuralist' explanation indeed. I argue however that this is neither accurate as an explanation of social movements, nor as a reflection of the claims and intentions of much PPT (Tilly, 2004, 34; Tarrow, 2004, 43; Meyer, 2004a, 55; Koopmans, 2004, 68).

PPT assessed

What kind of approach would argue that the choices that social movements make about when to act can be 'read off' of the political structures that constitute the world around them, such that social movements are like 'puppets on a string'? To argue this, we would have to employ the concept of 'political opportunity structure' and use it to determine how 'open' or 'closed' a polity was to political influence by studying its fixed political institutional arrangements. To determine the effect that these arrangements have on activists' choices, we would also need a fixed idea of whether closed or open political opportunity structures lead to collective action – or successful collective action – in all cases.

There is a problem with such fixed notions of political opportunity and their effects, however. Deciding whether the political opportunity structure of a nation (or region) is 'open' or 'closed' does not tell us 'for what or for who' (Meyer, 2004a). It may tell us some very general characteristics of the political regime, but not very much about the potential for a specific movement around a specific issue at a specific time. A movement that, say, campaigns for the environment in modern

America may find the political opportunity structure fairly open, whilst a movement campaigning for abortion may find the same structure fairly closed. This is also likely to vary across states, and across time. The point is that to read action from structure, we would have to assume that the 'political opportunity structure' could be, first, pinned down and, secondly, could be said to have deterministic and uniform effects. If we cannot make these assumptions then we have a lot more studying to do before understanding how political structures relate to people's action.

Most PPT scholars would agree with this, however. Koopmans (2004) and Meyer (2004a) contend that no one in the PPT tradition actually makes such general and universal claims about the political opportunity structure or its effects. Any argument that they did has been well and truly gazumped by McAdam, Tilly and Tarrow's more recent moves away from what they call 'invariant models' of political opportunity (McAdam et al., 2001; Tilly and Tarrow, 2006; McAdam and Tarrow, 2011) and towards more contextual understandings. Rather than fixed political structures, most PPT scholars talk about the shifting aspects of political opportunities, and there is extensive discussion about the multiple and sometimes contradictory effects that factors – like state repression for example – can have on mobilization (Koopmans, 1997; Carey, 2006). Political opportunities are, in Sidney Tarrow's (1998, 89) words, 'fickle friends', which come and go, sometimes in a flash. Rather than 'windows that are either open or closed', political opportunities refer to windows that are expanding and contracting according to specific situations that arise (Goodwin and Jasper, 2004b, 12). By approaching political opportunities in this way, PPT demands a much more situation-specific understanding of them. Political opportunities structures cannot be read from political regimes, but must be studied in relation to specific circumstances.

Estellés (2011), for example, includes the 3/11 Madrid terrorist attack in the 'political opportunity structure' of the anti-war movement in Spain in 2004. The media criticism of the government response to the attacks created mass public support and provided a 'political opportunity' for the anti-war movement to succeed in its aim of getting Spanish troops to withdraw from Iraq (Estellés, 2011). What a 'political opportunity' is, therefore, depends upon the case in hand. Whilst this removes the criticism of over-generalization, however, it also renders the concept of political opportunities rather vague. Political opportunities are what you label the favourable aspects of the external environment for the movement you are looking at, but presumably when it comes to this, everyone has their own list, and the factors involved are growing fast (Koopmans, 1999, 102). Gone is the ability to produce a list of six factors that constitute 'political opportunity' (Koopmans, 2004, 70). Karl-Dieter Opp (2009, 174) suggests that this should be the case since dimensions of the political opportunity structure should not be decided by 'a priori' lists but by empirical research.

Does the inability to create a list of the various dimensions of 'political opportunity' matter? Perhaps political opportunities are varied and the lists of factors involved as long as your arm. Perhaps they can only be deduced from the specific situations of the case in hand. If this is so, however, then some critics have argued that it is not properly accurate to link political opportunities to political 'structures'. Remember that structures exist prior to individual action and appear durable and immovable. Rootes (1999) suggests in response that PPT should narrow its agenda to these strictly structural aspects of the political environment – in other words, to the stable formal political system and its institutional arrangements. PPT should drop the other shifting, contingent, situation-specific factors from the picture. These are the result of strategic political *actions*, not political structures. With Rootes's (1999) solution, everyone would certainly know what was being talked about when 'political opportunity structure' is used, but because it remains at the general and abstract level of political regime type, there is a danger that no one would be able to do much with it. Clarity robs it of the sensitivity needed in analysis.

On the other hand, it is suggested PPT should embrace the fact that the political opportunities it is often most interested in are contingent upon strategic political action. Tarrow (1998) therefore seems to drop 'structure' from the picture to talk only of 'political opportunities' (Kurzman, 2004, 113) to ease the confusion of 'lumping', as Koopmans (2004) puts it, the structural and the shifting together. This approach has its weaknesses too, however. Critics argue that it leads to the concept being 'overstretched' (Goodwin and Jasper, 2004b, 27). As Gamson and Meyer (1996, 275) famously put it, the concept of political opportunity 'is in danger of becoming a sponge that soaks up virtually every aspect of the social movement environment'. This means that it ultimately loses its analytic utility, for if everything favourable about the world around a social movement can be labelled a 'political opportunity' then the concept becomes virtually meaningless (Gamson and Meyer, 1996, 275; Rootes, 1999; Goodwin and Jasper, 2004b). Retaining sensitivity therefore robs the concept of clarity. Political opportunity, I suggest, is caught in a conceptual Catch-22.

This leads, ironically, on to the another criticism of the political opportunity concept: it does not cover enough (it really cannot win it seems – McAdam, 1996). When scholars started to look at the aspects of the external environment that are favourable to social movement, they began to ask why there was such a concentration on political factors (Opp, 2009, 171). The world around the social movement is not just a world of political opportunity but a world of 'cultural opportunity' (McAdam, 1996; Koopmans, 1999), 'media opportunity' (Crossley, 2006), 'socio-economic opportunity' (Mees, 2004) and 'discursive opportunity' (Koopmans and Olzak, 2004; Giugni, 2011). If we include these then we have to get rid of not only the 'structure' bit of the concept, but the 'politics' bit as well. What we are left with then is simply a world of 'opportunity' (or threat, if anyone remembers that this was part of the original picture). Even 'opportunity' is, however, problematic.

Why so? Earlier, we saw that opportunities were thought to be important by PPT theorists because they affect the calculations (or emotions) of activists in a way that suggested to them that the 'time was right' (and ripe) for collective action. What does this really mean? Are opportunities to be seen as objective cues in the external environment that activists can seize hold of or miss? (McAdam, 1996). Or, does this suggest, as some critics have argued, that opportunities are purely subjective in that they only exist when people perceive them to exist? This would equate to something like 'an opportunity not recognized is no opportunity at all' (Gamson and Meyer, 1996, 283). Or further still, do activists themselves turn unfavourable environments into opportunities for action by their own action (something suggested, at least for some movements, in Tarrow's 1998 idea of cycles of contention)? In fact, some critics argue that this more often than not is the case. Activists do not take the chances gifted by political elites, but make their own chances by using their imaginations, passion, and creativity (Jasper, 1997). It is exactly the preserve of activists, for example, to dream that there are possibilities for change that others do not think exist, and to be optimistic about the chances for success, even if others are sure that they are staring down the barrel of defeat (Gamson and Meyer, 1996, 286).

If this is true then the distinctive claim that we started out with – that social movements rely on a favourable political context in order to emerge and succeed – disappears too. 'Good riddance', argue the main critics of PPT, Goodwin and Jasper (who, in a 'Brangelina'-esque twist, are referred to in the debate as 'Jaswin') (Goodwin and Jasper, 2004c, 82). I will return to the issue of whether we should wear a t-shirt supporting Jaswin, or McAdam, Tarrow, and Tilly (aka 'MTT') later, but for now the debate about opportunities raises a crucial point that demands our immediate attention: how do people perceive and construct opportunities out of structural, shifting, political, or otherwise aspects of the world around them, and translate these opportunities into collective action? In order to explore this question we will turn in the next section to the 'constructionist' approach to social movements – an approach that both criticizes PPT as we have understood it here, and, it seems fair to say, is also one that most so-called 'structuralists' now adopt in some measure for themselves (Kurzman, 2004).

The world of symbolic meaning: constructionist approaches to social movements

The debate over opportunities has actually brought us back to familiar ground. In Chapter 2, I suggested that collective behaviour (CB) imparted an important lesson: people act not because of their external environment, but because of the meaning that they give to this environment. Blumer (1951 [1946]) talked, if you recall, about the constructed nature of 'social problems' and Smelser (1962) about the role that 'generalized beliefs' played in shaping people's response to structural strains. This insight, we can see, is lost in the strong version of PPT which determines people's action from the nature of external political conditions (what could properly be called a 'structuralist' position). Political structures or changes in the configuration of power in the polity may provide some new openings for social movements according to the political analyst, but whether they are opportunities for collective action depends upon how activists themselves see the situation (Flacks, 2004; Kurzman, 2004).

Thinking about how activists see the situation immerses us not in the political world as such, but in the world of symbolic meaning. We need to know about the ideas of activists, their interpretation and definition of the situation, and the meaning that they attach to things in the world around them. It is no surprise to the sociologist therefore that constructionist approaches draw heavily upon the theory of symbolic interactionism that we encountered in Chapter 2. We saw there that symbolic interactionists urge the analyst to recognize that if people 'define situations as real, they are real in their consequences' (Thomas and Thomas, 1928, 572) (and presumably if they do not, then they are not). What this means is that political structures and shifts in power actually mean little *on their own* for collective action.

Despite his association with structuralism, McAdam (1982) had provided a sense of this in his study of the American civil rights movement by arguing that it was not just the existence of political opportunities that mattered, but a new way of recognizing the situation as one open to change – a 'cognitive liberation' – as he called it. McAdam (1982, 48) stated that 'mediating between opportunity and action are people and the…meanings they attach to their situations'. For mobilization to occur, activists must construct the meaning of things in ways that persuade themselves, and others, that collective action is right, necessary, and timely. The question then is how do activists construct and communicate the meaning of the world around them? This question is at the centre of constructionist approaches that point to the centrality of cultural processes in social movements.

Culture refers to the world of shared symbolic meanings out of which social action is constituted, and indeed, argue some constructionists, out of which all structures are constituted as well (Polletta, 2004). Constructionists have come up with interesting ways to explore the cultural processes of social movements in recent years as the approach has risen to ascendency, but if we want to understand one of the main ways that scholars include cultural factors in their analysis (and the limitations of them) then we need first to examine the concept of 'cultural framing' that was introduced into the field in the mid 1980s by David Snow et al. (1986). Not only does the framing concept continue to generate research and interest (Johnston and Noakes, 2005), but it is the one aspect of cultural processes that PPT has been more than happy to take on board (McAdam et al., 1996). In fact, by the mid 1990s, PPT scholars had been so convinced by the constructionist's calls for more attention to meaning and culture that they had broadened their model of social movements to include three factors that together constitute what is often called the 'political process model' (PPM). This model for explaining the

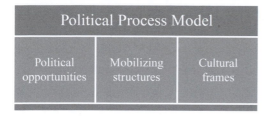

Figure 4.2
The political process model.
Source: McAdam et al. (1996).

emergence of social movements has achieved a position of dominance in social movement studies (see figure 4.2), with the factors used in combination to account for the specific case being researched.

We are already familiar with the first two factors in the political process model shown in figure 4.2: political opportunities have been discussed in the previous section, and mobilizing structures (the formal and information organizations through which resources are mobilized), in Chapter 3. Let us now turn our attention to the third.

Frames

The concept of a 'frame' comes from the work of the American sociologist Erving Goffman (1974) (whom we will revisit in Chapter 8). A frame is defined as:

> an interpretative schemata that simplifies and condenses the 'world out there' by selectively punctuating and encoding objects, situations, events, experiences, and sequences of action within one's present or past environment.
>
> (Snow and Benford, 1992, 137)

The idea of 'schemata' is made less abstract if we consider its definition within psychology as: 'a pattern imposed on complex reality or experience to assist in explaining it, mediate perception, or guide response' (The American Heritage Dictionary of English Language, 2000). As schemata of interpretation, frames are therefore ways of ordering experiences and events so that we can 'know' them and hence know how to react to them. It is only once the 'world out there' has been cognitively processed (mentally examined) that we can make any sense out of it. At its most basic, 'framing' therefore involves constructing the meaning of a given situation by selecting a culturally available 'frame' to put around it.

Goffman (1974) makes clear that this framing process is only made obvious to us when people select the *wrong* frame for the situation – something exploited on 'candid camera'-type television shows where people are set up to think that serious situations are unfolding, only later to discover that they are the victims of an elaborate prank. Our amusement comes from seeing the person interpret the situation wrongly. They are misguided in thinking things are 'serious' and they look embarrassed when they realize that something very different is actually 'going on here'. In this respect, frames are more situation-specific than ideologies (which are broader systems of beliefs about the world, which colour people's interpretations of all the situations they face). Ideologies are clearly very important to how activists see the world around them. Ferree and Merill (2000, 456) help us to appreciate the difference between frames and ideologies by suggesting that frames tell us *how* to think about things, while ideology tells us *why it matters*. Whilst ideologies cannot (and should not) be solely reduced to frames therefore (Oliver and Johnston, 2000), the frame concept can help us to unpack the process by which meanings and ideas are constructed.

When it comes to understanding the world around us, the answer to our question 'what is going on here' (Benford, 1997) is very often derived from our immediate contacts, personal experiences, and from the dominant 'frames' that are transmitted by the mass media and those with some authority. It is widely accepted in fact that the mass media play a crucial role in constructing and reproducing dominant frames of interpretation (McCarthy, 1994). These dominant frames generally include what Hirschman (1991) calls 'rhetoric of reaction' in that they produce understandings of reality that reinforce the status quo by con-veying the message that you should not act to change things, it could be bad if you did, and there is probably no point in trying anyway. Social movements, on the other hand, are involved in constructing alterna-tive frames of interpretation through 'rhetoric of change' (Gamson and Meyer, 1996, 285). They construct views of reality that convey the message that you can change things, *we* should do it now, and you will be pleased that you did. The alternative frames that social movements construct have been labelled 'collective action frames' by Snow et al. (1986), who contend that collective action frames provide a diagnosis of the situation (interpret what is going on); provide a prognosis (say what should be done about it); and provide the motivation for action (tell people why they should act).

To be persuasive to other people, collective action frames must convey ideas in a logical, convincing, and culturally resonant way. Movement activists try to find the best ways to package and present their ideas in order to get others on board (Benford, 1993a). This is an important part of the recruitment process which involves 'aligning' the frame of the movement with the ordinary, everyday frames of potential adherents – see Snow et al., 1986, who also suggest that frame alignment can be achieved by:

- frame bridging (linking two or more frames about an issue)
- frame amplification (clarifying existing beliefs and ideas within the frame)
- frame extension (broadening the issues that are important in the frame to incorporate those of a potential group of supporters)
- frame transformation (changing the frame radically or producing a new one).

Framing processes are ongoing and constantly negotiated. As Benford and Snow put it, frames are 'continuously being constituted, contested, and/or replaced during the course of social movement activity' (Benford and Snow, 2000, 628). Not only do activists dispute frames among themselves (Benford, 1993b), but movement frames must also contest official state and media frames (McCarthy, 1994).

Methods point: frame analysis

A common research strategy for frame analysis is to conduct a 'narrative analysis' of a 'representative text'. This analysis is used to reconstruct the frame of the movement (Johnston and Noakes, 2005). This text can be the spoken discourse of activists (e.g. interview transcripts, speeches) or movement produced texts (e.g. campaign material, leaflets, position statements on websites). Researchers have also looked at media frames of protest events by using newspaper articles or the 'official frame' communicated by government sources. The idea is to try and work out the content of the frame (the key ideas) and the structure of the frame (how these ideas are organized/related together). In other words, the method is interested in what they say, and how they say it. Both these elements organize social experience in a particular way, providing a particular 'interpretative framework' for events. Studies of movement frames tend to have a comparative dimension to research which aids the analytic value of the approach

(Johnston and Noakes, 2005). You can look at how social movement frames change over time within the same movement, linking changes in frames to the changing fortunes of the movement. Alternatively, you can compare frames across social movements within the same time period, exploring their differences and overlapping ideas, like for example, the 'rights frame' which became shared by many of the social movements of the 1960s (civil rights, women's rights, gay rights, and so on). Social movement frames can also be compared with the 'official' framing attempts of the media, to explore the nature of the contest between the two.

- Select a representative text of a social movement that interests you. Follow Johnston and Noakes's (2005) method of recreating the frame by looking for:
- the key issue in the frame
- responsibility/solution proposed in the frame (diagnosis and prognosis)
- the symbols used, like visual images, metaphors, historical examples, stereotypes, slogans
- the supporting arguments, especially about the historical roots of grievances and appeals to wider cultural values.
- Do you think that frame analysis is a useful method of social movement research?

The media and framing

The media – newspapers, radio, television, and social media – are central to how the public sees the world around them. Media, in fact, are central to people's perception of their environment and the 'political opportunities' that it affords. Roscigno and Danaher (2001), for example, show how the political messages communiacted via radio played an important role in the mobilization of textile workers in the south of the United States in the early 1930s, when thousands went out on strike. They suggest that radio affected mill workers' sense of collective identity, solidarity, and their perceptions of a 'political opportunity' to further their interests (Roscigno and Danaher, 2001). It is also the case, therefore, that if activists want to influence public perception then they inevitably have to engage with the media and shape the messages that are communicated. In other words, they must get their stories told and their ideas heard.

This often requires a conscious media strategy (Ryan, 1991). To get coverage, movements are at the mercy not only of the corporate and political interests shown to lie behind news corporations, but the journalist's requirement for stories that are 'newsworthy' (McCarthy et al., 1996, 297). The mass media have only a little space left to fill with extras (the 'news hole') and they select issues that fit the bill of a 'good story' – essentially, something that will grab the audience's interest (McCarthy et al., 1996). Good stories are dramatic spectacles, big important events, heart-rending tales of woe and adversity – which are all the better for a few famous faces, cute children, good-looking leaders, and innocent victims (McCarthy et al., 1996, 297). This means that the mass media tend to concentrate attention on the more violent protests. As Gamson and Meyer (1996, 288) put it, 'burning buildings and burning fires make better Television than peaceful vigils and orderly marches'. The mass media therefore tend to cover protest events if they are sensational, violent, emotive, celebrity-endorsed, and full of activist 'personalities'.

Whilst mass media attention can affect public perceptions of opportunity and bring vital resources to a movement (giving it the public status of an 'important player' on the issue) (McCarthy et al., 1996), the kind of attention bestowed may not be conducive to the movement's reputation, as found by the feminist group Riot Grrrl in the early 1990s. The mass media misconstrued aspects of the group and failed to give serious treatment to the issues it raised, like rape and abortion. Corin Tucker of the Riot Grrrl band Sleater-Kinney said that 'I think it was deliberate that we were made to look like we were just ridiculous girls parading around in our underwear.' As a consequence, the group refused to court the mainstream media at all, communicating through underground zines. Perhaps today the Riot Grrrl group would have spread their message via social media instead (Marcus, 2010). In this respect, new media have become a crucial platform not only for battles between movements and countermovements (discussed in the last chapter in the case of the internet feud between Anonymous and Scientology), but in providing activist-created media content that gives them journalistic control over the message, and a way to quickly diffuse their chosen frame to millions of users on sites like YouTube, Twitter, Facebook, and tumblR. Castells et al. claim for example that mobile communication (enabled by mobile phones and wireless networks) allows for a form of autonomous and personalized communication which, as they put it, 'effectively bypasses the mass-media system as a source of information, and creates a new form of public space' (Castells et al., 2006, 185). We will return to the role played by new media in Chapter 6.

Case point: the media framing of drunk-driving

Symbolic contests with the media are crucial in the ability of movements to communicate what Gamson calls 'injustice' frames (1992). To some extent, all movements are rooted in an interpretation of some aspect of the world around them as 'unjust' and in need of collective action. John McCarthy (1994) provides a useful example of how an injustice frame came to be constructed around drunk-driving in the United States in the 1980s. Unlike today, drunk-driving in 1970s America was pre-dominantly framed in terms of road traffic accidents and led to calls for better road safety. Individual agitators (like mothers who had had a child killed by a drunk driver) had tried to alter this interpretation to suggest that drunk-driving was a crime, with real victims, and should be publicly recognized as such. In the 1970s, this interpretation failed to resonate with the pub-lic's perception of the issue. In the 1980s however, there was a shift from what McCarthy calls the 'auto safety' frame to the 'killer drunk' frame. The 'killer drunk' frame enabled hundreds of anti-drunk-driving groups – like Mothers Against Drunk Driving (MADD) – to mobilize around the injustice by the mid 1980s. Interestingly, McCarthy shows how the media in this case played a key role in *enabling* rather than disputing the collective action frame by helping it to gain popular attention and appeal. The movement found it relatively easy to gain sympathetic media coverage because the stories of 'angry' 'mothers' who wanted to tell about the innocent child 'victims' of 'murdering' 'drunks' fulfilled the media's requirements for a 'good story'. The state authorities were also important to the framing effort, appearing on news broadcasts as 'experts' whose knowledge about the issue supported the activists' position.

- In what ways can mass media coverage hinder a social move-ment? In what ways could it help?
- What tactics could movements employ to challenge media frames?

Narrative and dramaturgy

Movements construct meanings not only through their texts, but through the stories that they tell and things that they do. Polletta (1998) for example points to the importance of narrative story-telling to the way in which social movements create understandings about what they are doing and why it came about. McAdam (1996) argues that movements also create meanings through the events they stage because 'actions really *do* speak louder than words'. Protest can be seen as a kind of drama, being played out before the eyes of the on-looking audience. This aspect of movement activity has been referred to as 'dramaturgy' (Benford and Hunt, 1992). McAdam (1996) argues that Martin Luther King was particularly skilled at using tactics to produce dramatic events in the American civil rights movement of the 1950s and 1960s. King adeptly employed tactics of peaceful protest in the face of violent reprisals from authorities, the images of which not only hit the front pages, but in themselves conveyed a sense of good, Christian Americans being persecuted by evil, violent racists.

The Israeli-Jewish group Women in Black provides another cogent example of dramaturgy. Every Friday between 1 pm and 2 pm, forty-plus women gather in a public square in Jerusalem, dressed in black to symbolize the tragedy of the Israeli-Palestinian conflict. They take up a position on a stage and remain there, silent. No words or great ideologi-cal statements are used to convey the message – just their presence in a public space usually dominated by men, wearing black to flaunt what is usually private grief. It was their silence, in fact, that 'compelled people to listen' to their anti-occupation message (Sasson-Levy and Rapoport, 2003, 385).

Framing and the political process model assessed

The concept of 'cultural framing' is primarily employed therefore to examine the process by which meanings are constructed and strategically communicated by social movements. PPT scholars adopt the concept as a kind of necessary supplement to the political opportunity approach. If the existence of political opportunities depends upon people 'defining' them as real in the first place, then attention must be given to how activists *see* the world around them. To this extent, the constructionists have won the day. Protest as a meaningful response to the structural conditions that people face, has to be *socially constructed* by them.

Cultural framing is used therefore as a device that can point to the cultural processes of meaning construction that 'mediate' between objective structural conditions on the one hand, and the action of social movements on the other. In other words, as McAdam and Tarrow put it, culture mediates between structure and agency (McAdam and Tarrow, 2011). No wonder then that PPT scholars so often reject the label of 'structuralism' (Tarrow, 2004). As Kurzman (2004) points out, there appear to be no self-confessed structuralists left in twenty-first century social movement theory.

Despite embracing what is called the 'cultural turn' in social movement studies (a cultural turn that was happening elsewhere in social theory from the mid 1990s), the political process model with its three key factors of political opportunities, cultural frames, and mobilizing structures (see figure 4.2) still came in for a great deal of criticism, both internally (from MTT themselves), and from more staunch constructionists like Jaswin. We will come on the MTT's self-criticism in the next section, but for now let us concentrate on the enemy from outside. This makes for lively reading. Jaswin's critique of PPT earned them the reputation of 'theory bashers', who have since taken their fair share of bashing in return (Goodwin and Jasper, 2004a). Much of this theory-bashing takes place in a Symposium on PPT in the journal *Sociological Forum* (19(1), 1999), and a later book that extended the debate, *Rethinking Social Movements* (Goodwin and Jasper, 2004a). Here, Jaswin accuse the political process model of an innate 'structuralist bias' in its approach to social movements, despite the inclusion of cultural framing. What are their main arguments?

First, Jaswin contend that retaining the concept of 'political opportunities' still suggests that activists *rely* upon some favourable external context in order to mobilize and succeed (Goodwin and Jasper, 2004b). It is clear, in their view, that this is not the case. Activists are not the puppets of structures, but themselves pull the strings. They do this first by using the emotional force of their moral arguments, something entirely overlooked by the rational actor model underlying PPM, which concentrates upon 'cold cognition' rather than 'hot' emotion (Ferree and Merrill, 2000). If activists are indeed the emotional actors I proffered in the last chapter, then actually their passion can take them further than political opportunities can. In her study of the AIDs activist group ACT-UP, Deborah Gould (2004; 2009), for example, found that AIDs activism was at its height in the US exactly when political opportunities were contracting (D. Gould, 2004, 164). Legal changes that contracted the rights of homosexuals at a time when the suffering of the AIDs crisis was so great created an emotional outpouring of anger and grief that drove people on to the streets in spite of – indeed *because of* – unfavourable political conditions.

Secondly, Jaswin argue that activists produce their own opportunities through their creative strategies (Jasper, 1997). It is wrong to see interpretative processes as mediating between objective political opportunities 'out there' and people's action, because people are, in fact, the sole creators of opportunities in the first place. Opportunities are entirely culturally constructed by the meaning-making processes of activists. They are not products of an external world around a social movement which frames render meaningful. To think otherwise is to retain a structuralist bias – namely a belief that people's actions are being determined by forces that lie outside their own control. Similarly, when PPM talks of 'mobilizing structures', such as networks, they are also viewed with a structuralist bias. Networks for example are seen primarily as pre-existing webs of relationships that structurally connect individuals to movements, without acknowledging that they only really matter because of their cultural contents, like ideas and emotions (Goodwin and Jasper, 2004b, 17). Again, emotions can compensate not just for a lack of political opportunity, but a lack of pre-existing structural connections too. Jasper, for example, argues that animal rights activists are not recruited through social networks but through 'moral shocks', which can be thought of as affronts to their moral sensibilities, which fill them with disgust and anger about the abuse of animals and motivate them to act.

Jaswin are right to criticize the rationalist bias in PPM. It is a bias that creates big problems with the framing concept. The framing concept suggests that activists strategically select and package together cultural symbols and ideas to manipulate potential recruits. This is a very 'voluntaristic' view of culture, as many critics have pointed out (Hart, 1996; Steinberg, 1999; Ferree and Merill, 2000; Polletta, 2004). The voluntaristic view of culture sees culture as like any other *resource* that can be picked up and used by a rational actor to achieve their goals (Steinberg, 1999). Rational activists select and order ideas so that they can create the most convincing arguments. This however, is criticized as a very 'top down' way of thinking about the importance of ideas, where meanings are communicated to potential adherents in order to manipulate them into participation (Ferree and Merill, 2000, 457), but how far can actors consciously put together schematic maps of their ideas as if they were devising a conscious PR strategy?

Steinberg (1999) offers an alternative to the framing approach which he terms a 'dialogic approach' in which meanings are constructed not like PR strategies, but in ongoing processes of social communication. For Steinberg, society consists of dominant discourses (powerful and accepted ways of talking about and thinking about things), and social movements, like anyone else, operate within these discourses. Whilst activists make efforts to subvert the dominant discourse and represent the world in a different way, they are nevertheless embedded themselves within the discourse and can only employ the categories and ideas that it provides (in other words, people cannot 'say the unsayable').

It is not the case therefore that activists can cherry-pick from different ideas and meanings at will – selecting and repackaging cultural symbols until they have the desired effect. Instead, Steinberg calls for a 'relational approach to meaning production' that sees the struggles around the production of meaning as part and parcel of social interaction between challengers, publics, and elites. This social interaction is the key to what Hart (1996, 91) calls 'culture-making practices' which are not simply about receiving a certain picture of reality (from a text for example) and assimilating the values and ideas it involves as an individual but, along *with others*, discussing, debating, challenging, and modifying discourses so that new collective understandings emerge:

> Only when we see cultural processes as part of the action, as part of what is quintessential both in formation and at stake, can we fully appreciate the cultural dimension of collective action.
>
> (Steinberg, 1999, 772)

Steinberg's argument reminds us that culture is not just about agency. It is not a tool used by activists to package meanings in ways that create commitment from individuals, but it is part of the wider social context in which framing processes take place. As Hart (1996, 94) puts it, 'culture is at least as often a source of constraint as of agency'. Where Jaswin are wrong then is in breaking from structuralism altogether. Instead, as Polletta (2004) argues, what is needed is an appreciation of the cultural dimensions of structures that render culture also as something that exists prior to people's actions, and appears to them as relatively durable and immovable. Jaswin, like frame theorists, come too close at times to suggesting that culture is individual consciousness – namely, the ideas and meanings that exist in individual people's heads and enable them to act creatively (Tilly, 2004). As Polletta puts it, however, 'culture is not just in your head' (Polletta, 2004). Culture is part of structures too (Laclau and Mouffe, 1985; Polletta, 2004, 97). Culture is the shared traditions that shape the nation state and its interactions with social movements (e.g. through the culture of political institutions, and the culture of policing (see Della Porta and Reiter, 1998)), and it is the 'collective memories' of past contention that shape current norms and practices.

It would be unfair to suggest that PPT had not considered culture as a constraining variable in this way at all. Tilly (1995) for example offered the concept of 'repertoires of contention', which refers to the way in which collective actors make claims (e.g. through street demonstrations, strikes, sit-ins, internet methods and so forth). The repertoire that movement activists employ is largely inherited from previous generations of struggle, which pass on a collection of culturally, and historically specific tactics and strategies from which to draw. Tilly states that 'repertoires of contention' is meant as:

> a cultural notion where you have collective learning going on through interaction and you have the residues of this historical process of struggle showing up as constraint on how people relate to each other next time they make claims.
>
> (Tilly, 1998, 203)

Although activists can play with the repertoires they inherit and come up with innovations, Tilly and Tarrow (2006) argue that modern protest movements have drawn upon what they call 'modular' performances when making claims, including demonstrations, petitions, and, increasingly today, internet-based methods.

If 'culture is not just in your head' (Polletta, 2004) then it should also warn us of another fallacy – emotions are not just in your heart. Emotions are also part of a wider culture that patterns the sentiments of a nation or group at a particular historical juncture. Emotion cultures for example, provide rules about feelings – what is appropriate and not, what is morally wrong and how you should feel about it. Shifts in emotion cultures can help explain the mobilization and success of social movements too. In his study of the anti-slavery movement, for example, Michael Young (2001) argues that a shift in the emotional culture surrounding slavery – from knowing it was wrong to *feeling* that it was wrong (because white people increasingly came into contact with black people) – enabled the anti-slavery movement to gain important middle-class allies that eventually led to success.

Despite Jaswin forwarding some valid criticisms of PPM, the idea of structures being important in shaping activist choices and strategies cannot be pushed aside. Hold off from buying your Jaswin t-shirt just yet. As McAdam (2004) continues to stress, structures place some limits upon the range of interpretations people can make. But these limits must be seen, as Polletta (2004) argues, not just as the products of political structures but as the products of their symbolic, cultural dimensions too. Culture, as well as politics, is responsible for creating an apparently immovable context outside activists' control. Jaswin would not disagree, when they claim that they are not arguing that action does not take place in what they call 'structured arenas' (Goodwin and Jasper, 2004b). The key question then is how can we best think of these 'structured arenas' in order to do justice to constraint and agency, structure and culture?

I suggest that we can best think of the 'structured arenas' in which social movements operate by employing the concept of 'relational fields'. Jack Goldstone (2004) for example calls for the concept of 'political opportunity structure' (POS) to be replaced by that of 'external relational fields'; a concept he sees better able to capture what POS was meant to designate (Goldstone, 2004, 356). A 'relational field' can be thought of as a space created by the interactions of actors and groups around a particular issue. There are fields composed of political elites, state actors, media actors, and corporate actors. What happens in these external fields and how they interact with social movement networks affects the fortunes of movements. Crossley (2005; 2006) for example understands movements themselves as 'fields of contention' (cultural and material spaces of contention populated by SMOs and structured by their interactions), and they are shaped in their interaction with external fields. He shows how the psychiatric field of contention was shaped by interactions with the mental health field, legal field, parliamentary field, and media field (Crossley 2005; 2006). Steinberg (1999) would add to this the 'discursive field' – namely the dominant cultural discourses that social movements work within which are constructed through the ongoing social interactions between movements and other players (elite actors, media and so on) and lead to the social production of meanings. The nature of these discursive fields can play an important role in movement success (Giugni, 2011).

The concept of 'external relational fields' therefore covers the aspects of the external environment that the POS concept had been referring to (Goldstone, 2004, 356). It stresses not structure, however, but interaction. Fields are the spaces in which strategic interactions between movements and other players take place. This means that rather than being stable, fixed, and outside the control of actors, the environment in which movements act is actually shifting all the time (Goodwin and Jasper, 2004b, 12).

Contentious politics (CP): developments in PPT

In the previous section, we explored the criticism of PPT that came from outside. Whilst this debate was raging, however, MTT were also reflecting upon, and critiquing, themselves (McAdam et al., 2001). They accepted the cultural turn and much of the constructionist critique of PPT. They accepted that the concept of 'political opportunity structure' had led to analyses that were static rather than dynamic; that cultural processes has been unduly limited to framing processes, and that not enough emphasis had been placed upon the fact that opportunities and threats have to be socially attributed (interpreted by people), and mobilizing structures socially appropriated (actively used by people). There was no longer point in debating whether the rationalists, structuralists, or culturalists were right, or whether they should be combined in this way or that (McAdam et al., 2001). Instead we should all move on to an approach that puts dynamic, interactive processes at its core, an approach which is, fundamentally, 'relational'. In order to do this, MTT suggested a radical break with what they called the 'classic social movement agenda' of political opportunities, mobilizing structures, and cultural framing. They replaced it instead with the 'contentious politics' approach. This approach was presented in *Dynamics of Contention* (McAdam et al., 2001), *Silence and Voice* (Aminzade et al., 2001), and *Contentious Politics* (Tilly and Tarrow, 2006; Tarrow and Tilly, 2009).

The contentious politics (CP) approach is new in two key respects. First, it included a much broader range of political contention than is covered by the label 'social movements'. MTT argued that the study of social movements had become unnecessarily divorced from the study of revolutions, rebellions, civil wars, industrial conflict, ethnic conflicts, nationalism, democratization, and even elections (on elections, see McAdam and Tarrow, 2012). By concentrating not on social movements, but on the 'contentious episodes' of claim-making between challengers and the state that constitute all of these, MTT hoped to reunite social movement studies with other disciplines that studied similar processes, and move beyond an undue emphasis upon the historically particular form of the 'social movement'. Contentious politics are:

> contentious in the sense that they involve the collective making of claims
> that, if realized, would conflict with someone else's interests; politics in
> the sense that governments of one sort or another figure in the claim
> making, whether as claimants, objects of claims, allies of the objects, or
> monitors of the contention.
>
> (Tarrow and Tilly, 2009, 438)

Secondly, CP adopted a different methodology for studying contentious episodes. Rejecting the 'invariant' models they had been accused of inventing (i.e. universal lists of conditions that scholars sought to correlate with their cases), MTT abandoned overarching grand explanations (McAdam et al., 2001). They argued instead that scholars should look to unearth the *processes* that shape social movement mobilization and dynamics, and, further, break these processes down into the *mechanisms* that cause them. CP argues that scholars should study *mechanisms* and *processes* involved in particular contentious episodes. Thus in *Dynamics of Contention*, MTT highlight a range of mechanisms including: brokerage, diffusion, polarization, repression, and radicalization, that have been found to play a role in contentious episodes from the French Revolution to South African anti-apartheid, to the Mau-Mau revolt and Swiss unification (in fact they take fifteen cases and explore the common mechanisms they contain by taking paired

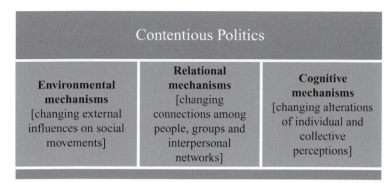

Figure 4.3
The mechanisms of contentious politics.
Source: adapted from McAdam et al. (2001).

comparisons of them) (McAdam et al., 2001, 76). There is a shift away, then, from looking at the three main factors in the political process model (see figure 4.2) as 'conditions' that should be 'correlated' with social movement activity, and towards looking at *processes* and *mechanisms* instead. The mechanisms are divided into three categories which we can see as loosely mapping on to those of the political process model (see figure 4.3). We will put some of these mechanisms to work in Chapter 6 in our explanation of global contentious politics.

Dynamics of Contention (McAdam et al., 2001) concentrated most of its efforts on relational mechanisms, leading to accusations that MTT retain a structuralist bias in the CP approach (Platt, 2004). This is undeserved considering that instead they see culture as a key part of all three of the mechanisms, especially the relational ones: 'if we did not invoke "culture" as a master variable, it was in part because we are suspicious of master variables and think of culture as being embedded in the relations among actors' (McAdam and Tarrow 2011, 6). So why was CP not seen as a resounding success? First, like PPT before it, CP contains an obvious *political* bias. The definition of contentious politics, for example, shows that it is premised upon contentious episodes that in some way involve the government. MTT (2001), and later McAdam and Tarrow (2011) acknowledge this 'statist' bias. While interactions between challengers and the state may well be central to a broad range of social movements, it is not to all of them. It is likely, for example, that CP, like PPT before it, will not apply well to movements who challenge cultural norms more generally and therefore take a counter-cultural rather than political form (we will look at these movements in Chapter 5) (Goodwin and Jasper, 2004b). Placing the state central to the picture is also problematic with the proliferation of movements who challenge corporations rather than nation states (Soule, 2009) (and we will pick this up in Chapter 6). Finally, Giugni (2011) argues that in non-Western contexts social movements have a different relationship to the state because there is not such a clear distinction between the state and civil society. In non-Western contexts therefore, social movements work more closely with the state and it is not as useful to think of social movements as external 'opponents' (see also, Goldstone, 2004).

Secondly, despite arguing on the one hand for a move away from overarching universal theories, some critics suggest that what CP gave us was another one in different clothes, which pulls out common causal mechanisms across an increasingly broad range of contention, even though they have different combinations and effects. In fact, because it engages with such a broad range and pulls out such a long list of mechanisms related to each, critics complain that it is unwieldy and unclear, again something that MTT admit. In wanting to integrate everything in a way that applied to everything (not only social movements but all episodes of contention), the CP agenda became squeezed of analytical interest as scholars drowned under the detail and yet also seemed to emerge on the surface with the kind of universal theory that they had wanted to get away from. Perhaps the most significant point we can take from the criticism that surrounds CP is captured by Ludger Mees: 'the search for an all-explaining general theory of contentious politics is something similar to the search of the Holy Grail: noble, but futile' (Mees, 2004, 328).

Summary

This chapter has critically engaged with political process theory. PPT argues that:

- RMT places too much emphasis on factors internal to social movements, like their organizational structure. The mobilization and success of social movements depends instead on external factors in the world around a social movement.
- The most important factors that are linked to social movement mobilization and success are political ones. The nation state and its political institutions are central to the opportunities for social movement mobilization. The

relationship between movements and this political context can be examined using the concept of 'political opportunity structure'.

- PPT largely accepts, however, that political opportunities are a matter of activists' perception – their existence depends upon how activists define the world around them. The concept of cultural framing is therefore a necessary compliment to that of political opportunities. Together with mobilizing resources, political opportunities and cultural frames constitute the 'political process model' of collective action (see figure 4.2).

If you scour social movement journals today, the continuing hold of the political process model is clear to see. Much research still adheres to MTT's description of a study which examines the ways in which their case 'fits the boxes' of political opportunities, mobilizing resources, and cultural frames, and then broadens the boxes to accommodate an increasing array of nuances thrown up by the case in hand (McAdam et al., 2001). This is perhaps because the single-case-study approach is still largely dominant in research, and fits better with this model than with the search for mechanisms, which requires large-scale paired comparisons (Mees, 2004). Where comparisons are used today, they tend to stay within the language of political opportunity structures, or cycles of contention (Jung, 2010). This is not to say that the mechanisms approach has made no impact (see *Mobilization* Special Issue, 2011). It seems to be particularly welcome as a way to move analysis from static variables to *mechanisms and processes*, urging the political process theorists to 'live up to their name' as Jaswin put it (Goodwin and Jasper, 2004b, 29).

Let us end, then, with some wider critical reflection. Rationalist, culturalist, and structuralist analyses, I suggest, are all moving in the *relational* direction that we first started to unpack in Chapter 3:

- The rationalists, as we saw last chapter, actually moved fairly quickly away from individual-level explanations of decision-making to a consideration of the relational context in which choices are made and strategies formed.
- Culturalists, as we have seen in this chapter, are also feeling the heat of criticism when it comes to overly individualist analyses of meaning and consciousness that place culture and emotion in people's heads and hearts rather than seeing them as woven into the very fabric of social relations.
- The so-called 'structuralists', with whom we started this chapter, have also driven forward the relational turn in their CP approach in which they see the actors, identities, and trajectories involved in contentious episodes as the ongoing products of the interaction between them. Gone is the image of an already constituted challenger opposing an already constituted nation state. Such an image is nothing but a static snapshot of a much bigger interactive process involving the both of them.

The world around a social movement is, then, no static place. It is no fixed place that lies outside social action and determines it. If this was the picture of structure that you started out with then it is well and truly gone. The world around a social movement is not some puppet-master that crafts its fortunes as suggested in the strong version of PPT (not that we could put anybody's name to it). Neither is it the invention of pure consciousness in which individuals can dream that literally anything is possible. Instead, the world around a social movement – like the social movement itself – can be thought of as a series of external relational fields (political, media, corporate, discursive), constituted by interaction, and which also interact with one another (Goldstone, 2004). These are the 'structured arenas' of action that Jaswin (2004b) talk about – and they place material, political, and symbolic boundaries around that action (Crossley 2005; 2006). The social interaction between the different players and fields, however, means that boundaries are always being negotiated, and possibilities for action always shifting. Structures have to be reproduced by action, and action, therefore, always has a chance to change them. Perhaps the key problem with the CP approach is that despite the relational turn, the mechanistic language employed still fails to resonate with this picture of agency. It is in relational processes that chances are made, and so too are the actors who will seize or thwart them.

We have not yet, however, given attention to this last question – which is made central by both culturalist and relational approaches – where do the 'social actors' implicated in various contentious episodes come from? To address this, we need to approach the issue of culture and social movements through a different lens – that of European NSM theory.

DISCUSSION POINT

- What influence does the national political regime have on social movement mobilization? Does the nation state always play a role in social movement fortunes?
- Can social movements emerge even if the political environment they face is repressive and unfavourable?
- Do opportunities for collective action only exist if people perceive them to exist?
- Why is 'framing' an important activity for social movements? Is this the only way, or the best way, to consider the role played by culture in movement mobilization?

FURTHER READING

For the work of MTT separately see: Charles Tilly's *From Mobilization to Revolution* (1978); Doug McAdam's *Political Process and the Development of Black Insurgency* (1982); and Sidney Tarrow's *Power in Movement* (1998). Doug McAdam et al.'s *Comparative Perspectives on Social Movements* (1996) presents the political process model's three concepts of mobilizing structures, political opportunities, and cultural frames. The CP approach is outlined in Doug McAdam et al.'s *Dynamics of Contention* (2001), and Charles Tilly and Sidney Tarrow's *Contentious Politics* (2006). For the lively constructionist critique of PPT see Jeff Goodwin and James Jasper's edited collection of the debate *Rethinking Social Movements* (2004a).

5 From old to new social movements: capitalism, culture, and the reinvention of everyday life

Culture is what we make it, yes it is
Now is the time,
Now is the time,
To invent, invent, invent.

(Riot Grrrl Band, *Sleater Kinney*, '#1 Must Have', 2000)

In this chapter, we will consider variations of new social movement (NSM) theory, which developed through the work of three European thinkers from the 1970s onwards: Jürgen Habermas (German), Alain Touraine (French), and Alberto Melucci (Italian). Each of these thinkers is involved in challenging the conceptualization of social movements as manifestations of 'class conflict' offered by Karl Marx, which had been extremely influential in European thinking. Instead, they pointed to fundamental changes in industrial society from the 1960s that had caused a decline in class-based mobilizations and the emergence of NSMs concerning identity, cultural values, and ways of living. They suggest to us that the battleground of social movements has fundamentally shifted from the workplace to culture, and our understanding of 'what social movements are', has to shift along with it.

NSM theory is also interesting because it provides a challenge to the rationalist approaches of the last two chapters. In contrast to them, it suggests that contemporary social movements cannot be viewed empirically as the organized, rational pursuit of shared interests. Nor do they involve making claims on the state and political institutions. Instead, they suggest that we should view social movements analytically as the construction of collective identities that express society's key conflicts, which are cultural in nature. As a consequence, conceptualizations of social movements as 'political struggle', give way to conceptualizations of social movements as 'cultural struggle'. This approach has several merits, not least the ability to refresh our very notion of what 'political protest' is, and looks like. Nevertheless, it generates its insights at a cost, leaving behind, for good, ideas on class struggle that, if contemporary Marxist scholars are anything to go by, can actually aid an understanding of the political significance of action taken to reinvent everyday life.

By the end of the chapter, you should know why NSM theorists left behind the Marxist view of social movements as working class-based mobilizations. You will understand why they think of social movements instead as the construction of collective identities. You will have knowledge of the arguments made by Habermas, Touraine, and Melucci, and be able to critically engage with their claims about the 'newness' of cultural struggle. You will also be able to draw out the conceptual advantages of the NSM approach, especially when trying to make sense of 'lifestyle movements'.

The background to NSM theory: class-based social movements

NSM theory developed through a critical engagement with Marxism. Cox and Nilsen (2005, 1) suggest that 'Marxism does not have a specific theory *about* social movements because it is in itself a theory *of* social movements'. In other words, the ideas of Marxism are fundamentally bound to the social movement whose struggle it predicts and analyses: the labour movement. To this extent, Alan Scott (1990, 2) states that 'Marxism may be said to be about little else other than social movements.' The social movements that Marxists are interested in are of a particular type: class-based mobilizations. This is because Marxists claim that the central struggle of capitalist society is 'capital versus labour'. Despite the appearance of other kinds of conflict (like those based around gender and ethnicity), the primary faultlines in capitalist society surround social class.

Class struggle

The two main social classes in capitalist society are the capitalist class and the working class, and they have an antagonistic relationship to one another. The capitalist class (bourgeoisie) own the means of production (the technology, machinery, land, factories, and so on with which goods are produced), and the working class (proletariat) only own their 'labour power' (their capacity to work). The working class sell this 'labour power' to the capitalists in exchange for a wage. The relationship between capitalists and workers is not a 'fair deal', however, but is based upon the exploitation of the workers. The goods that workers produce (e.g. in factories) are sold for more money than the worker is paid to make them. This creates a 'surplus value' which is extracted by the capitalist and reinvested into production, or translated into profit.

As competition between capitalist enterprises increases, however, commodities (the things that are bought and sold on the market) achieve a lower price on the market, meaning that capitalists have to make savings. They do this by increasing the exploitation of the workforce: wages have to be lowered, hours lengthened, or productivity increased. This makes the experience of work in a capitalist society a dull, repetitive, and alienating experience in which workers have little autonomy (Braverman, 1974). This experience was famously captured in Huw Beynon's 1960s study of workers at the Ford car factory in Halewood, UK. Beynon's study showed how being 'on the job' together galvanized the working classes with a sense of solidarity and fighting spirit as they attempted to wrestle back control over the workplace in 'a bloody war' with the bosses (Beynon, 1973). This antagonistic relationship is at the root of the conflict between capital and labour. Both are locked in a 'class conflict' that, for Marx, would provide an ever-present potential for class-based mobilization. Karl Marx and Friedrich Engels (1967 [1848]) therefore suggested that 'the history of all hitherto existing society is the history of class struggles'.

The class struggle is mobilized by the labour movement (consisting of trade unions, labour parties, and socialist movements), which first emerged in the wake of the industrial revolution in the mid nineteenth century. From the Luddites who smashed the new industrial machinery that rendered their skills obsolete, to trade unions striking for improved pay and conditions, to revolutionary socialist movements trying to instigate a whole new society, working class movements took centre stage in analyses of collective action in industrial capitalism (Hobsbawm, 1952; Thompson, 1991 [1963]). In fact, it is important to note that for Marxists the labour movement is *the* social movement of capitalist society. Social movements are defined in this respect as mobilizations that express the central conflict of society (capital versus labour), and have the ability to 'break the limits of the system', as

Melucci (1996, 25) describes it. The labour movement had the potential to break the limits of the system because it argued that workers could not fundamentally improve their position while capitalism remained intact. In the *Communist Manifesto*, written for the Communist League on the cusp of the 1848 revolutions in Europe, Marx and Engels called upon the 'workers of the world' to 'unite' in order to bring about a communist revolution and establish a socialist society in which private ownership of the means of production would be abolished, ending the antagonism between the classes (Marx and Engels, 1967 [1848]). They gave a flavour of historical inevitability to the process. Capitalism 'would produce its own grave-diggers': a social movement composed of workers who would overthrow the system once and for all.

Out with the old

Theories of NSMs arise out of a critical dialogue with Marxism. By the early to mid twentieth century it became clear that belonging to the working class did not necessarily breed a common class consciousness or a desire for revolution. Neo-Marxist writers, like Georg Lukács, Antonio Gramsci, Theodor Adorno, Max Horkheimer, and Herbert Marcuse reflected upon this problem when the communist revolution predicted by Marx and Engels failed to materialize. Neo-Marxists suggest that the power and control of capitalists over the working class does not just come at the point of production in the workplace, but through ideology and culture too, producing what Adorno and Horkheimer (1979 [1944]) call a 'totally administered society' in which class conflict is pacified. Through cultural (not just economic) domination, capitalism had won the ideological battle over people's minds, and had incorporated the working class as passive, compliant subjects rather than revolutionary ones. NSM theorists pick up this view to suggest that by the 1970s, working class-based mobilizations had 'lost their explosive power', as Habermas (1987, 350) puts it.

Evidence for this came from the declining trends in trade union membership and strike action. In the US, Europe, and Australia, trade union density (the percentage of all those employed who are members of a union) has steadily (and at times sharply) declined since the 1970s. In the UK, for example, union density peaked in 1979 during the 'Winter of Discontent' (which saw widespread strikes) at 55.4 per cent, but declined sharply in the 1980s and 1990s. This picture of decline in the

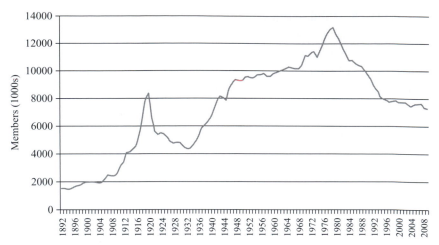

Figure 5.1
Trade Union membership in the UK, 1892–2009.
**Source of data: Brownlie (2012, 22), taken from 1892–1974 Department of Employment
Statistics Division, 1974–2010, The Certification Office. © CCSR, University of Manchester.**

UK since the late 1970s is revealed in figure 5.1, which shows trends in the numbers of workers who are members of a trade union from the late nineteenth century to 2009.

The latest figures show that in 2011, union density in the UK stood at 26 per cent. In the US, union density stood at 30 per cent in 1970, compared to 11.8 per cent in 2011 (Bureau of Labor Statistics). The number of working days lost to strike action has also declined. In the US, the early 1970s saw tens of millions of working days lost to strikes, compared to 124,000 in 2009 (Bureau of Labor Statistics). Some 12.9 million working days were lost to strike action in the UK in the 1970s, compared to 660,000 in the 1990s (Office for National Statistics). Figure 5.2 shows the trends in the number of working days lost to strike action in the UK since the late nineteenth century to 2009. This is the same time period as shown in the graph in figure 5.1. How do the trends in union membership and trends in strike action compare?

While trade unions did not completely disappear, and there was still some significant strike activity in the 1970s and 1980s, Habermas's (1987, 350) argument was that working class-based mobilizations had lost their 'explosive power' to really bring about fundamental change in society. Through their bargaining with employers, unions were able to reach compromises that meant that strike action was averted, or workers demands placated by monetary compensation (e.g. pay rises).

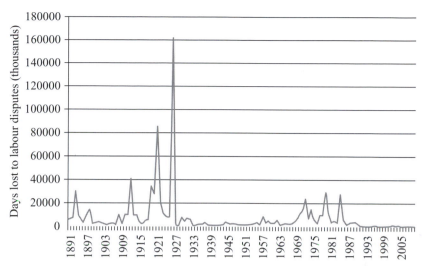

Figure 5.2
Number of days lost to labour disputes in the UK, 1891–2009.
Source of data: Guardian datablog (2010), taken from the Office for National Statistics.
© CCSR, University of Manchester.

The labour movement therefore lost the ability (or desire) to 'break the limits of the system'. Touraine furthermore suggests that even when strikes did appear in the 1970s and 1980s, they gained their impetus not from economic demands but a struggle to defend the way of life of a community, and these kinds of struggles involved non-traditional groups, like women, alongside male workers. Touraine has in mind here union action like the miners' strike in Britain 1984–5, where the closure of pits was seen as a danger to the whole way of life of working class communities. The miners' strike was also significant in that women joined men on the picket lines in the fight to save the pits.

In with the new

Further evidence for a shift in the nature of social movements came from observing the kind of social movements that appeared as significant forces in society from the 1960s onwards, and seemed to fill the gap left by the labour movement (Touraine, 1981). In the 1960s, the social movements that were making the headlines, for example, were the black civil rights movement, anti-nuclear movements, and the student movement (which was at the forefront of protests across the Western world in 1968) (Scott, 1990). These social movements were not led by the working class, but by minorities and middle-class intellectuals. They did not primarily make claims regarding the workplace and material redistribution, but instead made claims regarding human rights, quality of life, identities, and moral values. These kinds of claims were also found in the major social movements that followed in the 1970s and 1980s, like the women's liberation movement, gay liberation movement, and environmentalism. The second-wave feminists of the women's liberation movement (established in the US and UK in 1969 and 1970 respectively) claimed, for example, that the 'personal is political', pointing to the interconnection between political struggle and people's everyday lives, relationships, and identities, a theme that was echoed in the Gay Liberation Front of 1970.

Political struggle, then, was about trying to construct new identities, cultural values, and ways of living, and gain recognition and acceptance for them in society. Environmentalists too argued that social change had to start in people's everyday lives where their attitudes, values, and relationship to the natural environment needed to change. By changing your personal actions, like starting to recycle, grow your own food, use public transport, and so on, you could contribute towards wider efforts to protect the environment. What was different about these movements therefore was not only that their issues of concern had changed, but their way of pursuing social change had shifted too. Rather than targeting the state and political institutions with their claims, women's liberation, gay liberation, and environmentalism emphasized that social change had to start with personal change in what had been previously seen as the 'private' realms of everyday life, where shifts could be initiated in cultural values, the way people saw themselves and others, and the relationships that they had to each other and the natural environment.

This meant that the social movements entering the scene from the 1960s onwards also looked 'new' compared with the 'old' labour movement. Rather than formal, hierarchical organizations, the NSMs took the form of the decentralized 'polycentric' (many-headed) networks that we discussed in Chapter 3 (Gerlach, 1999). Furthermore, these networks among groups and individuals were often hidden from public view because they were part and parcel of people's everyday lives (Melucci, 1989). We will revisit this point later in the chapter. There are a number of ways in which social movements from the 1960s onwards therefore appeared to be 'new'. Four key dimensions of 'newness' are summarized in figure 5.3.

1. New Politics
- Post-material concerns
- Defend identities or gain recognition for new ones
- Challenge dominant definitions of who we are and how we live

2. New Site of Struggle
- Culture and everyday life rather than the workplace
- Seek to create cultural alternatives, i.e. new values, identities, and ways of living

3. New Composition
- Cut across classes and include groups previously marginal to the labour movement, like women, young people, ethnic minorities
- Not based in the working class, but led by middle class radicals (higher educated middle class)

4. New Organizational Form
- Decentralized, participatory and democratic networks rather than formal bureaucratic SMOs
- 'Submerged' in everyday life, less publicly visible

Figure 5.3
What was 'new' about new social movements?

NSM theory reflects upon this changing nature of social movements since the 1960s. Its main claim is that there has been a shift from 'old' social movements (working class-based movements that mobilize around the material effects of capitalism), to 'new' social movements (movements that mobilize around the cultural and psychological effects of capitalism). Social movements – argue the NSM theorists – have shifted from 'material' to 'post-material' concerns, reflecting wider value-shifts in capitalist societies from the 1970s onwards (Inglehart, 1977). This is the claim that we will critically engage with in the course of the chapter. Before we move on, however, there is one final point to be made regarding the particular conceptualization of social movements that we are working with here.

An analytical approach to social movements

While NSM theory criticizes the Marxist approach for being outdated in the context of modern capitalist society, it is nevertheless marked in its own approach to social movements by its dialogue with Marxism. This is especially clear in the way in which NSM theorists conceptualize social movements in the first place. Like Marx, NSM theorists view social movements as the vehicles that express the central conflict of society and have the ability to break the limits of the existing system.

Alberto Melucci calls this approach to social movements 'analytical' rather than 'empirical'. He states that 'I propose to transform the notion of a social movement from an empirical generalization into an analytical concept' (Melucci, 1996, 28). What he means by this is that social movements should be viewed as a particular subtype (or dimension) of collective mobilization, rather than all of the empirically observable instances of collective action (which is how RMT and PPT thinks of them). What the label 'social movement' refers to at this analytical level are the collective mobilizations that are orientated towards the *central conflict* of society, and hence threaten society the most. Social movements, as Melucci (1996, 30) puts it, 'break the rules of the game' in that their aims, ideas, and beliefs represent a fundamental challenge to the very way in which that society is organized. Melucci claims that:

> The notion of a social movement is an analytical category. It designates
> that form of collective action which (i) invokes solidarity, (ii) makes
> manifest a conflict, and (iii) entails a breach of the limits of compatibility
> of the system within which the action takes place.
>
> (Melucci, 1996, 28)

In the section on Melucci later in the chapter we will come to see why he thinks that invoking 'solidarity' (i.e. a sense of 'we' against 'them') is a key part of understanding what social movements are. For now, however, the point to take is that NSM theorists suggest – following Marx – that social movements can be separated on an analytical level from other instances of collective action that do not involve clearly identified social actors and opponents who address the central conflicts of society and who can therefore (potentially at least) break the limits of the system (Melucci, 1996, 25).

NSM theorists vary however in what they think the 'new' central conflict of modern capitalist society is that has come to replace 'capital versus labour'. In the sections that follow, we will take each of the three NSM thinkers in turn and critically engage with their ideas. What they share in common is the main claim that 'social movements' – thought about in analytical terms as the collective mobilizations that express society's central conflict and have the potential to fundamentally challenge society – have shifted away from the 'old' labour movement and towards the 'new' social movements. We will see, however, that there are variations in the reasons they give for this shift and the way in which they think about 'new' social movements.

Jürgen Habermas: NSMs as defensive reactions to the 'colonization of the lifeworld'

Jürgen Habermas (1929–) is a German critical theorist, and was the student of Theodor Adorno. Like Adorno, Habermas worked critically within the Marxist tradition and has broken from Marxist class analysis in fundamental ways. In terms of his overall work, he actually wrote relatively little about NSMs, although he did accord them a very important role in advanced capitalist societies. NSMs, he argued, are our hope for a more democratic society because they raise debates and moral issues to the level of public discussion, rejuvenating a 'public sphere' in society that has been in decline (Habermas, 1989 [1962]). This public sphere of debate is essential in Habermas's view for questioning the legitimacy of political institutions and calling them to account for their actions. NSMs therefore open up spaces for critical public deliberation on political and economic issues, and enable the public to form moral viewpoints on them.

The little that Habermas has directly written about NSMs appears in his short article 'New social movements' (1981), which is an extract from his larger work, *The Theory of Communicative Action*, volume 2 (1987). In this article, Habermas provides an explanation for the NSMs, which, he argued, had arisen out of the student protests and counter-cultural movements of the late 1960s. The examples Habermas gives of NSMs are the environmental movement, peace movement, student movement, educational reform movements, self-help movements, and feminism. For Habermas, these movements express the new 'post-material' politics that was referred to in the previous section. Rather than raising questions about material distribution in society, they raised questions about *who we are and how we live* (Habermas, 1981). They organized in non-hierarchical and decentralized ways, reflecting their concern with participation, inclusivity, and democracy. Habermas argued that NSMs also cut across social classes and involved a range of groups, like women, minorities, and students. Marxist theories of class struggle could not therefore aid an explanation of these 'new' social movements

(Habermas 1986, 60). Instead, Habermas (1981) argued that NSMs could largely be understood as 'defensive' reactions to economic and political interference in everyday life.

From capital/labour conflicts to system/lifeworld conflicts

Habermas suggests that class conflict has been integrated into Western capitalist societies through a 'class compromise' (Habermas, 1987). The 'class compromise' was achieved by the establishment of post-war social democracy in the West, in which the state plays a key role in redistributing material wealth to meet the demands for social justice advanced by the labour movement. The welfare state – a victory gained through the collective action of workers – promised to look after citizens 'from the cradle to the grave'. It staved off the worst effects of life in a capitalist boom-and-bust economy by providing unemployment benefits, sick pay, health and educational services, pensions, and care for the elderly. Occupying a key position in maintaining this social democratic compromise, trade unions, Habermas (1987) argued, became increasingly institutionalized. They established recognized systems of wage-bargaining with state and employers, resolving conflicts at work by negotiating around the table or, as is often the case today, by forging 'partnerships' with employers. Unions – which had been about issues of control and autonomy at work – became narrowed to a set of material demands over pay and conditions that could be met within the established system and *without* requiring radical changes to it.

Whilst the welfare state was an initial victory for the unions, it was also responsible, therefore, for a shift in the central social conflicts of capitalist society away from capital/labour and towards 'the seam between the system and lifeworld' (Habermas 1981, 36). Habermas (1987) uses the term 'system' to refer to the state and economy, and the bureaucratic power and money through which they are coordinated. The term 'lifeworld' on the other hand, refers to everyday life composed of familial and community relationships, personal identities, and the shared values, meanings, and understandings that arise from them.

Conflicts at the seam between system and lifeworld occur when everyday life has to absorb the strains created by the increasing interference of the state and the economy in cultural and personal realms, resulting in a lifeworld that is 'over-legalized and bureaucratized' (Habermas

1986, 58). Habermas gives us a 'strain' theory of social movements in this respect, by arguing that the crises created by capitalism are now shifted from the economic and political systems into the cultural and personality systems, creating conflicts that are felt well beyond the workplace (Habermas, 1976). In the process of capitalist development, for example, the state has intervened in the economy to off-set crises. An example of this is the establishment of the welfare state in Western European countries to prevent the 'social crisis' that would result from poverty and unemployment at times of economic recession (Habermas 1976, 46). Shifting problems from the economy onto the state, however, creates potential for other types of crisis. This includes a 'legitimation crisis', where the state fails to secure the democratic support for interventions in the economy, and a 'motivation crisis', where the state's interference in everyday life erodes community solidarity, traditions, and existing cultural values (Habermas, 1976). This creates a 'loss of meaning' for people, thus shifting the crises of capitalism from economic and political spheres into cultural and psychological spheres.

Habermas (1987) calls the interference of the state and economy in cultural and psychological areas of our everyday lives, the 'colonization of the lifeworld by the system'. He claims that the 'take-over' of the lifeworld by the state and economy is the new central conflict of advanced capitalist societies, replacing the conflict between capitalists and workers which is now successfully contained by the 'class compromise'. Colonization creates new conflicts that do not surround the workplace but our personal lives outside it. Our personal lives experience an 'attack' from above as we witness aspects of life that used to be within our control, taken away from us by becoming bureaucratized and commercialized. During this process, our existing values, understanding of the world, even our very sense of who we are, comes under attack too. This is because the state and economy have a certain way of doing things, operating via laws, bureaucratic rules, and profit-motives. When this way of doing things extends into people's everyday lives then it strips meaning and purpose away from communities and families. From the perspective of the state bureaucracy and market, for example, communities are sets of 'individual' clients and consumers. Client–consumer relationships come to replace relationships based on mutual understanding and trust, such that decisions about our lives are subject to red tape, expert knowledge, and market demand. Habermas (1987) refers to the result as one of 'cultural impoverishment' – where

the ability of communities to reproduce existing values and social relationships is eroded.

The real culprit here, according to Habermas (1987), is the spread of
an 'instrumental' rationality into our everyday lives. We have come
across 'instrumental rationality' before (see Chapter 3). Rational action
theorists argued that human beings employ instrumental rationality
when they pursue the most cost-effective means for their ends. Instrumental rationality is 'success'- or 'outcome'-orientated. The state and
the economy obviously have to operate on the basis of cost-efficiency,
finding a way to balance inputs and outputs – like state taxes and
expenditure, or market supply and demand. They employ experts to
control these processes, deciding what should be done on the basis of
'scientific knowledge' because it 'knows best' when it comes to how to
coordinate systems efficiently. The world of everyday life, however,
operates on a different kind of rationality, according to Habermas
(1987). In their everyday lives, human beings are not instrumental but
'communicative' in the way they go about things. They talk about what
should be done, draw upon their lay knowledge and understandings
(rather than expert knowledge), and raise and resolve moral dilemmas
through argument and debate. This 'communicative rationality' does
not seek success, but a mutual understanding between people, enabling
them to make decisions collectively.

Colonization, therefore, redefines the whole basis of everyday life:
the contours of social relationships, personal identities, ways of living,
and even the kind of logic we employ. More of our lives, for example,
are decided upon by expert, scientific knowledge which is instrumentally rational (seeking control and success with regards to outcomes)
rather than communicative (seeking mutual understanding and moral
grounding in debate). The case point presents an example of one area of
our everyday lives which has experienced colonization and resistance
to it: health and illness.

Case point: health-related new social movements

Although Habermas conducted little empirical research on NSMs,
his ideas have been widely employed by others, including scholars interested in the social movements that arise around health

and illness (Scambler and Kelleher, 2006; Crossley et al., 2012). Health services are bureaucratically organized and, increasingly today, privatized and profit-orientated. They are run by medical experts, who 'know best' when it comes to illness, our bodies, and the treatments we should receive. Medical science has an instrumental approach to the human body, intervening and manipulating biological processes to ensure successful results. As such, we can say that medicine belongs to the sphere of society that Habermas would call the 'system'. It is clear that expert medical knowledge has considerable power and influence over our everyday lives, and reigns supreme over our own (lay) understandings of illness that arise from our experience of it and our relationships with others. We could say, then, that in modern societies we experience a 'colonization' of health and illness by an instrumentally rational medical 'system' (Scambler, 1987). It has been argued by some scholars that this process has led to health-related NSMs, which seek to defend everyday understandings and experiences of illness and to reveal public concern about the growing power of expert scientific knowledge in everyday life (Kelleher, 2001; Scambler and Kelleher, 2006). Health-related NSMs, for example, seek to show how expert medical approaches to illness can create problems with social relationships and self-identity as people are forced to be treated, and understood, in different terms. We can see this particularly clearly in the case of being labelled with a 'mental illness' like depression. The label itself creates negative effects for the person's self-identity and the way others treat them. Health-related NSMs respond by constructing alternative identities for the sufferers of illness which have positive rather than negative consequences for them. The anti-psychiatry movement of the 1960s, for example, famously mounted a challenge to medical definitions of 'mental illness', arguing that they were imposed upon 'patients' from above (Crossley, 2006). In response, sufferers themselves established self-help groups in which personal experience was privileged and became the basis for new identities (Kelleher, 1994). The argument of health-related NSMs is, therefore, that experts do not always 'know best' compared to those who actually experience illness. In fact, social movements can form when medical science defines illness in a way that contradicts individual experience and as a result, becomes contested. This has been the case for example with disability movements (Oliver, 1990), movements around Aids (Epstein, 1996), and self-help groups for diabetes sufferers (Kelleher, 1994). Health consumer groups in the UK have also been established by the users of health services in order to gain better recognition of people's needs (e.g. relating to childbirth), and to construct positive personal identities out of their experiences of living with conditions ranging from cancer and arthritis to mental illness (Allsop et al., 2004).

Scambler and Kelleher (2006) suggest therefore that health-related social movements are particularly well understood as 'new' social movements. Not only do they react to a colonization of the lifeworld, but they also respond in distinctively *communicative* ways by starting a public debate and raising moral concerns about the influence of expert medical knowledge in everyday life. In this sense, they contribute to the creation of a public sphere. They do this in part by challenging the instrumental approach of scientists and raising the ethical issues associated with medical practices. The US environmental breast cancer movement, for example, conducts its own research to support alternative understandings of the causes of breast cancer by linking it to environmental hazards which are ignored by scientists, and also fights against treatments like mastectomies without consent, which approach women's bodies as objects of medical intervention and control without considering the 'whole person' (Brown, 2004). Other movements also raise public debate about medical practices, like genetic engineering, arguing that medical science is often less concerned about the ethical implications of treatments than it is with finding the most effective means to its ends.

- How does being defined by doctors as 'sick' affect your sense of who you are and what you can do in life?
- In what ways have health-related NSMs 'reclaimed' personal identities?
- What kinds of moral concerns arise for the public around medical treatments?

For Habermas, the new conflicts produced by advanced capitalist society are therefore cultural and social-psychological: we experience a loss of meaning in our everyday lives, and a loss of freedom and control over it. Nothing is untouched by state power or the market; nothing is 'private' anymore. Everything is up for grabs by the system – not just our workplaces, but *us*. NSMs must fight to protect the lifeworld from such an onslaught, to defend existing ways of life or to give life new meanings and values that are democratically decided rather than imposed from above. NSMs, Habermas (1987) argues, are united in a 'critique' of the growing system, and a critique of instrumental rationality. They operate in ways that raise debate and moral questions and reassert communicative rationality.

Habermas assessed

Habermas argues, then, that the 'colonization of the lifeworld' is a significant source of conflict and collective mobilization in contemporary society and has replaced class conflict. NSMs respond to colonization by reasserting communicative rationality (i.e. democratic debate and discussion about issues of moral concern). NSMs are therefore important to the rejuvenation of the 'public sphere' in contemporary society (the discursive arena of critical public debate that is vital to a democracy in that it provides a space away from state and business in which their activities can be critiqued and called to account). Despite being dated, these ideas have found contemporary support, and not only from the health field as we saw in the case point. Habermas's concepts have been used to show how social movements today – like environmentalism for example – are distinctive in their assertion of communicative rationality against the expert knowledge of government and scientists (McCormick, 2006). The colonization concept has also proved elastic enough to stretch to contemporary contexts. Lee Salter (2003, 2005) argues that it can be used to think about how the internet is subject to 'colonization'. Salter suggests that this happens through the extension of laws regarding the structure and use of the internet, which have the effect of eroding online freedoms and sparking NSMs who want to defend the communicative nature of the internet. Lincoln Dahlberg (2005) also claims that we can view the internet as a space subjected to 'corporate colonization' as it is taken over by the advertising of big business, which turns its users from active participants into passive consumers. We will see in the next chapter on global social movements that Habermas's colonization thesis has also been used to explain the increasing power of multinational corporations 'offline', showing how social movements have formed in response to the damaging effects that a 'corporate take-over' has on culture and social identity (Crossley, 2003; Edwards, 2004).

In spite of this support, Habermas has been very heavily criticized for his argument that there has been a *fundamental historical break* in the nature of society's central conflicts from capital/labour to system/ lifeworld. First, Jean Cohen (1995) points out that 1970s feminism can hardly be categorized as a straightforward identity-based movement, since it retained material demands like those surrounding equal pay. Feminists did not exclusively organize through decentralized leaderless networks either. They established formal organizations with bureau-cratic structures, like the National Organization of Women (NOW) (Freeman, 1973), showing that NSMs actually contained a mixture of formal and institutionalized methods and lifestyle methods. This mix of strategies has also been characteristic of the environmental movement.

Secondly, Kenneth Tucker (1991) and Craig Calhoun (1995) show how the labour movement is also not easy to categorize. They argue that labour movements of the past had similar concerns and orga-nizational structures compared with the so-called 'new' movements. Calhoun found identity and cultural dimensions to labour movements of the past, arguing that they had been 'obscured from conventional academic observation' by an over-emphasis upon workers' material demands (Calhoun 1995, 176). Tucker, meanwhile, shows that labour movements in the late nineteenth and early twentieth century like the Knights of Labour, the German Social Democratic Party, and revolution-ary French syndicalism, had surprisingly similar concerns to the NSMs. They wanted autonomy from state bureaucracy, and they engaged in moral critiques of capitalism and a defence of their cultural traditions. Tucker also observed that syndicalism adopted the same kind of demo-cratic structures supposedly distinctive of NSMs, which, in Habermas's terms, for example, asserted communicative (over instrumental) ratio-nality. Tucker states that:

> Participants freely debated all aspects of movement goals, respected one-another's opinions and autonomy (this was embodied in their very organizational structure), and attempted to create a new society based on the principles of a decentralized democratic socialism.
>
> (Tucker 1991, 92)

It is not just worker movements of the past that challenge the old/ new distinction. Trade unions in more recent times have launched new phases of mobilization that show overlaps with NSM concerns. 'New Unionism' for example, involves the American Federation of Labor (AFL) and the UK Trades Union Congress (TUC) in finding new ways of organizing from the grassroots up, improving participation, communication, and internal democracy (Wills and Simms, 2004). It also sees trade unions moving outside the workplace. Community trade unionism (also called 'social movement' unionism), aims to forge wider connections between unions and social justice campaigns in the community, finding a fusion between material issues of wages and moral concerns over quality of life by embarking on campaigns for a 'living wage' (Wills and Simms, 2004; Edwards, 2004). A 'living wage' is central, not just for economic survival, but for self-actualization, human rights, sustainable living, and many other issues considered 'new'. New Unionism also seeks to mobilize and represent non-traditional groups of workers like women, young people, and minorities. While the TUC has fought anti-racism campaigns since the 1960s (Barker and Dale, 1998), today they have an expanded set of campaigns around racism (Red Card to Racism) and homophobia, and local union branches in the UK have been involved in countering anti-immigration and far-right activity. This picture of contemporary concerns does not fit well with the narrow view of labour movements being only about clashes with the bosses. Interestingly, whilst old movements are looking more 'new', the new movements are moving in the opposite direction. From gay liberation, to the Campaign for Nuclear Disarmament, to the environmental movement, NSMs have become more formally organized, more bureaucratized, and follow the 'same pattern of institutionalization', as Offe (1985) puts it, that characterized the labour movement.

Habermas's student, Axel Honneth, therefore argues that Habermas overplays the 'newness' of system/lifeworld conflicts in capitalist society, suggesting that capital/labour conflicts encompass the idea that workers react to the negative effects caused in their everyday lives by the interference of a profit-driven state and economy (Honneth et al., 1981). Honneth also claims that issues of culture and identity are not distinct from class conflicts, but part and parcel of them (Honneth et al., 1981). Research with trade union members shows, for example, that material and cultural concerns are interconnected rather than distinct (Edwards, 2007). Questions of material distribution raise moral questions about self-worth, societal recognition, and human dignity (Fraser and Honneth, 2003; Edwards, 2007). Wages, for example, are not just used for the satisfaction of material needs; they are also symbols of identity and self-worth (Honneth, 1995). As striking workers in the early twentieth century put it, 'we want bread, but we want roses too' – notably a slogan also adopted by second wave feminists (McAfee and Wood, 1969).

In fact, there is a wider criticism here of the way in which Habermas fails to acknowledge the relationship between culture, class, and the NSMs. While NSMs may cut across different class categories in terms of their membership, it is widely recognized that they nevertheless tend to be dominated and led by middle-class intellectuals (Offe, 1985; Parkin, 1968; Bagguley 1992; Rootes, 1995; Eder, 1993; Rose 1997). It is not accurate therefore to suggest that NSMs are divorced from class politics. Through NSMs, however, the politics of the middle class – which are more 'post-material' than the working class – gain a cultural means of public expression. Honneth et al. (1981, 23) suggests that beneath this visible middle-class struggle, working-class struggles still exist, but lack the symbolic means to be publicly expressed.

It is clear that Habermas's idea of a fundamental break in the nature of social conflict from capital/labour to system/lifeworld is a problematic one. It is always going to be the case, perhaps, when a claim involves drawing firm conclusions about the direction of historical development. Rather than seeing history as moving in stages defined by *one central conflict*, social movement scholars have generally preferred to think about cycles, or waves, of conflict instead (as we saw in Chapter 4) (Tarrow, 1998). Colin Barker and Gareth Dale (1998) argue that trying to map out history in this way is, in fact, Habermas's major mistake. Instead we should avoid constructing theoretical explanations that link the nature of social movements to social structural change, not least because they leave plenty of scope for us getting 'caught' with our 'sociological pants down' (Barker and Dale, 1998, 97) at the next twist of history.

Alain Touraine: NSMs as a struggle over 'historicity'

Alain Touraine (1925–) provides us with the French variation of NSM theory, which has some similarities with Habermas's account, particularly with regards to the growing power and influence of system 'experts' in everyday life. Touraine (1981) investigates NSMs as a product of the transition from industrial to post-industrial society. In the late 1960s and early 1970s, the industrial character of capitalist societies began to change. Sociologists debated the coming of a new 'post-industrial society' (Bell, 1976; Touraine, 1971) in which surplus value did not accrue from the sector of industrial manufacturing, but from an expanding service and financial sector and culture industries (like the mass media), based on expert knowledge and new information and communication technologies. These new technologies became even more crucial for the accumulation of capital when the crisis of the mid 1970s hit, seeing profits, employment, and wages decline across the industrial sector of the economy and, with it, the strong position the trade unions had enjoyed. Henry Ford's system of mass production was giving way to more profitable niche marketing, 'just-in-time' production, and the rising dominance of the financial markets: all of which depended more upon the communication of information and the application of knowledge rather than physical hard graft (Lash and Urry, 1987).

Touraine (1992) refers to post-industrial society as 'information society'. He argues that the production of wealth now depends primarily upon circulating, utilizing, and controlling information and its meaning, rather than manufacturing goods in factories. This is reflected in the new knowledge-based economy, in information and communication technologies, the rise of banking and the financial markets, the mass media, and consumer culture – where goods are branded, advertised, and sold as 'symbols' of lifestyle and personal identity (Lash and Urry, 1994). Information has become a resource of prime importance, therefore. The information that people have at their disposal is used to construct their understandings of the world. If the meaning of information can be controlled, then things can be represented to people in particular ways and their understanding of the world, along with their place within it, can be controlled. According to Touraine, this desire to control the very meaning that things have for people – ranging from consumer goods, to the natural environment, to our bodies, and even our psychological 'needs' – is the key feature of post-industrial society. The new post-industrial economy is therefore very different from the industrial economy: it is somehow all-encompassing, according to Touraine, in that it controls not just the production of material goods, but the production of a symbolic world of meaning (in other words, 'culture') as well. 'Culture' is exactly what is produced and manipulated for the sake of capital accumulation in post-industrial society. Touraine states that 'industrial society had transformed the means of production: post-industrial society changes the ends of production, that is, culture' (Touraine 1988, 104).

Touraine (1981) argues that the increased ability of society to produce itself materially *and culturally* has gone hand in hand with the growing power of 'technocrats'. Technocrats are experts who employ the kind of 'instrumental' rationality that Habermas talked about to manipulate and control not just the economic and political system, but the cultural system too. They use their expert knowledge to manipulate signs and symbols for their own ends, modifying as Touraine puts it, human 'values, needs, and representations' (Touraine, 1988, 104). This total control over cultural production creates what Touraine (1971) terms a 'programmed society'. The effect of the programmed society is similar to Habermas's (1987) notions of cultural impoverishment and loss of freedom: human existence is hollowed of meaning, or has meaning imposed on it from above. The only way to escape this, according to Touraine, is to attempt to define things for yourself, to come up with alternative understanding of human existence and ways of living – in short, to become a 'rebel subject'. Touraine states:

> the individual is merely a screen onto which the desires, needs, and imaginary worlds manufactured by the new communications industries are projected … The subject is formed in the will to escape the forces, rules and powers that prevent us from being ourselves, that seek to reduce us to the condition of a component of their system and their sway over everyone's activity, intentions, and interactions … The only subject is a rebel one, divided between anger and hope.
>
> (Touraine, 2007, 101)

Touraine (1981) investigates whether the 'rebel subjects' of post-industrial society were potentially to be found in NSMs like the student movement, anti-nuclear movement, and women's movement. Touraine saw that these protest groups potentially involved:

> the reactions of cultural actors who are trying to keep, or to recover, control over their own behaviour, in the same way that workers once did with respect to their working conditions.
>
> (Touraine, 1981, 150)

For Touraine, this struggle was represented by the women's movement. Feminists in the women's liberation movement (1969/70), for example, mobilized around the notion that the 'personal is political' and constructed themselves as 'rebel subjects' by rejecting the dominant meanings, expectations, and labels attached to being a 'woman'. They sought to regain control over the meaning of their existence away from subordinated housewives whose purpose was to be the object of male desire, by redefining female bodies, sexuality, and reproduction on their own terms. New cultural values formed the basis of a counter-culture which was conducted through alternative media, music, art, and poetry, providing women with an alternative way of knowing, representing, and relating to themselves and to men (Rowbotham, 1997).

The struggle over 'historicity'

Touraine suggests that we should understand the struggle of the NSMs for personal freedom in an all-dominating 'programmed society' as a struggle over what he calls 'historicity' (Touraine, 1977, 1981). Touraine's theoretical approach is referred to as 'action theory' because he argues that in all phases of history, social actors are at the centre of social and historical processes, creating them through their collective action. Hence, social movements are central to an understanding of society in his eyes. Through their collective action, human beings 'produce' society, akin to Marx's notion that 'people make history'. The term 'historicity' therefore refers to the collective processes by which society produces itself. Reid defines 'historicity' as: 'the capacity [of society] to produce its own social and cultural field, its own historical environment' (Reid, 1979, 91). Historicity involves a struggle, however, and it is this struggle that can be seen as the 'central social conflict' of society (Touraine, 1992, 125). The struggle is between 'those who direct the self-production and transformation of society' (i.e. the technocrats who dominate and control social and historical processes) 'and those who are subjected to its effects' (i.e. social subjects in their role as consumers, members of communities, families, and so forth) (Touraine, 1992, 125). Let us unpack this struggle in more detail.

In post-industrial society, the ability of human beings to produce society through their action is enhanced. This is due to the ability that actors in post-industrial society have to produce society not only materially, but culturally too. Material and cultural production (and reproduction) is in our hands. Touraine states that:

> societies are less and less 'in' history; they produce themselves their
> historical existence by their economic, political, and cultural capacity to
> act upon themselves and to produce their future and even their memory.
> (Touraine, 1981, 155)

The point of conflict comes, however, from the way in which technocrats are increasingly controlling the production of society. Rather than democratically deciding upon the cultural values that will guide social production and thus historical development, decisions are being taken out of our hands and placed in the hands of the so-called industry 'experts' (the technocrats). In Touraine's (1981) view, NSMs emerge as a critical response to technocracy and can be understood as attempts to take control back over historicity. NSMs, not the labour movement, have the potential therefore to express and engage with the central social conflict of post-industrial society (Touraine, 1981). They are potentially *the* social movement that can break the limits of the system by engaging in a struggle with technocrats over the direction of social and historical development and the cultural values that underpin it.

Touraine's work on NSMs is about investigating the potential that they have for becoming the replacement for class-based mobilizations in post-industrial society (Scott, 1990). If the new movements, like women's liberation, environmentalism, and peace movements, could be understood to relate to the central social conflict of post-industrial society and to offer an alternative model of society, then they could meet the analytic definition of a 'social movement' drawn from Marxism. To qualify, the movement must: define a social group that it represents; define its enemy; and develop an alternative idea of social development, which is not based upon the current technocracy (Scott, 1990, 63). In order to see whether the new movements of the 1970s and 1980s fulfilled these criteria, Touraine (1981, 1983) closely researched the way in which they developed an understanding of their struggle. We consider his distinctive methodological approach in the methods point.

Methods point: sociological intervention

Alain Touraine developed a novel method for studying the NSMs, called 'sociological intervention'. This method was widely used at his research centre for social movements in the 1970s and 1980s (CADIS). The method was called 'sociological intervention' because it involved sociological researchers intervening in the discussion and self-analysis of social movements by setting up meetings between activists and researchers. The purpose of the meetings was to set up a conversation between activists and researchers so that researchers could analyse the meaning of the movement and how it relates to the central social conflict of society (i.e. the struggle over historicity). This intervention was necessary because Touraine argues that social movements contain many layers of 'meaning', and it is the job of the researcher to analyse what the movement means in relation to the society in which it arises. In the 1970s and 1980s, interventions were therefore employed to 'test' whether the NSMs, like the student movement, women's movement, and anti-nuclear movement, expressed the central social conflicts produced by the transition from industrial to post-industrial society (Dubet and Wieviorka, 1996, 55).

Touraine's researchers asked movement activists to discuss who they think they are (*Identity*), who they think they are against (*Opponents*), and their understanding of the social field that gives rise to this opposition (*Total*) (Dubet and Wieviorka, 1996, 56). Touraine thought that investigating 'IOT' could get to the heart of a social movement and what it means. Using their analytic skills, the researcher uses the knowledge produced by the interventions to distinguish the 'highest level' of meaning that the movement expresses (Touraine, 1981). This was not necessarily what the activists said themselves, but the researcher's own analysis of how the movement might connect to the central conflicts of society. Touraine argued, for example, that student and women's movements – whilst they had different aims and agendas – were, at the 'highest level' of meaning, social movements which challenged the technocratic way that decisions were made in modern societies by government and corporate elites. This 'hypothesis' was then fed back to the activists in more meetings as a way of testing the analysis and helping the movement itself to develop. In terms of the anti-nuclear movement, however, Touraine (1983) concluded that it ultimately failed to fundamentally challenge society because it was clear that while activists critiqued the expert scientific knowledge behind the nuclear energy policy in France in the 1970s, they did not identify 'technocracy' as the key target of their struggle, and

did not develop a coherent sense of the wider social group whom they represented (Scott, 1990, 64–5).

- Are social movements 'what they say they are' or do they have a 'higher
  level' of meaning that can be uncovered by the researcher?
- How do you think activists might respond to being part of a 'sociological
  intervention'?
- Should research on social movements always consider the way in which
  movements understand themselves?

Touraine assessed

Touraine argues that the new post-industrial economy produces a new
set of social conflicts. These conflicts can no longer be explained in
terms of class struggle. Touraine makes it really clear that in his view,
there is one central social movement in each phase of society that
comes to express the central social conflict of that society. In post-
industrial society, NSMs look as if they could take over and 'occupy
the central position held by the workers' movement in industrial society' (Touraine 1981, 24). Touraine's view of history as one of definite
stages of social development (i.e. industrial to post-industrial) which
correlate with one central social conflict in each case is therefore open
to the same criticism that we encountered in Habermas's version of the
NSM theory.

Alan Scott (1990) provides us with some more specific criticisms
of Touraine's theory. First, Touraine seeks to find a common struggle
among a wide variety of NSMs – from women's liberation to the anti-
nuclear movement – which are actually so diverse in their ideological viewpoints that, as Scott (1990, 67) states, 'there is little realistic
possibility' of finding a common thread. This relates to a criticism
that applies to NSM theory generally: they lump together very diverse
movements under one umbrella, wrongly suggesting that it is possible
to sum up the concerns, class base, and structure of extremely varied
and fluid sets of social movements (Bagguley, 1992). This is an impulse
that Melucci, it has to be said, tries to refrain from.

Secondly, and most significantly, Scott (1990, 69) criticizes Touraine
for a contradiction in his theoretical approach. We have seen that

Touraine emphasizes the self-production of society, the way in which social action is central to shaping society and its historical development. Touraine suggests in fact, that structural strain theories of social movements suck agency (the ability of human beings to affect the world around them) out of the picture by establishing a functional or automatic relationship between structural strains and social movements. Instead, historical development according to Touraine is all about agency. Modern societies in fact are marked by the capacity of human beings to be reflexive about society's choices and to affect and control the direction of social change. Touraine refers to this in his concept of 'historicity'. History, argues Touraine (1992, 144), is *made* by a society which 'debates its choices'. To leave reflexive social actors out of the picture is to be left with no picture to analyse at all. While this is a useful corrective, argues Scott (1990, 67), to some of the structuralist theories that we looked in Chapter 4, Touraine nevertheless undermines the central role he gives to social action. What Scott means by this is that Touraine appears ultimately to put social structures first in his analysis by arguing that there is only one social movement in each type of society (Scott, 1990, 69). If this is true, then it means ultimately that social movements arise as a response to social structural strains and the conflicts they create. Action is a response to the structures that shape it. This sounds little different from the structuralist accounts that we encountered in the last chapter and heavily criticized.

Finally, we should note that Touraine's methodology has been criticized by Alberto Melucci (whom we are about to discuss in more detail). Melucci (1989) also made use of sociological intervention in the case studies he conducted in Milan in the 1970s and 1980s into youth movements, women's movements, environmental movements, and self-help/ spiritual groups. Melucci video-taped and analysed numerous meetings between researchers and activists. He challenged Touraine's approach to the use of interventions, however, because he argued that it was wrong to translate activists' own understandings of the struggle that they were involved in, into the 'higher meanings' of the researcher. To do so implied that the academic researcher had some privileged role in the development of the movement, helping activists to see the 'true nature' of their struggle. Instead, Melucci (1989) argued that interventions should be a two-way exchange of knowledge between sociologists and activists. Researchers offer their analytical knowledge of society and where social movements fit into it, and activists offer their understanding of the struggle, providing mutual benefit to both. Observing discussions between activists is also crucial in Melucci's view for giving researchers insight into the interactive processes of 'collective identity' construction that lie behind all social movement activity. It is to the issue of collective identity that we now turn.

Alberto Melucci: NSMs as the creation of new collective identities

Melucci (1943–) provides us with the Italian version of NSM theory, and is similar to Habermas and Touraine in highlighting the cultural and psychological nature of contemporary social conflict. Although Touraine and Melucci do make reference to Habermas's work (and vice versa), they have a closer relationship in that Melucci had been Touraine's student. Like Touraine, Melucci (1996) views post-industrial societies as 'information societies'. He argues that living in an information society has an upside and a downside. The upside is that people can use the contents of the vast symbolic system created by information society to construct an autonomous sense of self. Previously, a person's way of life and self-identity was set out for them in advance because they belonged to identity categories that were established through the structure of industrial society itself (like social class categories). In post-industrial society however, these group memberships have dissolved because material needs are largely fulfilled, and the experience of work no longer gives rise to class-based collective identities (Melucci, 1996). In the vacuum left, people are 'individualized'. They are increasingly well-educated, knowledgeable, and skilled at work, and increasingly self-reflexive and able to make their own choices outside work. With fixed social categories removed, people construct their own sense of self through their life-projects (their lifestyles and leisure activities). This increase in individual freedom is seen as a key feature of 'post-modern' society.

The downside, however, is that society depends upon us being *certain kinds* of individuals, ones who have life-projects that are compatible with advanced capitalism. To ensure this conformity, social control is increasingly targeted not at the workplace but at the personal lives of individuals outside it through the operation of 'dominant cultural codes' (Melucci, 1996). These dominant cultural codes create meanings and understandings that are used to construct identities, bodies, needs, and desires that serve the dominant interests. In order to ensure the conditions for social reproduction, for example, people's behaviour relating to 'consumption, sexuality, education, and interpersonal relations' has to be controlled from above, not just by imposing socially prescribed norms and values, but through what Melucci calls 'the hidden operation of *symbolic* forms, patterning people's thoughts, emotions and feelings' (Melucci, 1996, 180). So much for being an individual: life in post-industrial society forces us all to be the same. We have to conform to the same values, the same desires, the same needs. The search for difference – or an 'autonomous' sense of self – therefore becomes sharpened. Put another way, individuals struggle to be just that: an individual, who is truly free to decide who they want to be for themselves. Melucci states that:

> Personal identity – that is to say, the possibility on the biological, psychological, and interpersonal levels, of being recognized as an individual – is the property which is now being claimed and defended.
>
> (Melucci, 1980, 218)

Like Touraine, Melucci developed these ideas based on studies of the women's movement, youth movements, environmental movements, and peace movements. He sees in these movements 'forms of collective action based on the affirmation and defence of one's identity' (Melucci, 1996, 186). He also sees in them the crucial role played by information. Like the health movements and women's movements already discussed, NSMs attempt to gather and use information for the purposes of developing oppositional forms of knowledge that can give an alternative understanding of reality (Melucci, 1996, 223).

Collective identity

Out of all the NSM theorists, Melucci gives us the most comprehensive account of how the 'social actors' who respond to the conflicts of post-industrial society form (Opp, 2009). These social actors no longer arise automatically out of the conditions of industrial society as 'classes as real social groups are withering away' (Melucci, 1996, 234). Instead, Melucci argues that new social actors have to invent themselves, and they have to do so in the course of their everyday lives in which the new conflicts over cultural codes are encountered. In what he calls the 'submerged networks of everyday life', people fight to regain control over the symbolic resources of information society, and they use them to invent themselves as new kinds of individuals. Importantly, these new personal identities can also become the basis for new collective identities which make explicit the existence of a new 'we' who is in conflict with 'them' over 'this'. In other words, creating new collective identities means creating NSMs to replace the class-based mobilizations of the past.

The focus for social movement theory should therefore be upon the process by which new collective identities form. This is a process that is missed in other approaches to social movements according to Melucci (1985). While he applauds its emphasis upon human decision-making and strategy, Melucci argues that, for all that is written about the 'doing' of collective action, RMT fails to actually give much of a sense of *how* those who share common interests because of their structural location (class, gender, and so forth) come to develop a shared sense of purpose. Instead, they are just individuals participating together because of their self-interest (Melucci, 1996, 18). This raises a question about how a common *consciousness* (a sense of 'we') actually develops. This is not a question about how rational individuals can be coaxed into acting together (Olson, 1965), and it is also more than the question of how solidarity can be built through emotional attachments (Blumer, 1951 [1946]), it is about how a bunch of individuals come to think of themselves as a 'social actor'. In other words, how a group develops a sense of who they are, who they are against, and what the struggle is all about. To understand how social actors in these terms form, we need to understand how a 'collective identity' is constructed.

A common consciousness, argues Melucci, has to be constructed by social actors themselves and this is essentially what they do when they 'build' a social movement (as opposed, or in addition, to mobilizing resources for example). The implication of this is that activists build social movements not primarily, or even necessarily, by establishing formal organizations (SMOs), but by constructing a 'shared collective identity'. Melucci states that:

> A collective identity is nothing else than a shared definition of the field of opportunities and constraints offered to collective action; 'shared' means constructed and negotiated through a repeated process of 'activation' of social relationships connecting the actors.
>
> (Melucci, 1985, 793)

Collective identities, then, are not pre-given but arise out of the social relationships between people in which shared definitions and understandings of the circumstances in which they find themselves are created, negotiated, and reproduced. This shared definition of the situation involves three key elements essential to a social movement: a shared sense of who the challengers are, who the opponents are, and what is at stake in the struggle. In other words, a collective identity refers to a sense of 'we' who are against 'them' in a conflict over 'this'.

Melucci is keen to point out that if we view social movements essentially as collective identities in this way, then the kind of structure and organization they take is very much an informal 'network' structure composed of social relationships that give rise to 'aims, beliefs, decisions and exchanges' (Melucci, 1980, 793). This is a very different empirical entity compared to the formal SMO with its hierarchical bureaucratic structure and, crucially for Melucci, it means that social movement activity happens more often than not away from public view. The construction and reproduction of new collective identities is 'submerged in everyday life' where 'cultural innovation' is practised (Melucci, 1980, 800; 1989). This is not to say that more formal SMOs do not develop, and that groups at times become visible by, for example, engaging in a public confrontation with their adversary, but that these more submerged processes of identity building are always there in the background (Melucci, 1980, 800). Lying out of view, they are very often forgotten or missed by movement scholars who have their gaze firmly set on the glittering lights of public protest. Nevertheless, informal interactions in which a shared definition of the situation – a sense of 'we', of 'them', and of the 'stakes' – is constructed, lie behind all visible, public, instances of collective action. In Melucci's view, identity-building has become of prime importance to NSMs in contemporary 'information society' exactly because social class categories can no longer be relied upon to supply an automatic sense of collective identity.

Melucci assessed

Melucci's work on collective identity is the main way in which European NSM theory has influenced mainstream social movement studies. While arguments about a break in the nature of society and its central social conflicts have been well criticized (as we have seen in relation to Habermas and Touraine), social movement scholars have welcomed the focus upon collective identity building. It is accepted, for example, that the construction of collective identity is a process which is relevant to *all* social movements, and is not especially correlated with the NSMs as Melucci suggests (Polletta and Jasper, 2001, 287; Opp, 2009). It is not a case of 'strategy or identity' because both are necessary and compatible processes (Cohen, 1985). Constructing a sense of 'we' who are against 'them' in a conflict over 'this', is what social movements have to do in order to be effective at mobilization. Melucci should note that this includes labour movements as well. Class categories – even in industrial capitalist societies – did not somehow automatically create collective identities either. They too have to be constructed in a process that involves building 'cultures of solidarity' among workers as Rick Fantasia (1989) puts it.

Melucci goes further than this however: constructing collective identities is not just what social movements *do*, it is what they *are*. Social movements in these terms can be conceptualized as the process by which new collective identities are constructed. I want to suggest that this conceptualization of social movements has merits which are twofold: (a) it helps us to identify forms of political protest that do not fit our conventional understanding of 'political' action; and (b) it helps us to recognize circumstances in which individuals embark upon collective action 'on their own'. Let us unpack each of these in turn.

(a) *A new idea of political protest*

Melucci's conceptualization of social movements fundamentally challenges the image of 'political' action that many of us hold. The process of constructing new collective identities is *itself* the political action (and not what the group does once it has formed, e.g. stage a public campaign). This means that political protest can look very different compared with formal SMOs, trade unions, or political interest groups. It does not, in fact, need to be formally organized, or publicly visible, at all. Instead, cultural struggles can be considered to be 'political' challenges in post-industrial society because they involve making a bid for freedom in a system which seeks only to control. Melucci (1996) calls NSMs 'prophets in the present' who reveal that different ways of life are possible – not after some revolution – but in the here and now. The politics of NSMs in this respect can be called 'prefigurative': they live the change that they want to see in the future.

Alongside SMOs, we can also think of social movements therefore as counter-cultural spaces – or 'submerged' networks – as Melucci (1980, 800) calls them. Counter-cultural spaces have been variously labelled 'free spaces' (Evans and Boyte, 1992; Polletta, 1999), 'oppositional subcultures' (Johnston, 1991), 'cultural laboratories' (Mueller, 1994), and, most recently, 'social movement scenes' (Leach and Haunss, 2009). Social movement scenes have a complex relationship to politics. The scene can be understood as an alternative community, including alternative media, music, shops, hang-outs, ways of dressing, and living (e.g. squatters and communes). It fosters alternative personal and collective identities – which may or may not be mobilized by SMOs. Its primary purpose however is to achieve autonomy through the very nature of its activity. Leach and Haunss (2009) use the example of the 'autonomous movement' which emerged in the 1970s in Europe out of the squatter and anti-nuclear movements. The scene still exists today and focuses upon inventing oppositional identities and values in daily life, reflected in clothing, punk music, and collective living (Leach and Haunss, 2009, 62). Mirroring Melucci's (1989, 60) contention that for NSMs the 'form is the message', the slogan of the autonomous community is 'the way is the goal' (Leach and Haunss, 2009, 258).

(b) *Doing collective action on your own*

Melucci's conceptualization of social movements is also valuable in helping us to acknowledge that collective action does not always have to involve a 'physically present' group of people. What I mean by this is that, sometimes, individuals can do collective action 'on their own'. They do so by taking direct action in their everyday lives (referred to as 'DIY politics' – 'do it yourself'), while seeing this action as contributing towards the construction of a wider collective identity. This is made clear in the environmental movement, for example. From the 1970s, Greenpeace, Friends of the Earth, and Earthfirst! argued that the way to resist the damage to the natural environment caused by a growing capitalist state and economy was to change the way in which people lived their everyday lives. Individuals could choose to live in more environmentally friendly ways by recycling and growing their own food (Veldman, 1994).

The notion that the way to achieve political change is through personal change helps us to understand a range of contemporary forms of collective action that Haenfler et al. (2012) call 'lifestyle movements'. Lifestyle movements involve individuals focusing upon their personal identity and everyday practices as a 'site of social change' (Haenfler et al., 2012, 5). Lifestyle activists adopt different ways of doing things – from veganism, to virginity pledges, to buying fair trade – in order to construct a sense of self which for them is 'ethical'. While lifestyle activists 'imagine' a wider community in which other people are doing the same thing as them, they are not necessarily physically co-present. While Haenfler et al. avoid calling lifestyle movements 'new social movements', it could be argued that without Melucci's ideas (and NSM theory more widely) social movement scholars would be much less able to look at the political importance of personal lifestyle choices. This is perhaps why Melucci in particular has been employed to understand contemporary lifestyle movements like 'voluntary simplicity'. The debate point explores how well Melucci's ideas can be applied to this case.

Debate point: does NSM theory help us to understand contemporary lifestyle movements?

Voluntary simplicity is an international movement of individuals who adopt a way of life which rejects the materialistic nature of our existence, like the constant emphasis upon consumption (i.e. the value we place on buying things, having things, and wanting more things). Hélène Cherrier (2007) argues that voluntary simplicity can be viewed in Melucci's (1996) terms as a challenge to the dominant 'codes' of consumer culture. Rather than build a formal SMO, this challenge is manifested in the everyday personal lives of individuals, who express their post-materialist values through their consumption choices in order to construct an 'ethical' sense of self. Voluntary simplifiers do things like buy less (e.g. 'Buy Nothing Day'), work less (to enjoy life more), downsize, reuse and recycle, sell their car, ride a bicycle, buy fair trade, grow their own, boycott unethical products. Drawing upon Melucci, Cherrier argues that voluntary simplicity is not merely about individual preferences and identity. Instead, the personal identities of ethical consumers are intertwined with the collective identity they construct through their interactions. Individuals help to construct a collective identity for voluntary simplicity through their involvement in its social networks (virtual, like websites, and face-to-face, like conferences). These inter-actions generate shared definitions, values, beliefs, understandings, and alternatives to the dominant culture of consumption. Individuals draw upon these to construct their own sense of an 'ethical self'. Voluntary simplicity is, as Melucci suggests, the co-construction of a counter-cul-tural space within people's everyday lives where new identities and new ways of living can form. Haenfler et al. (2012) however argue that it is problematic to analyse lifestyle movements like voluntary simplicity as 'new social movements'. Not only does the term 'new social movement' imply false assumptions about the historical novelty of lifestyle activ-ism, but NSM theorists still focus more upon collective action rather than individual action. Haenfler et al. (2012), 5) argue that participation in lifestyle movements 'occurs primarily at the individual level with the subjective understanding that others are taking similar action'. It also involves personal identity work rather than collective identity work in that individuals seek to construct through their lifestyle practices a 'morally coherent' sense of self which is meaningful to them.

- In what ways are 'lifestyle movements' 'new social movements'? Would you label them NSMs?
- Is it beneficial to analyse 'voluntary simplicity' using Melucci's ideas on 'collective identity'? Give reasons for your view.
- Can NSM theory help us understand *individual* action directed to-wards social change?

Class struggle and cultural struggle

While Melucci may be useful in pointing to the political significance of cultural struggles in everyday life, it is not the case that we need the 'newness' argument in order to enable us to conceptualize the relationship between cultural struggle and politics. Marxist scholars have also drawn a relationship, for example, between class struggle and efforts on the part of individuals to reinvent everyday life. Barker and Dale (1998) suggest that NSM theorists miss the more cultural aspects to class struggle by concentrating simply upon economic dimensions:

> For Marxism, 'class struggle' is not simply the struggle of the exploited
> for already given 'material interests' within capitalism, but is at its heart
> a struggle with the potential for transcending the limits of that mode of
> production. It is not simply economic, but equally political and cultural.
>   (Barker and Dale, 1998, 82–3)

Picking up on the cultural dimensions of class struggle, Alf Nilsen (2007, 2009) argues that the essence of Marx's approach is the idea that society is the ongoing product of 'conscious human activity', reflected in the statement, 'people make history'. Marx argued, for example, that what is distinctive about human beings as a species is their ability to consciously transform their environment through labour in order to satisfy their needs. This labour is not only about producing tools to satisfy material needs, but about producing 'symbols and signs' to satisfy the human need for everyday life to have meaning and value (the bread *and* the roses). Conscious human activity does not just transform external nature therefore, but 'inner' nature too, creating new needs and new capacities for human beings all the time.

Nilsen argues that this conscious human activity becomes contained however when it is socially organized into a particular system, for example, capitalism. Human activity within capitalist society gives rise to a set of 'dominant' needs and capacities that thwart the ability of human beings to be truly free in shaping both the world and themselves. In other words, 'people make history' but 'not in circumstances of their own choosing'. This focus upon the domination of individuals, shaping their very needs and 'inner life' in the interests of capital accumulation, sounds very similar to Melucci's argument, except it is not historically specific to post-industrial society. It is the general human condition under capitalism.

This does not mean that the dominant set of human needs and capacities contained within capitalist society are the only ones. Day-to-day life throws up new problems and people invent and learn new ways to address them (Cox and Nilsen, 2005). These new practices lead them to develop new needs and new capacities. When people's daily practices develop needs and capacities that are 'oppositional' to the dominant ones (which Nilsen 2007 calls 'radical needs and capacities') then they can be the source of new kinds of human activity, new meanings, and new social relationships. In other words, Nilsen (2007) argues that human beings who develop 'radical needs and capacities' through their everyday practices, are able to change the structure of society in the here and now. What is interesting is that the image that Nilsen constructs can apply to NSMs and contemporary lifestyle movements like 'voluntary simplicity', as well as labour movements:

> The practice which transcends the given society would then be … oppositional collective action that consciously, explicitly, and actively seeks the transformation and transcendence of a dominant structure of enacted needs and capacities and the social formation in which it is embedded so as to fully satisfy the radical needs and capacities that are frustrated and contained within this structure and formation.
>
> (Nilsen 2007, 20)

There is an ongoing conflict, then, between human practices that foster a dominant set of human needs and capacities, and alternative or oppositional practices that foster radical sets of human needs and capacities. The latter, oppositional practices are invented by human beings themselves through their conscious attempts to survive: materially, psychologically, and emotionally. Nilsen shows, therefore, that there is no 'new' 'cultural' conflict, opposed to the 'old' 'material' one that Marx was talking about. Neither are cultural conflicts distinct from 'class struggle'. We will return to this point in Chapter 6.

Summary

This chapter has critically engaged with NSM theory. NSM theory is a perspective on social movements that developed through the work of three European thinkers from the 1970s onwards: Habermas (Germany), Touraine (France), and Melucci (Italy). NSM theory presents us with the claim that there has been a fundamental shift in the nature of Western, capitalist societies, summed up as a shift from industrial to post-industrial society. Post-industrial society has a 'new' central conflict, and 'new' social movements that respond to it. NSMs are 'new' in the following ways:

- They have new political concerns, which are post-material and arise from the cultural and psychological effects of capitalism.

- They have a new site of struggle, not the workplace but culture and everyday life.
- They have a new composition, made up of a mix of social classes, and including more women, young people and minorities than had been seen in the labour movement (although there is an over-representation of middle-class intellectuals).
- They have a new organizational form, which is decentralized, participatory, and democratic.

NSM theory has made some positive contributions to the way in which social movements are conceptualized. First, NSM theory brings home to us why Sleater Kinney's opening assertion in this chapter that 'culture is what we make it' is a *politically* provocative statement, and why attempts to reinvent identities, meanings, values, language, and representations are *political* actions. They offer us many reasons why struggles around culture and identity are created in contemporary societies: from the power of technocrats, to the assault of state bureaucracy and capitalist markets, to domination through cultural codes.

Secondly, this understanding of culture, not just as a resource for social movements but a battleground on which they act, helps us to see that counter-cultural struggles aimed at constructing alternative identities and lifestyles (and sometimes involve individuals acting outside SMOs) *are* social movements. This is difficult to do through the lenses of the more 'politically' orientated theories of social movements as formal organizations that publicly target the state in the pursuit of shared interest. NSMs largely call for autonomy from the state rather than more interference. Thirdly, NSM theory is also very strong when it comes to analysing the process by which the 'social actors', who constitute movements, form in the first place, employing techniques of 'sociological intervention' to see how a sense of 'we' against 'them' in a conflict over 'this' is constructed by activists. In this respect, it has brought to light the role of collective identity in the mobilization process, which should enrich the analysis of any social movement (Polletta and Jasper 2001, 287; Opp, 2009).

NSM theory, however, offers us these insights at a cost. It analyses the cultural struggles that took prominence in the transition to post-industrial society – women's, peace, and environmental movements, and so forth – by drawing a distinction between them and the 'old' material struggles of class-based movements. It claimed that culture as a battleground was, somehow, not just more publicly visible at this time, but entirely 'new' to the emerging post-industrial society, and signalled a shift in the central contradictions and conflicts of capitalism.

Just as we can point to three positive contributions of NSM theory therefore, this 'newness' argument has three major flaws:

- It feeds us a false claim in suggesting that material and cultural conflicts are distinct when they are actually interconnected (and old and new movements contain both).
- Because it glosses over this interconnection, NSM theory perpetuates an economistic reading of the class-struggle.
- NSM theorists therefore fail to see that Marxism understands class struggle as cultural as well as material, as about the control of external nature and its effects on inner nature, as about everyday life and identity, as well as work and wages (Nilsen, 2007).

What this more continuous picture of social conflict gets rid of are the problematic assertions about history – about what is 'old' and what is 'new'. It is crucial that we are rid of this, if only to prevent us being 'caught with our sociological pants down' (Barker and Dale, 1998, 97) in the next two chapters. For if the real point of NSM theory is to identify the 'new social actors' of contemporary society then even Touraine (2002) admits that he might have got the identity of those social actors wrong. Today, 'even newer' social actors (Crossley, 2003) mobilize to express the central conflicts of 'global society' and to show that 'another world is possible' – from the alternative globalization movement (AGM) fighting for social justice, to the 'anti-social movement' of terrorism (Touraine, 2002). In the next two chapters, we take each of these cases in turn and ask what they tell us about the nature of social movements today.

DISCUSSION POINT

- Do you think of yourself as belonging to a social class? Would you ever join a trade union? Can class identities be a source of collective identity today?
- Can struggles aimed at reinventing culture by giving alternative meaning to human existence really be considered 'political'?
- Do you ever buy Fair Trade? Grow your own? Recycle? Are individual actions like this part of *collective* action in your view?
- Has class struggle got anything to do with individual efforts to reinvent everyday life?

FURTHER READING

It is worth engaging with the NSM theorists in their words. Habermas's (1981) short article entitled 'New social movements' in *Telos* is a good place to start, although for wider context read it alongside his theoretical work *The Theory of Communicative Action*, volume 2 (1987) in which it also appears. For Melucci, *Nomads of the Present* (1989) and *Challenging Codes* (1996) are interesting reads, and for Touraine either *The Voice and the Eye* (1981) or his more recent *A New Paradigm for Understanding Today's World* (2007). For contemporary Marxist approaches to social movements see Colin Barker et al. (eds.), *Marxism and Social Movements* (2013).

6

From national to global social movements: network movements, alternative globalization, and new media

> Our protests have erupted on continent after continent,
> fuelled by extremes of wealth and poverty, by military
> repression, by environmental breakdown, by ever-
> diminishing power to control our own lives and resources. We
> are furious at the increasingly thin sham of democracy, sick of
> the lies of consumer capitalism, ruled by ever more powerful
> corporations. We are the globalization of resistance.
>
> (Notes from Nowhere, 2003, 21)

In this chapter, we will consider the challenges to conceptualizations of social movements and protest that come from three interlinked sources: globalization, the growing trend in 'transnational activism' (Tarrow, 2006), and the rise of 'new media' (by which I mean ICTs, including mobile communications and social media). Globalization has involved the spread of 'people, capital, goods, and ideas' (Adamson, 2005, 31) across national borders in ways that have provided social movements with a growing infrastructure to 'go global'. This trend – like globalization itself – is not, historically speaking, 'new'. Since 1989 (and the collapse of communism), however, globalization of a particular kind has stepped up its pace, extending a capitalist economic model and Western consumer culture across the globe, which is driven by multinational corporations and international political and economic institutions (Waters, 1995; Smith and Johnston, 2002; Cohen and Kennedy, 2013). This 'dominant mode' of globalization has been seen to provide a new issue environment for social movements, and new targets of activism (Sklair, 1998).

The scholarship on 'global social movements' and 'transnational contentious politics' is vast (see Della Porta and Tarrow 2005; Della Porta 2007). It is not possible here to pick up and consider all aspects of the debate, and there will be necessary omissions. Instead, we will consider two key questions: first, what processes and mechanisms are involved in shifting contention from the national to the global level? Secondly, how can we conceptualize 'global social movements' and do they – and their relationship with new media – require us to understand social movements in very different terms? To engage with these two questions, we will concentrate our attention on the most significant 'global social movement' to date: the alternative globalization movement (AGM).

By the end of the chapter you should have some knowledge of the AGM's history, organization, and activities. You will understand some of the mechanisms and processes related to transnational activism – like externalization, domestication, diffusion, brokerage, and identity-shifts – and how they can aid our understanding of why and how the AGM mobilizes. You will be aware of the ways in which the structure, tactics, and targets of the AGM stretch and challenge the conceptualizations of social movements that we have encountered so far in the book. You will also understand how the AGM simultaneously challenges and reinforces aspects of political process theory (PPT) and new social movement (NSM) theory, depending upon which 'camp' within the movement you look at.

Global social movement processes and mechanisms

We begin by considering our first key question: what processes and mechanisms are important in shifting social movements from the national to the global level? By invoking the language of processes and mechanisms, I refer you back to the 'contentious politics' (CP) approach that we encountered in Chapter 4, which was a development within PPT (McAdam et al., 2001; Tilly and Tarrow, 2006; Tarrow and Tilly, 2009). CP offers us a range of fluid 'processes and mechanisms' that recur across episodes of contention (like radicalization, diffusion, brokerage, democratization, identity-shifts, repression) and which can be drawn upon to understand social movement mobilization. These are divided into three main categories (McAdam et al., 2001, 25–6, phrasing below is theirs):

- environmental mechanisms – 'externally generated influences on conditions affecting social life'
- relational mechanisms – 'alter connections among people, groups, and interpersonal networks'
- cognitive mechanisms – 'operate through alterations of individual and collective perception'.

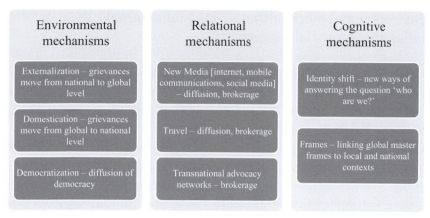

Figure 6.1
Processes and mechanisms involved in scale-shifts.
Source: adapted from the mechanisms and processes presented by McAdam et al.
(2001), and Tarrow (2006).

Although we raised criticisms of the CP approach in Chapter 4 – which mainly surrounded its (perhaps unintended) status as a general theoretical model for all forms of contentious politics – its focus upon the fluid processes and mechanisms that drive social movement mobilization is particularly helpful for thinking about the shift from national- to global-level contention. Although it is not entirely clear how we should think of 'processes' and 'mechanisms' theoretically (e.g. what makes something a 'process' and something else a 'mechanism'?), we can nevertheless, pick out some specific examples of the processes and mechanisms that McAdam et al. (2001) refer to as valuable for understanding how contention spreads from one place to another. The mechanism of 'diffusion' for example is widely invoked in studies about how social movement activism, ideas, and tactics spread beyond a particular locale to new geographical areas (McAdam and Rucht, 1993; Hedstrom, 1994; Soule, 1997; Given, et al., 2010; Wood, 2012; Edwards, 2014).

Furthermore, Sidney Tarrow (2006) has highlighted specific mechanisms and processes that can aid an understanding of transnational contention by explaining how issues, ideas, and activists can shift between the national and global level. In this section, we will apply CP's three categories of mechanisms, alongside Sidney Tarrow's insights. Figure 6.1 highlights the processes and mechanisms that we will discuss. These are necessarily selective of the range of processes and mechanisms that we could have chosen, but they nevertheless provide us with a good place to start.

Environmental mechanisms – changing external influences on social movements

Let us begin with 'environmental mechanisms'. Environmental mechanisms refer to changing external influences on social movements (McAdam et al., 2001). The rise of a 'global society' since the 1990s has been a significant development in the environment of social movements. 'Global society' refers to the way in which the movement of 'people, capital, goods, and ideas' across national borders (Adamson, 2005, 31) creates political, economic, and cultural interdependence among countries. As a result, they begin to form 'one society' that exists at the global level, rather than many separate societies bounded by nation states (Cohen and Kennedy, 2013).

A global society has been a long time in the making. National society – with the nation state at the centre of power and government – has increasingly given way to the global level since the end of World War II (although we must be critical of accounts of its total demise, as we will see later in the chapter). An array of international political and economic institutions, for example, has arisen since the Bretton Woods Conference in 1944, which gave rise to an international monetary system. Bretton Woods established the 'World Bank' (WB), and the 'International Monetary Fund' (IMF). In 1945, the United Nations (UN) became an international peace-keeping force, working in areas of peace, human rights, and international law. In 1993, the European Union (EU) was erected among countries in Europe. The EU established a single market, which enables money, people, and goods to move freely between member states. Located in Brussels, the EU Parliament also decides European laws regarding economic, social, and fiscal policies. There is a 'Central European Bank', and a common currency among some member states (the euro).

In 1995, the World Trade Organization (WTO) became a part of the picture of international economic governance, tasked with ensuring the free movement of money and goods by expanding and protecting the freedom of corporations to trade across national borders. On the political side, the 'Group of Eight' (known as the G8, who first met as a group of eight in 1997) consists of political representatives from eight of the largest and most powerful national economies: US, UK, Japan, France, Germany, Italy, Canada, and Russia. They come together to discuss and decide upon policies relating to global concerns like climate change, poverty, third world debt, health, food, the economy, and terrorism.

The political environment in which social movements operate has therefore been transformed with the rise of global society. The idea of the 'political opportunity structure' of social movements (Tarrow, 1998) must subsequently be stretched to include 'supranational' political opportunities (Giugni et al., 2006), which, we will see, are important in shifting social movements to the global level. The nation state – the traditional target of political claims – has become 'de-centred' from our picture and instead exists as one 'node' in a network of global governance (Castells, 2004a). Importantly, in the network of global governance, there are other powerful players alongside nation states. Among them, multinational corporations (MNCs), and a range of civil society groups and non-governmental organizations (NGOs) (like charities, churches, and human rights organizations, who work within and around international institutions like the UN) (see the 'case point' for an example).

What mechanisms and processes, then, shift social movements from national society to global society? The first process stated in figure 6.1 is one that Sidney Tarrow calls 'externalization' (Tarrow, 2006). 'Externalization' drives contention from the national to the global level when problems experienced within national borders become displaced onto the global level. The process of externalization can, for example, be driven by the mechanism of 'repression'. A repressive or unresponsive nation state (with a 'closed opportunity structure' for activists) can, in effect, shift contention that arises within its borders to the level of global society as social movement activists seek a listening ear. Movements may find this beneficial in two respects. First, they may find *opportunities* for greater success at the global level. International political institutions, for example, may provide activists with opportunities that they would not otherwise have, seen in the appeals that are made to international courts, like the European Court of Human Rights. Secondly, the global level may provide an injection of *resources* that activists would not otherwise have, like, for example, the resources gained when movements link up with international NGOs and other civil society groups.

Activists have taken nation-based grievances, ranging from poverty and oppression to debt and health concerns (like HIV/Aids), to the international level in recent years, where they seek opportunities and resources that are not open to them on a domestic level. It is worth noting that if they have some success, and a formerly repressive regime is pressured into becoming more responsive, then this can create a 'boomerang effect' (Keck and Sikkink, 1998), which shifts contention back to the national level. We will look at an example of this later in the chapter.

The process that Tarrow (2006) calls 'domestication' shifts contention the other way. Contention that arises within global society is shifted to the national level when activists decide to target their nation state for assistance or intervention. Globalization, for example, has been connected with the rise of a new issue environment for activists, which we will look at more closely in the next section. This means that grievances that arise in global society are taken up by social movements within their own borders. Climate change is a good example of where a global issue has produced activism at a domestic level and benefits the cause substantially. Climate change is a global issue, but it cannot be addressed without targeting and pressurizing nation states to lower the levels of carbon emissions taking place within their borders.

This point is important because it shows that, even in a global context, the nation state is still an important part of our social movement picture (Tarrow, 2006). Nation states, like those who belong to the G8, do have some political influence within global society, and may be able to use their position to exert pressure for reform or new policies. In these cases, social movements renew their claim-making efforts on the nation state. We have seen this situation in European countries when it comes to opposition to EU-level laws on agriculture and genetically modified food. Activists have mounted protests within their own countries in order to exert pressure on their own government to act in a way that influences EU policy, or expresses citizen dissatisfaction with it. Protests calling for multinational corporations (from Starbucks to Google) to adhere to national tax laws have also been targeted by activists at their nation state's failure to clamp down on tax avoidance.

The other process I have identified in the first column of figure 6.1 is 'democratization'. Globalization sees the flow of political ideas, as well as people and goods, across borders. In this respect, the Western model of the 'democratic nation state' is spreading across the globe, bringing with it an upsurge of contention which aims to reform or overthrow authoritarian regimes and claim democratic rights (Goldstone, 2004). 'Diffusion' is an important mechanism in spreading democratization from one national context to another, creating a 'wave' effect (Tarrow, 1998). A good example of this is the wave of rebellions in 2011–12 known as the 'Arab Spring'. Tunisia was the 'early riser' in the protest cycle, overthrowing the government in January 2011. It sparked a wave of rebellion across the Middle East, including (not exclusively) countries like Syria, Oman, Jordan, Egypt, and Algeria. The Tunisian pro-democracy protests were communicated to other countries via mass media and social media (e.g. satellite television, Twitter, and Facebook). Through these channels, democratic ideals, symbols, and – importantly – examples of success, spread to other countries, which then had pro-democracy protests and revolutions of their own. We will come back to the role of Facebook in protest in Chapter 8.

Relational mechanisms – changing connections among people, groups, and interpersonal networks

Relational mechanisms refer to changes in the patterns of connection between people and groups (McAdam et al., 2001). In Chapter 3, we saw that the networks of interpersonal ties among activists – which are created, for example, by their overlapping memberships, cooperation on campaigns, and existing family and friendship connections – play an important role in providing an infrastructure of communication and interaction on which mobilization depends. Globalization has expanded these activist networks considerably by enabling activists to connect beyond their geographical locale.

The first reason for this is the rise of 'new media' (ICTs, including mobile communications and social media). The internet and mobile phones, for example, have provided activists with the means for easy and instant communication over spatial and temporal distances (Pickerill, 2003; Donk et al., 2004; Castells et al. 2006; Gillan et al., 2008). Castells et al. (2006, 185) look, for example, at the way in which new media have transformed the nature of communication. They claim that information and communication can no longer be controlled 'top down' by the state or mass media because people can directly communicate with one another via the internet and social media in ways that are instant (in real time), interactive (many-to-many), and credible (personalized, you know its source). They call this kind of communication 'person-to-person, horizontal, mass communication' (Castells et al., 2006, 211). *Mobile* communication (i.e. mobile phones in particular rather than the internet per se – although they converge through wireless technology) also plays an increasing role in the mobilization of protest events. This can be seen in the case of 'flash mobs' (mentioned in Chapter 3), where protest events can be *spontaneously* and *autonomously* organized via text messaging (Rheingold, 2002).

Mobile phones also allow for communication of different kinds, a feature that Castells et al. call 'multi-modality' (image, sound, text), enabling them to become 'living eyes and ears...to observe events in real time and share them' in a communication network that is 'always on' (Castells et al., 2006, 211). Activists no longer depend therefore upon the proximity of face-to-face encounters for communicating grievances, sharing information, and generating emotional bonds. Once established via new media, communication channels can become conduits for the *diffusion* of grievances, ideas, and events not only from one person to another, but also from one country to another.

The second reason for the development of transnational activist networks is the free movement of people (e.g. within the EU), and the availability of cheap international travel, which has seen increases in migration (e.g. for work and education purposes). As they travel, activists become 'brokers' who link up previously disconnected concerns, ideas, and groups.

The third reason for the development of transnational activist ties is related to the new environment of global governance, and we will detect the importance of this factor in the mobilization of the AGM in the next section. The network of global governance involves a range of civil society groups and NGOs (e.g. charities, churches, human rights organizations), many of which have their roots in the global south, and play a role within and alongside international institutions, like the UN. Their work involves raising awareness of issues like global poverty, third world debt, human rights, health, material inequalities, and gender inequalities. This has created a network of political actors who link up across countries in order to exchange information and coordinate campaigns. They are referred to as 'transnational advocacy networks' because they 'advocate' (argue) on behalf of globally aggrieved groups (Keck and Sikkink, 1998). These networks act as important brokers in global society, linking previously disconnected activists who share similar concerns with one another. The case point below discusses an example of a transnational advocacy network (DAWN) which was started by feminists in India in the 1980s. Transnational advocacy networks like DAWN are not usually considered 'social movements' in themselves, because, for example, while the activists involved link up for a common cause, they do not share a sense of 'collective identity' (Tarrow and Della Porta, 2008). In other words, the activists involved in the network retain their own varied understandings of the issues, problems, and solutions. Advocacy networks do, however, provide infrastructural resources, and play important brokerage functions. In this respect, they can be useful sources of information and allies for those who do want to mobilize social movements on the global level.

Case point: Development Alternatives with Women for a New Era (DAWN)

A good example of an advocacy network is DAWN (Development Alternatives with Women for a New Era) (see Mayo, 2008), which was founded in 1984 in India at a meeting of women from across the global south (Africa, Asia, Latin America, and the Pacific) and launched at the United Nations Third World Conference of Women in 1985. Today, DAWN is a network of feminists from the global south who campaign about, and conduct research on, the damaging effects of economic globalization and religious fundamentalism on women's lives across the world, particularly for poor and marginalized women in the south. DAWN advocates on issues like third world debt, environmental sustainability (with nuclear power and deep-sea mining among its current campaigns), marketization, militarism, reproductive rights, and HIV/Aids. They feed back their research findings to international conferences and world summits, working both with national governments and the United Nations and outside them with NGOs and other civil society groups. Like other transnational advocacy networks, DAWN acts as an important broker by linking up previously disconnected political actors (social movements, NGOs, feminists, academics) and forging links between the global north and south in the process. They run workshops, provide training, coordinate via a website, hold face-to-face meetings of regional coordinators, and participate in international summit meetings. Email exchange has, in fact, been vital to the communication of research papers and the exchange of ideas across the different

regions (Mayo 2008, 314). Since 2003, DAWN has also run training institutes in which expertise can be shared with the next generation of young feminist activists.

- What kind of issues do transnational activists network around?
- What do advocacy networks like DAWN actually do?
- Are transnational advocacy networks 'social movements'? How
  do you decide?

Cognitive mechanisms – changing alterations of individual and collective perceptions

'Cognitive mechanisms' refer to changes in the way in which activists
construct and perceive the world, themselves, and their chances for
success. An important cognitive mechanism is the 'identity-shift'. This
refers to changes in the way in which activists answer the question
'who are we'? (McAdam et al., 2001) In order for a social movement to
mobilize at a global rather than a national level, there needs to be some
way of answering this question which can construct a sense of collective identity beyond local and national boundaries (although we will
critically engage with this idea later in the chapter). It has been argued
that the shift from national to global contention, for example, requires
the construction of global 'frames' of reference and meaning (Bayard
de Volo, 2000).

Considering the great variety of national and cultural differences
in identity and experience, this can be extremely difficult to achieve.
This perhaps explains why global social movements are rarer forms of
'transnational political contention', compared, for example, with transnational advocacy networks like DAWN (Tarrow, 2006), who form a
network between different actors but do not seek to construct a collective identity among them. We will pick up this issue again in relation
to the AGM in the next section.

Before we move on to the AGM, however, one further point needs
to be made regarding identity-shifts. Shifting social movements from
the national to global level does not have to mean that local/national
identities are *replaced* by global ones, and in fact, argues Sidney Tarrow, this is just not the case (Tarrow, 2006). Instead, the national and
local contexts of social movements remain vital linchpins of identity

and mobilization. Giugni et al. (2006) caution us against seeing global society as an arena that is capable of providing the symbolic material for the construction of collective identities. Instead, activist networks at the national and local level remain the spaces within which identities are framed. Identity-shifts are about linking exercises, then, rather than replacement exercises (Giugni et al., 2006). Social movements must find ways to link local grievances to global 'master frames', which on their own have little resonance for activists.

The alternative globalization movement (AGM)

In this section, we look at one of the most discussed global social movements – the AGM – in order to apply and critically explore the processes and mechanisms outlined. The AGM is also sometimes called the 'global justice movement', as well as overlapping with what people call the 'anti-globalization movement', the 'anti-capitalist' movement, and the 'anti-corporate' movement (Ibrahim, 2009). There are political reasons for these different labels, with each one reflecting a different interpretation of the main issues and solutions. Following Pleyers (2010), I adopt the label of 'alternative globalization' ('alter-global' for short), because this is the most widely used term for the movement by activists worldwide.

The AGM is not 'global' in the sense that it literally exists everywhere in the world. It has, however, involved huge swathes of activists from the global north and the global south, has staged global protest events like 'Global Days of Action', and has targeted global-level institutions. To that extent, it is certainly the most 'global' of social movements we have yet seen (except for international terrorism perhaps, which we consider in relation to globalization in Chapter 7). In what follows, we apply the mechanisms and processes highlighted in the previous section to understand the origins and mobilization of the AGM.

Environmental mechanisms: contesting global governance

The AGM first emerged in the mid 1990s in the global south. In 1994, the Zapatistas, an army of indigenous people from the Chiapas area of Mexico, led a rebellion in which they seized control over rural villages, setting up autonomous zones within the region (Castells, 2004a).

They were contesting the introduction of the 'North American Free Trade Agreement' (NAFTA), which expanded free trade between North America, South America, and the Pacific. In order to create the conditions for free trade, changes were planned to how the land was owned and used in Chiapas. In particular, communally owned land was set to be privatized so that it could be bought and sold for commercial purposes (e.g. to attract MNCs). In staging a rebellion against NAFTA, the Zapatistas announced a struggle against the dominant mode of globalization emerging in the 1990s, which had at its heart the interests of 'business over people' (Starr, 2000), and which, the Zapatistas argued, had devastating consequences for communities, the local economy, and the natural environment.

The Zapatistas' concerns were not unfounded. They were based upon the growing discontent that had been building up in the global south for decades (Walton and Seddon, 1994). In the 1970s, the IMF started to administer 'structural adjustment programmes' (SAPs), lending money to developing countries in order to help them develop new infrastructure so that they could modernize their economy and attract foreign investment from MNCs (Klein, 2007). In return, they had to 'restructure' to create favourable conditions for free trade by, for example, clearing land of forest so that it could be used for commercial purposes, removing price protections on locally produced goods, allowing foreign imports, building dams and power stations, and so on (Klein, 2007).

Debt has been a key source of concern following on from SAPs. Some IMF loans were paid to corrupt leaders or were made illegally, others are so large and incur so much interest that developing countries cannot afford to pay them back without plunging their own citizens into poverty and diverting funds from essential public services and welfare (George, 1988; Stiglitz, 2003, 2006). The charitable organization, Jubilee, states that together developing countries owed $3.7 trillion in debts in 2008, and that year repaid £602 billion. Not only were developing countries crippled by the debt repayments, but the end of regulation in the domestic market and the influx of cheap imports undermined local economies, while established labour rights were lifted to create a cheap and flexible workforce attractive to MNCs (Starr, 2000; Josselin, 2007).

In 1999, at a protest against the meeting of the WTO in Seattle, the level of concern around free trade became visible. Over 75,000 protesters took to the streets of Seattle on 30 November 1999 to disrupt the meeting of the WTO (Smith, 2001), which was holding the 'Millennium Round' of talks aimed at expanding free trade. The WTO's primary aim is to administer 'the global rules of trade between nations…to ensure that trade flows as smoothly, predictably, and freely as possible' (www. wto.org, 2012). Protesters – who included a wide array of groups from socialists and trade unionists, to anarchists, feminists, farmers, human rights organizations, and churches – surrounded the WTO conference venue, marched in the streets waving anti-WTO placards, partied to the sounds of samba bands, and some – who came to be known as the anarchist 'black bloc' – smashed the windows of the premises belonging to MNCs, like Starbucks and Nike, spraying graffiti on the walls of the banks, and as the day wore on, rioting with local youths locked in confrontation with the police (Juris, 2005b).

Why target the WTO? AGM activists argue that the WTO – alongside the WB and IMF – have an agenda of expanding and protecting free trade, which means that they operate in the interests of MNCs and global elites rather than the majority of the world's population. In essence they argue that the WTO (along with the WB, IMF, and G8) put the desire to make profit above labour standards, the environment, human rights, and social justice. They argue that the G8 do not do enough to address global problems ranging from poverty, to third world debt, to climate change. In addition, they claim that international institutions like the WTO and G8 suffer from a 'democratic deficit' (Hertz, 2001; Monbiot, 2003; Stiglitz, 2003). They make important decisions, but the people who are affected by those decisions lack representation or say in the discussions that take place at international meetings and summits.

The World Economic Forum, for example, excludes civil society groups and NGOs from discussion about the global economy. The G8 consists of only the eight most wealthy and powerful nations, excluding countries in the global south (who suffer the worst effects of debt, poverty, and environmental destruction), as well as any country that does not have significant power. As such, the G8 maintains the current hierarchy between nations. Nobody has voted MNCs, the WTO, or G8 (directly at least) into their position of power over the global economic system, yet they are shaping the future of people's lives, environments, work, and life-chances. A battle is on, argue the activists, over nothing short of 'the fate of the earth' (Castells, 2004a).

Since Seattle, AGM activists have frequently mobilized around the summit meetings of international institutions, as well as organizing

January   November   November
1994   1999 the   July 2001 G8   2002,   April 2009
Zapatista   'Battle of   Protest,   Florence   G20 Protest,
uprising   Seattle'   Genoa   Protest   London

          June 1999   January   March 2002   2004 World   September
          'Carnival   2001 First   European   Social   2011 Occupy
          Against   Social   Summit   Forum, India   Wall Street
          Cpitalism',   Forum,   Protest,
          London   Porto Alegre   Barcelona

Figure 6.2
Timeline of selected AGM events, 1994–2011.

'global days of action'. They protested against the IMF and WB in Prague in 2000, against the G8 in Genoa in 2001, against the WTO in Cancun in 2003, against the G8 in Evian in 2003 and in Gleneagles in 2005, and against the G20 in London in 2009 (see figure 6.2).

Figure 6.2 mentions 'Social forums' alongside protests as AGM 'events'. When the World Economic Forum meets every year, activists establish an alternative 'World Social Forum' to provide a space for democratic debate for those who are excluded from the official process (Tormey, 2005). Social forums have been held in many regions of the world, and in many cities, and consist of a series of meetings organized by different groups of activists to provide 'open spaces' for discussion and debate about the issues arising from globalization and free trade (Keraghel and Sen, 2004; Gillan, 2006). Through these discursive spaces, activists aim to construct alternatives. The slogan of the social forum process is: 'is another world possible?' We explore this question in the debate point.

Debate point: is another world possible?

In Western democratic systems we are used to an electoral process in which each citizen votes for a party candidate as their representative and the party with the most votes gets into power and runs the country. Our lives then are, by and large, decided for us by the elected leaders. Are there other ways to go about things, however, that involve everyone who is affected in a more direct and meaningful way? In other words, can there be a process by which each human being is an equal participant in deciding their own fate, and has the future in their own hands? Consensus-based decision-making (CBDM) is a method of doing things 'for yourself' (i.e. self-organization) that is employed by a wide variety of communities and groups, including by anarchists in the AGM, in social forum meetings, in the People's Assemblies run by the Zapatistas in Mexico, and in the Occupy movement (2011). Other examples include housing co-ops (like Radical Routes in the UK), neighbourhood collectives, workers' collectives, Quaker meetings, eco-villages, and the online free software community (Open Source) (see www.seedsforchange. org). CBDM techniques can be used when a group already agrees on a particular agenda and meets to make a decision about what to do. The decisions that are reached in the meeting have to be ones that everyone in the group is happy with because the group cannot resort to a majority vote. Should even one person disagree with the proposed action then a decision cannot be made. Instead, the group must work to find a solution that every single person can agree upon. It is argued that this process is more democratic than majority voting, which effectively silences minority voices. Furthermore, it forces groups to be inventive and creative in coming up with better solutions to problems. The main principle on which consensus meetings run are that all the participants are equal. They all must discuss and debate the issues, each one contributing verbally or by using hand signals. The hand signals include the veto (raised fist), used when you object to a proposal, the 'I agree' (waving hands), and the 'I wish to contribute' (raised finger). The meeting does not have a leader but a 'facilitator', who takes no part in the discussion or decision-making themselves, but helps to make sure that everybody is contributing and the meeting is progressing.

There are a number of problems with consensus methods and the idea of 'direct democracy', however. The first is a question of whether CBDM can be an effective strategy for actually coming to any agreements at all. There is a lot of discussion and debate, but this can go on for a long time in the absence of a majority vote, leading some to argue that CBDM is flawed. Secondly, everyone involved in the discussion is treated equally and has the right to their own opinion and cannot silence others, such that issues of sexism, racism, or homophobia that arise within the group are difficult to deal with. Thirdly, the spaces of debate are not divorced from the power inequalities of society at large. Men tend to outnumber women and to dominate the discussion. Similar dynamics have been noted regarding race, class, and region in the AGM social forum process (Levidow, 2004; Juris, 2005c).

- Consider whether you think the following could be run using consensus based decision-making:
    ○ a seminar
    ○ the university
    ○ your local community
    ○ your country.
- What are the merits and limitations of consensus methods?
- Could you imagine life 'without leaders'?

Although its initial wave of activism – marked by summit protests and social forums – has since waned (Pleyers, 2010), the AGM nevertheless remains an important part of the contemporary movement scene, reflected in the Occupy movement (2011–). This movement is concerned with the growing gap between rich and poor in the wake of the global banking crisis and austerity measures and can be seen as the latest manifestation of a struggle that has, since the mid 1990s, contested global governance, and (for some activists) the very system of global capitalism. Occupy is the latest movement to express the idea that the global order is increasingly, as Manuel Castells puts it, 'sensed as disorder by people around the planet' (Castells, 2004a, 72). This captures the basic message that the alter-global movement has had since its inception.

AGM environmental mechanisms assessed

Globalization has therefore become a source of contention for social movements, and this in itself has shifted their focus and activity to the global level. The new environment of global society, with its institutions of global economic and political governance and MNCs, has provided activists with new targets of attack that are well beyond the nation state. We have seen, for example, that the network of global governance provides activists with 'supranational level' political opportunities (Giugni et al., 2006) and targets of collective claims-making, like the WTO, WB, IMF, and G8. Significantly, in global society, political institutions are no longer the sole locus of power and influence. Instead, MNCs have also become important nodes in the network of global governance. MNCs

Name these brands   Name these plants

Figure 6.3
Adbusters 'culture jamming' advert.
Source: © Adbusters, spoof advert by 'Kevin', 28 February 2011, published in Adbusters
issue #84, www.adbusters.org/content/name-these-plantsbrands. Courtesy of Adbusters
Media Foundation.

have therefore formed new targets for activists, with some strands of the
AGM being specifically 'anti-corporatist' (Starr, 2000).

We can see two main ways in which the AGM targets corporations.
First, activists *attack the brands* of MNCs, which symbolize corporate
power in our everyday lives and are the basis of corporate identity
and profit (Klein, 2000). In attacking brands, AGM activists are also
engaging in a broader critique of capitalist consumer culture and the
values that underpin it. Activists employ novel tactics to attack brands
and these wider consumer values. The alternative media group based
in Canada called 'Adbusters' is a good example. Adbusters employ a
technique called 'culture jamming' (Carducci, 2006), which involves
subverting the intended message of corporate communication so that
the audience is forced to adopt a critical attitude and see the world
from an alternative viewpoint. With this in mind, Adbusters produce
a range of 'spoof adverts', which lead audiences to question corporate
power and legitimacy and emphasize the damaging personal, environmental, and cultural effects of consumerism. Figure 6.3 shows one of
their spoof adverts. Can you name more of the brands or more of the
plants? What critical messages do you take from this advert about contemporary society?

Another group worth mentioning for their creative tactics are 'The
Yes Men' (The Yes Men, 2004). The Yes Men are a pair of impersonators

who employ culture-jamming techniques through spoofs and pranks. They are famous for staging media 'stunts', which contest corporate power and gain mainstream coverage for the stories that corporations and the international institutions who protect them (like the WTO) would rather never got heard. One of the tactics they employ is 'hactivism' (Jordan and Taylor, 2004). This involves hacking into the websites of corporations to change the messages that they contain, or creating 'spoof websites' on which they post spoof public announcements highlighting corporate scandals, or faking promises of long-awaited action on issues like climate change (The Yes Men were famous for creating a spoof website of the WTO).

In 2004 a Yes Man appeared on BBC news in the UK pretending to be a representative for 'Dow Chemicals', the company who had been responsible for the Bhopal disaster in India in 1984 (when thousands of people were exposed to harmful chemicals after a gas leak at the plant). He took responsibility for the disaster on behalf of the company, and announced a $12 billion compensation package for the victims, thus highlighting the moral course of action that should have been taken and causing the real company the embarrassment of a U-turn. In this respect, The Yes Men are best described as 'political pranksters'. They use society's reliance upon the information given by official institutions and the mass media against itself, subverting the meanings we receive because we habitually ignore the credibility and trustworthiness of the source. Their tactics are effective because they also make people laugh (see Chapter 8 for more on humour and protest). Their slogan is 'The Yes Men are Revolting!' and they run a web-based 'Yes Lab' to aid AGM activists in the creative use of protest tactics (www.theyesmen.org).

The second way in which activists increasingly target MNCs is through directing their collective claims directly at the door of the corporation, rather than the nation state. There are a growing number of campaigns around 'global corporate responsibility' (Soule, 2009), which aim to create pressure on corporations to act in more ethical and moral ways when it comes to the sources of their investment, the treatment of the labour force, the local community, and their impact on the natural environment (Carty, 2002; Shurman and Munro, 2010).

It is clear therefore that there are new targets of activism, which do not involve making claims on the nation state. The 'powerful opponents' with whom social movements engage have shifted to include supranational political institutions, MNCs, and the more diffuse cultural values which underpin consumer society. The case for a shift in activism from the national to the global level should not, however, be overstated. Studies of alter-globalization activists show that local and national contexts (including local activist networks, frames, and resources) remain central to their mobilization (Della Porta, 2007). We have also seen that the externalization and domestication of issues can create a 'boomerang effect' between the national and global levels (Keck and Sikkink, 1998, 13), and that the nation state – while decentred from our picture – by no means disappears (Castells, 2004a; Tarrow, 2006). The global level has opened up a new arena of struggle, but one which interacts with, and continues to be shaped by, the national arena (Giugni et al., 2006).

Sidney Tarrow (2006) also cautions against a straightforward explanation of the AGM as a response to 'globalization' and the grievances it has caused. Although global society provides a new issue environment that has clearly shaped activist concerns and targets, we should know better than to think that social movements can be explained by structural strains and grievances arising from social change *alone* (see Chapter 2). The question then is 'how does the AGM mobilize'?

Relational mechanisms: a network movement of the information age

AGM mobilization can be traced to changes in the patterns of connection among activists. In the mid 1990s, for example, the initial mobilization of the AGM was aided by the brokerage role played by the Mexican Zapatistas. What was significant in the Zapatista rebellion was the way in which the movement used the internet to publicize its campaign to the rest of the world, leading Castells (2004a) to name the Zapatistas 'the first informational' social movement (i.e. a social movement of the information age, which relies heavily upon ICT). Through the internet, news of the Zapatista struggle was able to escape censorship and diffuse to other regions, including to activists in the global north who felt sympathy with the campaign.

In 1995, the Zapatistas sent out a worldwide 'global call for action', and invited activists from other countries to come and participate in political meetings held in Mexico. Activists from the global north travelled to attend these meetings (Ibrahim, 2009) and, in doing so, became brokers who linked previously disconnected social movements in the south and the north into one network. The Zapatistas are therefore a good example of what we encountered earlier as the 'boomerang effect' (Keck and Sikkink, 1998, 13). The Zapatistas 'externalized' their local land struggles by linking them to global resistance against neoliberalism, thus gaining international attention, support, and resources. Once they had international attention and support, they were able to make stronger land claims domestically.

The Zapatista meetings gave rise to a new transnational network of activists called the 'Peoples' Global Action' (PGA) (1997). PGA became a crucial 'hub' of the AGM movement in its early phase, providing a communications channel through which activists in different countries could find one another and coordinate global protest events. The PGA was not, however, a social movement organization (SMO) in the traditional sense that we encountered in Chapter 3. In fact, it consciously acted as a 'broker' rather than a central organization, with no offices or resources of its own (Chesters and Welsh, 2011). Instead, the PGA's existence depended largely on new media. This is characteristic of other important AGM 'brokers', some of which exist solely online, like Protest. Net and Climate Action Direct. It is also a characteristic of social forums, which conceive of themselves as 'open spaces' rather than organizations, and consciously state that while they bring actors together in networks around a common concern, they are not there to mobilize or coordinate campaigns in the traditional sense (Nunes, 2005; Gillan, 2006). In this respect, we can see that the organizational form of the AGM is shaped by an ideology which rejects formal, hierarchical organization and celebrates the diversity and freedom of political viewpoints and strategies that is allowed for by a decentralized network structure (Juris, 2005a).

The network structure of the AGM is also shaped, however, by its relationship to new media (van Aelst and Walgrave, 2002). Just like the internet itself, the AGM takes the shape of a sprawling web of autonomous nodes that are linked by communication and information sharing, and can connect together in a myriad of ways (Graeber, 2002; Juris, 2004; Routledge et al., 2007, 2008). In the AGM, therefore, local actors are able to act in a global network to which they can connect, yet still retain their autonomy. This creates a movement based on 'many-to-many' grassroots networks that are able to deliver improved forms of democracy (Maeckelbergh, 2009).

Drawing upon the work of Deleuze and Guattari (1987), Chesters and Welsh (2006) have talked about the organizational structure of the

AGM using the terms 'rhizome' and 'plateaux'. 'Rhizome' is usually a word used to refer to the mass underground roots of plants, out of which new shoots appear. Chesters and Welsh (2006) see the word 'rhizome' as a fitting metaphor for the sprawling network structure of the AGM, which has become a mass of nodes and connections that shoot in different directions and create a complex and unpredictable web. The word 'plateaux' refers to the spaces in which these networks form, in the case of the AGM, networking spaces include protest events and online forums (Ibrahim, 2009).

Chesters and Welsh (2006) see this network structure in positive terms. They argue that it enables an improved form of democracy and self-organization, especially compared with traditional hierarchical organizations. The network exchanges in the AGM are, for example, *horizontal* and multi-directional rather than 'top-down', and the AGM network is *decentralized* (it organizes around many nodes rather than a few central ones). Chesters and Welsh (2006) argue that this structure is highly beneficial because it allows local actors to have autonomy, whilst linking to wider networks of exchange, which are always open, flexible, and adaptable to their needs. This is an essential configuration for a movement in which the actors involved have seemingly so little in common, even to the extent that they disagree on how to 'name' the movement. Having to operate as part of the same formal SMO would therefore stifle global resistance rather than help mobilize it (Castells, 2004a). For Chesters and Welsh (2006), this network is able to grow by itself, forming a complex emergent system that no one particular node within it can know, control, or predict.

How do we actually go about researching these sprawling AGM networks, however, especially when they often form and exist online? The methods point engages with this challenge by looking at internet-based research methods for studying social movement networks.

Methods point: researching online social movement networks using hyperlink analysis

The networks of the AGM exist on the internet, as well as 'offline' during summit protests, social forums, and global days of action. While the offline events have been researched using ethnographic methods (like participant observations of AGM events and meetings, and interviews with AGM activists), how can we research social movement networks when they exist online? Researchers have been meeting this challenge by experimenting with new methods for tracing online networks between activists. Kevin Gillan (2009), for example, employs software called 'Issue Crawler' to conduct a 'hyperlink analysis' of online social movement networks. Hyperlink analysis enables the researcher to capture, trace, and map the pattern of links between different activist web-pages. Gillan uses hyperlink analysis to research the UK anti-war movement. Although the anti-war movement is not normally classed as an AGM group, anti-war activism has formed an important phase in AGM campaigns (Pleyers, 2010). The anti-war movement has, for example, been an important part of the AGM since the wars in Afghanistan (2001) and Iraq (2003), when AGM activists turned their attention towards issues of militarism and American imperialism. Gillan traces the use of ICT by the anti-war movement. These uses leave behind a virtual footprint of the movement. Gillan employs a hyperlink analysis alongside a more traditional ethnographic study of the anti-war movement's 'offline' practices in order to compare the two. This comparison revealed that the offline anti-war movement very much operated within national boundaries and was affected by domestic political divisions. Online, however, the anti-war movement was able to 'routinely transcend national and political boundaries' (Gillan, 2009).

- How can activists use the internet to mobilize transnational struggle? Does it make 'offline' protests less important?
- How can we study social movement networks when they exist online?
- Are virtual activist networks and offline activist networks the same thing?

Castells (2004a) argues that the AGM is very much a movement of the 'information age' not only in its organization through horizontal ICT-mediated networks, but also in its tactics which use these ICT networks in order to protest. When the 2001 planned Washington protest against the WTO was cancelled because of the events of 9/11, some activists staged a 'virtual sit-in' instead by crashing the WTO website. Another tactic – that of electronic civil disobedience – sees activists targeting the mass networks of horizontal communication (like the internet) on which global elites now depend so heavily (Castells, 2004a). Following attempts to censor wiki-leaks, for example, Anonymous (whom we came across in Chapter 3 in relation to Scientology), carried out 'denial of service attacks', where websites of corporations and/or governments are crashed through a sudden increase in traffic.

AGM activists are also involved in the creation of independent media (indymedia) in which they can produce their own message about events in order to oppose the dominant message received from the mass media (Bennett, 2003; Kahn and Kellner, 2004; Juris, 2005a; Pickerill, 2007). Gillan et al. (2008) show how AGM activists assisted the development of interactive, user-created web content. The Independent Media Collectives, first established at the 1999 Seattle protests, wanted to create websites that allowed for different groups and individuals to contribute to the creation of their own content – like, for example, posting user-created videos. In this respect, they make the important point that as well as utilizing developments in new media (e.g. mobile phones and social media), social movements have also been at the forefront of developments in new media, like web 2.0 technology (Gillan et al., 2008, 173).

AGM relational mechanisms assessed

Chesters and Welsh (2006) suggest that the sprawling, leaderless network of the AGM is a new manifestation of social movements, which requires us to adopt a new language for understanding 'what social movements are' (like 'rhizome' and 'plateaux'). The old picture of formal, hierarchical organization, with leaders and top-down communication, can no longer capture the complexity of the global web, which has no master, and which social movements have, to their advantage, become. Can we therefore speak of the AGM as a 'social movement' with respect to our previous conceptualizations?

There are certainly ways in which the rhizome networks of this information age movement challenge our previous ideas of what social movements actually look like. The AGM exists not as a formal organization but as something else again. Castells (2004a) for example calls it a 'network movement'. It exists as a global information and communication network that connects already existing and autonomous social movement networks together. Like the internet itself, it is a complex mass of connections that is leaderless and impossible to control and coordinate in its entirety (Chesters and Welsh, 2006). For some, this new manifestation of struggle contains a new potential for what social movements *could* be: democratic, decentralized, flexible, diverse efforts at change (Maeckelbergh, 2009).

We need to be careful however in the extent to which we claim that the AGM is a 'new' manifestation of social movements. In fact, the internal diversity of the movement means that whether it confirms or challenges our previous conceptualizations of social movements depends upon which part of the movement you actually look at. Pleyers (2010) has argued, for example, that we can detect two 'camps' within the AGM (each one consisting of diverse groups and individuals in themselves). These camps have very different ways of achieving social change.

One camp – which Pleyers calls 'the way of subjectivity' – eschews political channels. It sees social change lying in the creation of cultural alternatives outside neoliberal capitalism and therefore puts efforts into networking and creating autonomous spaces, radical practices, even different values for living (e.g. pleasure and fun that oppose values of work and rationality). This camp may fit very well into the language of 'rhizome' and 'plateaux'. It also fits well with the argument that the AGM is no longer interested in targeting the nation state. Coming from a perspective known as 'autonomous Marxism', John Holloway (2010a [2002]), for example, calls for anti-capitalist protesters in the alter-global struggle to 'change the world without taking power'. They can do this, he argues, not by getting together to put collective claims on the state (or international political institutions for that matter), but by refusing to continue to 'make' capitalism in their everyday lives. The experience of everyday life itself is enough to highlight the 'cracks' in capitalism – such as the growing gap between rich and poor, cuts to essential public services, having to pay for higher education while still funding nuclear weapons programmes, and so on. These produce in the average person a 'scream' of rage that can be channelled into a rejection of capitalist values and practices. The way to achieve social change in this view is very much connected to those individuals who in their daily lives 'decide to stop making capitalism and do something sensible instead' (Holloway, 2010a [2002]).

The second camp, however – which Pleyers calls 'the way of reason'– is more suggestive of the conceptualizations of social movements we have looked at previously. This camp within the AGM, for example, involves formal organizations. A good example is ATTAC (the 'Association for the Taxation of financial Transactions and Aid to

Citizens'), which was established in 1998 in France and has branches and local organizations in forty countries. ATTAC is famous for campaigning for regulation of the global economy and for a 'Tobin tax' on the profits of corporations which is to be used for global humanitarian and environmental initiatives. Organizations in this camp, according to Pleyers, do still target nation states and international political institutions with collective claims (like those surrounding democratic rights). Each camp therefore takes a different organizational structure and draws a different relationship between social movements and the nation state/political institutions: one targets the state and politics in order to change the world, the other sees this as mere distraction from the real struggle of changing the world from the bottom up (Holloway, 2010a [2002]).

Due to this diversity, we can perhaps best understand the AGM in terms of a 'social movement network', which we looked at in Chapter 3. A social movement network consists of informal ties between activists who cooperate on campaigns and share a sense of collective identity (Diani, 1992, 13). We saw that social movement networks can involve SMOs which are organized in different ways, including formal organizations (like NGOs, trade unions, ATTAC), and more informal groups (like anarchist 'leaderless' networks, or friendship groups), plus individuals (who can be considered part of the movement to the extent that they carry out actions in their daily lives that they connect to the collective efforts of the movement). The idea that individuals can be part of a social movement network is particularly important for conceptualizing the AGM. Counted among AGM activists, for example, are people who strive to create alternatives to neoliberalism in their daily lives. These can be collective efforts within a community to establish an alternative economy outside the capitalist market, to grow and sell their own local produce, to establish social centres in which people can think, act, and cooperate freely outside the dominant system (Yates, 2013). They can also, however, be acts undertaken by individuals who do not belong to any SMOs. Geoffrey Pleyers refers to these individuals as 'free electrons' (Pleyers, 2010, 48). Their acts of protest can include 'political consumerism' (also called 'ethical consumerism' and 'anti-consumerism') whereby they boycott the brands of multinational corporations (Klein, 2000).

We can, therefore, imagine visualizing the AGM as a map of connections between different groups and individuals, similar to the network graph (or sociogram) that I presented in the methods point on social network analysis (SNA) in Chapter 3. Indeed, it has become customary to do so in research on the AGM, with SNA used as a methodological approach (Della Porta, 2007). The concept of a social movement network is, however, premised upon the idea that the groups and individuals involved share a 'collective identity' (Diani, 1992, 13). In the case of the AGM, can this criterion be maintained?

Identity-shift: a struggle against 'neoliberalism'

Identity-shift mechanisms have been seen as crucial to the mobilization of alter-global activists into a social movement. Recall that McAdam et al. (2001) described the identity-shift mechanism as finding new ways to answer the question 'who are we'? If we are to accept the idea that a 'social movement' involves people who not only interact and communicate around a common concern (like DAWN) but also share a 'collective identity' (Diani, 1992), then the AGM has to find an effective way to 'frame' the struggles surrounding globalization so that a sense of 'we' against 'them' in a struggle over 'this' can form. It has been suggested that the AGM has been able to do this by constructing a global 'master frame' (Benford and Snow, 2000), which enables different activists to link their local experiences to one central source: neoliberal globalization.

The Zapatistas played a part in creating this master frame by arguing that their struggle was best cast as part of a global struggle against 'neoliberalism'. Neoliberalism refers to 'rule by the market' and was a philosophy linked in the 1980s to Margaret Thatcher (UK) and Ronald Reagan (US). Neoliberals argue that principles of free market competition, and supply and demand, will produce wealth for society and help to 'deliver the best goods to the most people' (Starr, 2000). Neoliberalism is seen as a way of summing up the dominant mode of globalization, which has 'free trade', 'free markets', and the interests of corporations at its core. For many, therefore, the spread of neoliberalim goes hand in hand with the spread of consumer capitalism (Callinicos, 2003).

The master frame of opposition to neoliberalism has proved sufficiently broad and elastic to enable activists in very different contexts to connect their local struggles to it. It has been able to unite anti-capitalist, anti-corporate, pro-democracy, human rights, feminist, charity, church, and NGO groups (who would not see eye to eye on many other points) under its broad umbrella. Some scholars therefore argue that the master frame of resistance to neoliberalism has successfully enabled an identity-shift in the way in which people in the global south and people in the global north answer the question 'who are we'? To refer you back to the opening quote of the chapter, 'we' are 'the globalization of resistance' to consumer capitalism, the power of corporations, and the failure of democracy (Notes from Nowhere, 2003, 21). This master frame has been connected to the emergence of a collective identity among AGM activists, which turns their transnational networks into what we can properly call 'a social movement' (Pleyers, 2010).

AGM cognitive mechanisms assessed

The construction of a collective identity has been especially difficult for the AGM, however. I have already referred to the political disagreement that exists over the most basic issue of how to name the movement itself. At the Seattle protests in 1999 against the WTO the sheer diversity of the activists involved in the 'movement' was made clear. Socialists, trade unionists, feminists, anarchists, farmers, human rights groups, NGOs, churches, charities, and so forth, have all had their part to play in global protest events and social forums. Many AGM activists have a prior political identity and some of these prior identities clash in fundamental ways when it comes to defining the issues, the enemies, and the solutions.

Socialists and anarchists within the AGM, for example, have had noticeable tensions, reflected in different 'styles' of activism that have become learned and ingrained in their different groups (Tormey, 2005; Ibrahim, 2011). Furthermore, we have also seen that the AGM involves activists from the global south alongside those from the global north. Such regional differences also lead activists to have very different experiences and interpretations of global problems (Juris, 2005b). The master frame of resistance to neoliberalism has caused difficulties because whilst it has been able to unite people in what they are *against*, it does not actually prescribe ideas about what they are *for* (something seen as essential to injustice frames in Chapter 4). We have seen previously in the book that solidarity and a sense of collective identity form through a common interpretation of who belongs to the group, whom the group is against, and what needs to be done. The AGM clearly lacks this unity.

Importantly, the extent to which the AGM does have a 'collective identity' to speak of has therefore been challenged (Chesters and

Welsh, 2006, 2011). The AGM is a movement of 'one no, many yeses' as Kingsnorth (2004) puts it. In short, it is a 'movement of movements' (Mertes, 2004). The lack of unity within the AGM has been seen as its very strength and its very vulnerability (Escobar, 2004; Pickard, 2006). It can be seen as a vulnerability when it comes to problems with sustaining a collective challenge and formulating common lines of action. For those who point to the rhizome nature of AGM networks, however, the lack of unity is a strength. Rhizome networks are not premised upon a collective identity, but upon the possibility of many identities that can keep their own local autonomy while linking up with others for the purposes of struggle against neoliberal globalization. This is where the new conceptualization of social movements really comes from: not from the network structure of organization in itself, but the idea that this network cannot achieve a 'collective identity', and does not desire it either. In a context of such diversity, defining a sense of 'we' against 'them', in a battle over 'this' could be the death knell of mobilization, not its impetus. We are left with two possible positions therefore: either the AGM lacks a 'collective identity' and on the basis of that criterion does not properly count as a 'social movement'; or global social movements like the AGM show us that collective identity is an overrated criterion in our conceptualization of what social movements are.

Summary

This chapter has looked at the challenge to conceptualizations of social movements that has come from globalization and the rise of new media. It has tackled two key questions. The first was 'what processes and mechanisms shift contention from the national to the global level?' We have seen that:

- Externalization and domestication are important mechanisms in shifting grievances between national and global contexts, and there can be a 'boomerang effect' between the two.
- Transnational networks of activists are formed by processes of diffusion and brokerage, enabled by new media, cheap travel, and the rise of transnational advocacy networks.

- Identity-shifts (changes in the answer to the question 'who are we?') are connected to the development of master frames, but local framing processes remain central in linking activist grievances to global issues.

The second key question asked whether global social movements, like the AGM, require us to adopt a different conceptualization of social movements. We found that:

- The nation state is decentred as a target of activist claims as it becomes one node in the network of global governance, but it does not disappear. New targets of claim-making include supranational political and economic institutions, MNCs, and the values of consumer society.
- The targets, structure, and tactics of the AGM are shaped by its relationship to new media. In this respect, the AGM is a movement of the 'information age' (Castells, 2004a).
- The structure of the AGM has been called 'rhizome', a metaphor that likens it to a mass of underground roots that shoot in different directions, is leaderless, and grows by itself. We should not overstate this view, however. One 'camp' within the movement fits this well in seeking change from the 'bottom-up' through autonomous efforts, but the 'other camp' adopts formal organization and targets political institutions (Pleyers, 2010).
- The major sticking point for previous conceptualizations of social movements is the question of collective identity. While for some a master frame of resistance to neo-liberalism enacts the necessary 'identity-shift', for others the lack of basic unity in the AGM means that a collective identity is not achievable, and nor is it desirable.

I also want to end by summarizing how the AGM relates to the conceptualization of social movements that we received from PPT in Chapter 4, and NSM theory in Chapter 5, for this comparative exercise yields an important observation. First, the AGM proves NSM theory wrong in several respects. Protest and social movements today do not revolve around 'post-material' concerns *rather than* concerns about material distribution. Not only do global activists cite 'extremes of wealth and poverty' as one of their key concerns, but some of them actually *are* the trade unionists and socialists that NSM theory had written off. In addition, one 'camp' within the movement adopts 'political' claims-making rather than the 'cultural' strategies associated with NSMs. 'We were convinced' argues Alain Touraine − one of the key NSM theorists − 'that at the end of the twentieth century and beginning of the twenty-first century, the social and political scene would be dominated by the growing role of these new social and cultural movements' (Touraine, 2002, 91–2). Even he admits that the prominence of conflicts surrounding globalization instead has proved NSM theory wrong. There is an 'even newer' (Crossley, 2003) or 'newer still' (Touraine, 2002) historical agent of change on the scene, and it challenges many elements of how NSM theory understood contemporary social movements.

Having said this, NSM theory may actually be very helpful in understanding the other 'camp', which engages in the defence of identity and ways of living, and seeks to invent new ones on the basis of alternative cultural values. There are parallels to be drawn, for example, between the 'corporate take-over' of our everyday lives (Hertz, 2001; Klein, 2000), and the 'colonization of the lifeworld' that Habermas (1987) talks about as a source of social movement activism (Crossley, 2003; Edwards, 2004). Furthermore, we have also seen that some alter-global activism takes place outside SMOs, can be done by individuals 'on their own', and involves experimenting with new forms of personal relationships, practices, and identities (Holloway, 2010a [2002], 2010b).

I suggest therefore that the AGM both confirms and challenges NSM theory. PPT meets a similar fate. On the up-side, we have used the contentious politics approach here to good effect to consider the processes and mechanisms that shift social movements from the national to the global level and which help to explain the mobilization of the AGM. We have also seen that for all the talk of a 'global society' in which nation states have become decentred, the state and the national context still remain an important part of the picture of mobilization (Tarrow, 2006). If we are willing to accept that alongside the state, there are international political institutions that now count as the 'opponents' of social movements, then perhaps we can continue to apply political theories.

There are two sticking points, however. The first is what to do about corporations, who have now become part of the network of global governance and therefore a key target of attack for social movements. The second is, what to do with the 'other camp' within the AGM, who make contentious politics ideas of protest sound 'way off the mark' by consciously rejecting the notion that the state is, or should be, at the centre of the struggle against capitalism (Holloway, 2010a [2002]). Perhaps the answer to this quandary is that while both PPT and NSM theory contain useful analytic insights, neither is equipped to sufficiently make sense of the AGM. The AGM challenges the division we find between political/instrumental struggle and symbolic/expressive struggle, essentially because it is both. The AGM is, then, caught between political and cultural conceptualizations of social movements. Indeed, the question of whether social movements should adopt political, state-centred strategies, or build cultural alternatives, continues to be debated within the AGM itself, reflected among other contexts in the Occupy movement (2011–).

Occupy, according to Todd Gitlin (2012), is caught between a political and a lifestyle movement. For Castells (2012), it is the creation of autonomous spaces within cities for experimenting with alternative cultural and economic values. For David Harvey (2012), it raises important questions about whether autonomous cultural spaces can really remain in a position of 'autonomy' from the capitalist system when that system stays, politically, intact, and how change worked from the 'bottom-up' can be 'scaled up'. We are at a particularly interesting moment, then, in our effort to probe conceptualizations of social movements, which has brought us to the question of 'how do they conceptualize themselves?' Conceptualizing global struggle is, therefore, itself a struggle, which shows little sign of abating.

DISCUSSION POINT

- How has globalization changed the environment in which social movements operate?
- What processes and mechanisms are involved in shifting political contention between national and global levels? How do these apply to the AGM?
- What is the relationship between the AGM and new media?
- In what ways does the AGM challenge and confirm previous conceptualizations of social movements you have come across in the book?

FURTHER READING

Sidney Tarrow's (2006) *The New Transnational Activism* provides a valuable introduction to transnational contentious politics and processes and mechanisms that can be used to analyse it. Geoffrey Pleyers (2010) *Alter-Globalization* is a comprehensive account of the different phases in the history of the AGM, and outlines the 'two camps' I have talked about in the chapter: 'the way of reason' and the 'way of subjectivity'. Manuel Castells (2004a) *The Power of Identity*, volume 2, connects the AGM to new media and 'information society'. Edited collections provide a useful range of AGM case studies from different national contexts, see Donatella Della Porta (ed.) (2007) *The Global Justice Movement: Cross National and Transnational Perspectives*, and Donatella Della Porta and Sidney Tarrow (eds.) (2005) *Transnational Protest and Global Activism*.

7

From the pretty to the ugly:
terrorism, social movement theory, and covert networks

> I like the *Zapatistas*, I dislike the American militia, and I am horrified by the *Aum Shinrikyo* and *al-Qaeda*. Yet, they are all…meaningful signs of new social conflicts, and embryos of social resistance and, in some cases, social change. Only by scanning with an open mind the new historical landscape will we be able to find shining paths, dark abysses, and muddled breakthroughs into the new society emerging from current crises
>
> (Castells, 2004a, 74)

This chapter explores the challenge to conceptualizations of social movements that comes from a consideration of terrorism. We will look at theories of political violence, but focus especially upon the kind of violence that targets 'non-combatants', like civilians, and therefore attracts the label of 'terrorism' (Goodwin, 2004). World events have placed terrorism on the agenda for many social science disciplines. The September 11th 2001 attacks on the World Trade Center in New York and the Pentagon in Washington DC by Al-Qaeda raised questions about why 'ugly' social movements (Tarrow, 1998, 6), like terrorist movements had not been on the list of cases studied by social movement scholars. Is it because terrorism is a 'special case' of collective action, best left to 'terrorism studies'? Or can social movement studies help us to understand terrorism?

This chapter will make three points about the value of social movement theory for the study of terrorism: first, social movement theorists from different persuasions are adept at explaining *political violence* as one of the possible repertiores employed by social movements, viewing its adoption largely as the result of an interaction between the movement and its political context (Della Porta, 1995; Tilly, 2003; Smelser, 2007). On its own however, this analysis does not explain the political violence particular to terrorism. As Jeff Goodwin (2004) argues, terrorism requires us to explain how activists come to employ violence *against* *civilians* as a political strategy. This, he suggests, necessitates the kind of cultural constructionist approach which we looked at in Chapter 4.

Secondly, social movement theory is not only useful for understanding domestic terrorism but has insights to offer the study of contemporary international terrorism because it already analyses the link between globalization processes and the development of global social movements (see Chapter 6). While we have identified the 'alternative globalization movement' (AGM) as a global social movement fighting for democracy and justice, Islamic terrorism reflects the 'dark-side' of globalization (Bill Clinton, cited in Kellner, 2002, 152), and has been termed a global 'anti-movement' (Touraine, 2002). Both can be conceptualized as transnational 'network movements' of the information age that assert the 'power of identity' against the logic of the global order (Castells, 2004a). This said, there are challenges to the view that globalization adequately explains Islamic terrorism.

Thirdly and finally, I will suggest that the biggest challenge for social movement theory in explaining terrorism lies in the 'underground' or 'covert' nature of terrorist movement networks. When movements adopt more violent and illegal means, they become more covert in their operations. This not only presents major methodological challenges, that we will discuss, but also raises the question of whether social movement theories usually focused on 'public' networks can be easily transferred to 'covert' networks.

By the close of the chapter, you will understand the nature of the challenge that terrorism poses to current conceptualizations of social movements. You will be aware of the strengths of a social movement perspective on terrorism, as well as the limitations that arise – both theoretically and methodologically – when trying to comprehend the workings of 'covert' social movement networks.

What is 'terrorism'?

It is widely acknowledged that 'terrorism' falls into the category of what Gallie (1956) calls 'essentially contested concepts' (Crenshaw, 2000; Goodwin, 2006, 2027–8; Smelser, 2007, 239). As it is so often used as a term of political and moral condemnation of violence, the question of what terrorism is, and who therefore is a 'terrorist', is very difficult to answer. Reaching agreement on its 'essential' characteristics is fraught with difficulty, as each criterion reflects a value-judgement. Academics and governments alike have therefore found it difficult to define 'terrorism', making the criteria either too narrow or too broad. The UK is a good example of the dangers of being too broad in the legal definition of terrorism. The UK Terrorism Act of 1999 defines 'terrorism' as 'the use or threat, for purposes of advancing a political, religious, or ideological cause, of action which involves serious violence against person or property' (Whittaker, 2003, 4). Section 44 of the act gives police powers of 'stop and search' over anyone they suspect of terrorism under this definition. A number of cases have been taken to the European Court of Human Rights – and upheld – involving political activists who have been stopped, searched, and arrested while participating peacefully in protest events.

For academics, the problems of defining terrorism are similar to those that have arisen when we have tried to define 'social movements' in this book. If we look back historically at all the groups that have been labelled 'terrorist' then they are so varied that it becomes almost impossible to select common criteria to be used to define them (Laqueur, 2001, 7). Furthermore, the meaning of terrorism is historically situated and changes over time. Today we may associate terrorism with international and religious dimensions, but we are probably invoking specific contemporary examples that are at the forefront of our minds when we do this (Smelser, 2007). As in social movement studies more generally, definitions seem to be constructed with some group or other most specifically in mind, and generalizations or claims to have found 'essential characteristics' rarely hold beyond the temporal and spatial limitations of that case (Smelser, 2007, 230). Walter Laqueur therefore suggests that a universal definition of terrorism will not be achieved (Laqueur, 1999, 5–6).

Martha Crenshaw raises further difficulties. 'Terrorism', she argues, is a label capable of de-legitimizing a political cause and is often employed by opponents to do so (Crenshaw, 2000, 406). The groups labelled 'terrorists' on the other hand, do not call themselves 'terrorists' but 'Liberation Armies' and so forth (see figure 7.1). Labelling a group 'terrorist' also has political consequences in terms of how other parties deal (or refuse to deal) with them (Whittaker, 2003). We often hear declarations from politicians, for example, that 'they will never negotiate with terrorists', making it difficult to bring certain groups into formal political discussions at a later point. Crenshaw (1995, 9) thus argues that labelling a group as terrorist is a 'political process' in which normative judgements are made.

The normative component in defining 'terrorism' is summed up in the famous saying: 'one person's terrorist is another person's freedom fighter' (see debate point). The waves of violent conflict between Israel and Palestine offer a good contemporary illustration of this. Hamas is an organization labelled 'terrorist' by Israel because of its rocket attacks into Israeli territory, but some within Gaza consider Hamas to be their 'freedom fighters' against Israeli occupation of the Gaza strip. Others, including the Turkish prime minister, have declared that Israel is a 'terrorist state' for its missile attacks on Gaza (Reuters, 19 November 2012). On both sides, civilians have been amongst the victims of violence.

This raises another important question about whether terrorism applies only to groups that mobilize outside the state, or to states themselves as well. This question – of state terrorism or terrorism 'from above' – is not the subject of this chapter. As is usual in social movement studies, it is left aside because it invokes different dynamics, and is treated elsewhere (Jackson et al., 2009). Here, we concentrate upon a particular kind of terrorism that has been called 'oppositional terrorism' (Goodwin, 2006) – in other words, terrorism carried out 'from below' (Smelser, 2007, 13) by social movements seeking often revolutionary social change.

Debate point: were the suffragettes 'freedom fighters' or 'terrorists'?

A fierce debate was sparked amongst historians in the UK in 2007 over claims made by Christopher Bearman that the suffragettes, who campaigned for 'votes for women' at the turn of the twentieth century, would today be thought of as 'terrorists', akin to Islamic terrorists. The debate was published in the *BBC History Magazine* in February 2007 (see also Bearman, 2005). Although the suffragettes employed largely peaceful methods before 1912 (predominately including deputations to Parliament to present petitions to the prime minister, the disruption of Liberal Party meetings, and arrests and imprisonments in order to gain publicity for the cause), there was an escalation in the period 1912–14 when tactics became more clandestine and violent. Suffragette militants, for example, committed arson, often targeting empty properties. They set fire to Bristol University's new sports pavilion, producing an angry backlash from students. Alongside arson, they were involved in bombings, stone-throwing and window-smashing campaigns, poured tar in letter boxes, and caused damage to golf courses and works of art (MacLeod, 2006). Bearman argues that because of these acts, we can liken the suffragettes to the Islamic terrorists that we observe today. They have both employed violent methods to achieve their political aims and, therefore, the suffragettes should rightly be labelled 'terrorists' as well.

Calling the suffragettes 'terrorists', has, however, angered other historians. Notably, June Purvis (2007) rejects Bearman's claim, arguing that the suffragettes were unlike terrorists as they were only employing violent methods because they lacked formal political representation, and that they carefully chose targets to avoid causing harm to civilians (no civilians were killed as a result of suffragette violence). Furthermore, the period of suffragette violence in 1912–14 followed on from instances of repressive government action towards suffragettes, in particular the brutal policing of peaceful protest events. The government had, according to Purvis, already used violence against the suffragettes, both on protest events like 'Black Friday' in 1912, and when they force-fed suffragettes in prison by forcibly inserting feeding tubes. In this context, the response of Suffragettes can be understood. Purvis maintains therefore that the suffragettes were not terrorists, but 'freedom fighters' in the feminist cause whom we should all be proud of.

- Why does labelling the suffragettes as 'terrorists' generate anger and debate?
- What criteria would you use to decide whether a group of activists were 'terrorists'?
- Is it appropriate to use contemporary understandings of 'terrorism' to describe social movements of the past?

In spite of these difficulties, it has been argued that a historically specific definition of oppositional terrorism needs be found, and is even more necessary considering the practical applications sought by security forces from knowledge about 'terrorism' (Goodwin, 2006; Smelser, 2007, 240). At its most basic, people need to know what the subject matter under investigation is before they can study it. On this basis, Colin Beck (2008, 1566) suggests that three key characteristics mark out the subject matter of 'terrorism':

Organization	Dates
National Liberation Front (FLN), Algeria	1954–62
Palestine Liberation Organization (PLO)	
Popular Front for the Liberation of Palestine	
Hamas	
Palestinian Islamic Jihad	1964–present
Liberation Tigers of Tamil Eelam (LTTE), Sri Lanka	1983–2002
Al-Qaeda	1988–present
Chechen separatists, Chechnya/Russia	1996–present
Sandinista National Liberation Front (FSLN), Nicaragua	1961–79
African National Congress (ANC), South Africa	1961–90
Basque Homeland and Freedom (ETA), Basque Country/	
Spain	1968–2006
Irish Republican Army (IRA), N. Ireland/UK	1969–97
Farabundo Marti Front for National Liberation (FMLN),	
El Salvador	1980–92

Figure 7.1
Key 'terrorist' organizations since World War II.
Source: adapted from Goodwin, Jeff (2006), 'A Theory of Categorical Terrorism' in *Social Forces* 84(4): p. 2032. By permission of Oxford University Press and the author.

- violence, or the threat of violence
- violence aimed at 'non-combatant' targets (like civilians, politicians, business people, property)
- violence used in the pursuit of political goals and political claims-making.

Jeff Goodwin (2006) argues that the second of these characteristics is an important defining feature of terrorist violence as opposed to other forms of political violence. He suggests that what we need to explain in order to explain terrorism is not primarily the use of political violence by social movements, but the use of a particular kind of violence that targets *civilian* populations (Goodwin, 2004). Terrorist movements vary, Goodwin argues, in the extent to which they do this (targeting politicians, the state, and property as well), but nevertheless, attacking, or being willing to attack certain 'categories' of civilians who can be cast as complicit with the enemy, is an essential feature of terrorist movements (Goodwin, 2006). Examples of the terrorist movements that Goodwin highlights since World War II on the basis of this criterion are shown in figure 7.1.

The third characteristic of terrorism shown in the bulleted list of criteria is also important for our purposes: terrorism involves the use of violence targeted towards civilians in order to make political claims and to achieve political goals. Terrorism is therefore a strategy employed when it is per-ceived that violence will help to shift the balance of power in favour of the group who uses (or threatens to use) it. Bruce Hoffman states that:

> Terrorism, in the most widely accepted contemporary usage of the term, is fundamentally and inherently political. It is also ineluctably about power: the pursuit of power, and the use of power to achieve political change. Terrorism is thus violence – or equally important, the threat of violence – used and directed in pursuit of, or in service of, a political aim.
>
> (Hoffman, 2006, 2–3)

This recognition is important because if terrorism is used by groups involved in struggles which are essentially about power and politics then it falls into the same analytical category as social movements, and we should be able to use social movement theory and concepts to understand it. Within terrorism studies, however, there has been some suggestion that the use of violence is a 'special case' where we need to focus attention on how certain individuals have developed an irrational ideology and pathological personality traits which make them prepared to kill civilians, or themselves, in pursuit of their goal (Juergensmeyer, 2003). There has been a tendency in this respect to 'psychologize' ter-rorism and terrorists, looking at their personal problems and family history to locate the source of their cold-blooded ruthlessness (Della Porta, 1992). Security forces therefore 'profile' terrorists, trying to spot the common psychological characteristics that are related to the use of violence against civilians.

This kind of research has, however, been unreliable when it comes to providing evidence or predications. There are mixed results as to whether terrorists come from deprived backgrounds or are well edu-cated; come from broken families or close-knit ones (Krueger and Mal-ecková, 2003). If this sounds somewhat familiar then it is because there are overlaps here with some of the criticisms of collective behaviour (CB) that we forwarded in Chapter 2. For instance, many more individuals share biographical and psychological traits associated with terrorism than become terrorists (just as many more people experience the strains and grievances associated with social movement participation than become activists). Social movement scholars have subsequently argued, as they did in relation to CB, that we cannot rely upon psychological explanations of terrorism but require a more sociological account that conceptualizes terrorism primarily as a *tactic* employed in the course of political claims making (Tilly, 2003). Tilly thus tells us that:

> terror is a strategy, not a creed…it is a serious but common error to assume that a class of people called terrorists, motivated by ideological extremism, perform most acts of terror.
>
> (Tilly, 2003, 237)

Social movement scholars, and some terrorism scholars, have therefore argued that terrorism is a rational strategy employed by collective actors to pursue political aims (Tilly, 2003; Crenshaw, 2000; Goodwin, 2006; Hoffman, 2006). Even though we challenged the rational actor model in Chapter 3 by acknowledging the importance of emotional actors, this point plays the useful corrective role that it once did in relation to CB, because, as in CB, terrorism studies tends to overstate the emotional/ideological side of terrorism and associate this with irrational group behaviour which reflects the pathologies of individual participants. We are told that terrorists have been driven mad by social problems like deprivation, poverty, social disconnection, cultural divisions, and so on, and a psychological account of grievances can explain their CB (Juergensmeyer,2003).

The rational critique of this kind of approach (which we encountered in chapters 2 and 3) is useful then for reinserting terrorism into social science agendas that treat it as 'politics by other means' and, in that sense, as strategic collective action in pursuit of political goals. Even suicide missions can be cast as 'rational action' when martyrdom is the ultimate individual goal (Coleman, 1988; Pape, 2003), although we might want to challenge the value we get from explaining them as such. We may not agree with terrorist movements therefore, and personally think the individuals involved must be 'mad' (just as CB theorists did when they reflected upon their cases, like Nazism and Fascism), but it is important that we provide terrorism with the same analytical status as we do other social movements for the purposes of research and understanding (Castells, 2004a). This is the lesson we were already taught by resource mobilization theory (RMT): collective action has political aims and is not primarily a psychological phenomenon. Some social movements we like, some we do not, but these are 'normative distinctions' rather than analytical ones. '*From an analytical perspective*', argues Manuel Castells, 'there are no "good" or "bad"' social movements (Castells, 2004a, 4). If we only treat those movements we like as 'politics by other means' then we lose the ability to *understand* those we do not.

From this perspective, if the question is 'what is terrorism?' then the answer is that terrorism is a tactic of violence, waged against 'non-combatant' targets, like civilians, and used by some social movements to achieve their political aims. Although social movement scholars have most of the time overlooked terrorist movements in the cases they study, terrorist movements are not therefore qualitatively different forms of collective action compared to social movements (Tilly, 2003). In this respect, social movement studies may be 'uniquely positioned' as Colin Beck (2008, 1565) puts it, to contribute to an understanding of terrorism, a position shared by other movement scholars whose names will be familiar to you from previous chapters (Neil Smelser, 2007; Jeff Goodwin, 2006; Anthony Oberschall, 2004; Charles Tilly, 2003; Dona-tella Della Porta, 2008). They suggest that the concepts and models for explaining non-violent and largely public protest may also have some-thing to contribute to the study of terrorism, which employs violence (or threats of violence) and often operates covertly. In the next three sections of this chapter we will look at how this might be achieved.

Why social movements adopt terrorist tactics

In this section, we will look at the first reason why social movement theory is valuable for studying terrorism: it is already adept at explain-ing why social movements may come to adopt political violence in order to achieve their ends, and this can be (and has been) stretched to include terrorist tactics. Social movement scholars have explained the use of violence on the part of movement activists by invoking three factors: the interaction between a social movement and its political environment (political opportunities); organizational splits, factions, and countermovements (mobilization processes); and the social con-struction of violence against civilians as an appropriate tactic (cultural framing). Will we look at each of these in turn.

Political opportunities and interactions with state authority

The political environment of a social movement plays a role in shaping its emergence, strategies, and success by affecting the costs and rewards for activists. In Chapter 4, we encountered this viewpoint in the 'political process' approach, which argued that the external political environment *is the most important* factor in explaining social movements, although this statement was quickly watered down by the recognition of other important factors, not least the ability of activists themselves to 'perceive' their environment as either facilitative or inhibitive of their goals (Gamson and Meyer, 1996).

The idea that the political context of a movement however may shape its trajectory is a valuable one for starting to think about why social movements may come to adopt political violence and terrorist tactics. On one level, this is because movements that adopt political violence are more likely to appear in certain kinds of political contexts compared to others.

While there is no simple correlation, those 'mixed' and unstable political opportunity structures that Eisinger (1973) talked about – for example, formerly repressive regimes that are beginning to open up and provide limited political rights but are not yet democratic – do seem to foster the use of violent tactics, either to fight for the full realization of democracy, or against it (think of the Italian Red Brigades in the 1970s as the former, and contemporary Islamic terrorism as the latter). Democratic regimes that remain exclusive towards a movement's political aims can also be related to terrorist activity when their lack of responsiveness can be perceived by politically weak groups to leave them with no other option but violence (think of the British government's response to the Irish Republican Army – IRA). Just as we found in Chapter 4, however, relating incidences of terrorism to political opportunity structures is a difficult exercise because little about the *fixed* political structures of a regime necessarily invites terrorism, or inhibits it. Political structures are not determining of a movement's course, but are one factor amongst others.

Having said this, there is good empirical evidence to suggest that a certain type of state response towards social movements does facilitate the radicalization and escalation of their struggle, including the radicalization of their tactics towards more violent repertoires. Rather than referring to political *structures* per se, these are the opportunities and constraints that arise from the interactions between movements and political authorities. In her work on the political violence among German and Italian left-wing militants in the 1960s–1980s, Donatella Della Porta (1995) finds, for example, evidence to suggest that when states respond to social movement claims by excluding them from the political process, and protest events are heavily policed (e.g. resulting in police violence and brutality against protesters) then movements and their activists can become radicalized and pushed towards the use of violence themselves (see also Tilly, 1978; 2003).

Della Porta argues, for example, that in the case of German and Italian militants in the 1970s, '*state "repression" created martyrs and myths*' (Della Porta, 1995, 191, her emphasis) that helped to construct 'injustice frames' and motivate participation in more radical and violent activities against the state. By allowing repressive policing of protest events and committing violence against the protesters, the Italian state and the German state had effectively sanctioned and legitimized the use of violence for political ends. Violence, then, had become 'fair game' in the context of the rules that the political authorities and police had themselves presented in their interactions with leftist activists. By the 1980s, however, violent protests subsided in Germany and Italy as policing became increasingly tolerant and the political system became responsive to the democratic claims of movement activists. The interaction between movements and political authorities therefore explains the dynamics of a 'protest cycle' (Tarrow, 1998) and the oscillation between violent and non-violent tactics. Movements adopt violence and terrorism if they are weak when it comes to resources and political leverage (Della Porta, 1995, 198).

The link between state repression and the use of *terrorist* violence in particular finds support in other contexts. In his study of the Irish Republican Army (IRA), Robert White (1989) explains the cycle of violence perpetrated by the IRA by arguing that each act of violence (e.g. setting off bombs) was a direct response to state repression. State repression took the form of the brutal policing of protest events, like Bloody Sunday for example where demonstrators were killed by police during a peaceful march; the policy of internment (which enabled police to arrest and detain suspects without charge); and the treatment of IRA prisoners, like Bobbie Sands who died on hunger strike in 1981. State repression therefore elicits violent acts of revenge, but it can also help to radicalize struggle in other ways. The imprisonment of activists, for example, can lead to the unintended creation of networks of radicalized prisoners whose prison connections become the basis of covert terrorist networks (as was the case in the IRA) (Stevenson and Crossley, 2014). Similarly, the threat of arrest (rather than actual imprisonment) can send activists 'underground' where they become increasingly drawn into radical activities (Della Porta, 1995).

Further support for the importance of political opportunities and state response is found from what might seem a rather unlikely source: the work of Neil Smelser (2007). We discussed Smelser (1962) in Chapter 2 in relation to CB theory, but his more recent work on terrorism shows that it would be wrong to simply associate him with structural strain theories of social movements. Smelser offered us, even in Chapter 2, a 'value-added model' to explain the emergence of social movements which included five other factors alongside structural strains. In his latest work, Smelser suggests that a similar 'value added' explanation can be used to account for terrorism, which results from the interaction between multiple causes and conditions (see figure 7.2). One of these conditions, which he had termed 'structural conduciveness' in his original 1962 model, is now more explicitly discussed in terms of 'political opportunities'.

Smelser argues that political opportunities (alongside the other factors listed in figure 7.2) play a crucial role in the emergence of terrorist movements. Like Della Porta (1995) and White (1989), Smelser highlights the repressive response of the state and police towards social movements as a factor in the turn towards terrorism. Terrorism results, he suggests, when opportunities for violent protest open up and opportunities to protest in non-violent ways are blocked off. Movements adopt violence, then, when they have no other option left.

Political opportunities that arise in the short term, Smelser argues, are also particularly important to explaining the timing of terrorist attacks. Moments of setback, or success, for a movement can motivate particularly violent attacks because they act as the 'trigger events' that he outlined in his original model. Smelser cites the example of the Italian Red Brigades, who kidnapped and killed Aldo Moro in 1978 after he played a role in striking a deal between the Communist Party and the Christian Democrats, leaving the militants with the feeling that the left was 'selling out'. They dumped his body halfway between the headquarters of each party (Smelser, 2007, 35).

Although structural strains are still considered vital to an explanation of terrorism (and include factors like poverty, dislocation, and cultural division that create feelings of deprivation and dispossession for people), Smelser argues that the response to these strains is not automatic or straightforward: 'whether this action occurs at all, and if

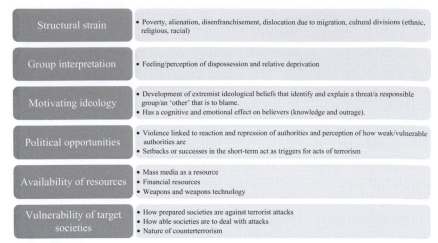

Figure 7.2
Smelser's six-point model for the emergence of terrorism.
Source: adapted from Smelser (2007).

it does, what form it takes, are largely a function of the opportunity structure (which includes both facilitative and inhibitive forces) confronting the movement' (Smelser, 2007, 28–9). You can see from the table in figure 7.2 that the kind of 'opportunities' he considers important in relation to terrorism are political ones, but also ones relating to mobilizing resources (media publicity, money, weapons) and the vulnerability of the societies that terrorists intend to attack (in other words, societal resources for counterterrorism).

Organizational splits, radical factions, and countermovements

We have seen, then, that repressive responses towards social movements by the state and police can lead to a radicalization of their tactics and a turn towards political violence. Radicalization of movement tactics can also happen during the process of mobilization. For example, the interactions – especially the competitive ones – between different social movement organizations (SMOs) who mobilize on an issue can lead to a radicalization of collective action frames and tactics for some groups as they seek to find a 'niche' in the movement market (Della Porta, 1995).

This is because when resources are particularly scarce, competing for recruits and financial support requires SMOs to become increasingly dissimilar. Taking a radical stance on an issue can be one way of differentiating your group from the others. As a result, some groups become more moderate and others more radical and militant (Della Porta, 1995, 196). This was the case for the militant suffragettes when they set up the Women's Social and Political Union (WSPU) in the UK in 1903 amidst competition with a whole host of non-militant suffrage organizations who had been campaigning for votes for women for decades. The WSPU argued that they were different because of their use of militant tactics, with members prepared to get arrested, go on hunger strike and, later in the campaign, throw stones, set bombs, commit arson, destroy letters, slash works of art in galleries, and cut up sports grounds. This 'stepping up' of the campaign by employing militant tactics was attractive to many women who had become impatient with the non-militant suffragists.

Smelser offers further support for the importance of organizational dynamics. He suggests that SMOs also become radicalized by internal splits, which create radical factions. This was the case for the Weather Underground in America – a group of radical students who split off from the Students for a Democratic Society (SDS) (Gentry, 2004). For Della Porta, radical factions break away from more moderate SMOs and become underground militant groups. In the case of German and Italian terrorism, 'small radical organizations espousing violence evolved within and then broke away from the larger, nonviolent social movement organizations' (Della Porta, 1995, 195). Della Porta also points to the interactions between movements and countermovements as a source of radicalization. Violent confrontations between armed members of radical left groups (like students) and radical right groups (like neo-fascists) during protest events in Germany and Italy meant that activists became socialized into the use of violence for their cause at an early stage in their activist careers (Della Porta, 1995, 191).

I have made two points so far that suggest that the radicalization of social movements and the turn towards political violence arise from interactions with political authority, and from competitive interactions within and between movement organizations. The nature of interaction in the 'relational fields' (see Chapter 4) in which movements operate can therefore help us to explain their trajectory and choices with respect to non-violent or violent forms of protest. This makes it clear that social movement studies and terrorism studies should not be distinct subject areas. Non-violent and largely public social movements can turn into violent and covert movements employing terror at some point in the protest cycle, and it should be said, vice versa. They are both the outcome of similar interactive dynamics, in the course of which possibilities for the form of protest are shaped. As Charles Tilly puts it: 'the same sorts of political processes that generate other forms of coordinated destruction produce the special forms that authorities and horrified observers call terrorism' (Tilly, 2003, 238).

Resource mobilization theory and political process theory approaches to terrorism assessed

While the previous two factors may help us to explain why some groups turn towards political violence in the course of their struggle, there is still some explaining to do with regards to why they may adopt the particular kind of violence that is associated with terrorism. As Jeff Goodwin (2004) argues, terrorism requires us to explain how activists come to employ a certain kind of political violence targeted against non-combatants, like civilians. Theories of state repression in this respect may help us to understand why violence might be targeted towards the state (e.g. political assassinations and kidnappings), but not necessarily why activists come to target members of the general public with violence, or threats of violence (Goodwin, 2004). In order to do this, Goodwin suggests, we need to employ the cultural constructionist approach which we looked at in Chapter 4.

Although terrorism may be a strategy available to all social movements, many social movements decide never to employ it. Many are against violent strategies per se (e.g. the peace movement) or against violence targeted at, or at least potentially harming, non-combatants, like civilians. While some terrorist acts do not harm the general public but specifically target politicians or property instead, the most widely used terrorist tactic in recent times – bombings – clearly does (Tilly, 2003).

Employing terrorist tactics therefore necessitates an interpretative process in which some 'categories' of civilians, as Goodwin (2006) puts it, are constructed as legitimate targets of attack. This interpretative process points to how activists (and moreover, militants) construct their picture of reality. It involves those 'meaning-making processes that we referred to in Chapter 4 through the concept of 'cultural framing'. Terrorism, in other words, has to be successfully framed by movements as a legitimate and justified strategy.

So how do militants construct the frames that legitimize violence against some groups of civilians? Della Porta's (1995) work on German and Italian left-wing militants who were part of the underground movements of the 1960s and 1970s is again illustrative in this respect. This is because she was able to draw upon biographical accounts from militants about their experience of participation, and through these accounts probe the way in which they perceived reality at the time (see methods point). Della Porta notes that militants tend to interpret their own actions in terms of frames of honour, injustice, revenge, and heroism. They see themselves as the 'elite warriors' who are the true defenders of a cause. Crucially, they construct a dichotomous view of the world, which divides people into two categories only: those who are with them, and those who are against them. Anyone who is not actively pressing for their cause can be viewed therefore as complicit with the enemy: there is no 'grey area' in which to escape responsibility.

This dichotomous view of the world is effective, as Blumer (1951 [1946]) highlighted, in generating a strong sense of collective identity, solidarity, and emotional commitment to a cause. It also enables militants to 'dehumanize' their victims, thus diminishing their feelings of personal responsibility when it comes to the harm they inflict.

Goodwin provides a further example from Al-Qaeda to illustrate the way in which movements who employ terrorist tactics socially construct civilians as complicit. In his speeches, for example, Osama Bin Laden referred to the tacit support shown by American civilians to the American government, in the form of voting for the president and paying taxes, which makes them responsible for the actions and policies of the government towards Muslims (Goodwin, 2006, 2043). Goodwin also quotes Mohammed Sidique Khan, a suicide bomber in the London 7/7 bombings in 2005 who said 'your democratically elected governments continuously perpetuate atrocities against my people all over the world. And your support of them makes you directly responsible' (BBC News 2005, as quoted in Goodwin, 2006, 2043).

Goodwin argues that highlighting this interpretative process in which certain categories of civilians are constructed as complicit with the enemy is essential if we are to understand why some social movements adopt terrorist tactics and others do not. He suggests that political process theories – although they point out relevant 'push' and 'pull' factors with regards to the how worthwhile it is for activists to employ violence – fail to fully account for this difference. Many social movements face unstable or unresponsive political environments, many are weak in terms of resources and political leverage, and many have found little success with non-violent methods. This does not mean however that they will all turn to terrorist tactics. Some may adopt armed struggle against the state, some guerrilla warfare, some may remain with non-violent repertoires of protest. Only for those who are able to successfully construct and maintain collective action frames in which certain categories of civilians can be perceived as complicit with their enemy will the turn to terrorism appear an appropriate and justifiable strategy.

Globalization and international terrorism

Social movement studies can be useful, then, in explaining why some movements adopt political violence and terrorist tactics. When it comes to the political process argument, however, references tend to be made to the *national* context, which may help to explain instances of domestic terrorism (e.g. as responses to state repression), but can social movement theory explain the dynamics that lead to *international* terrorism? In this section I suggest that because it already analyses the link between globalization processes and the development of global social movements (see Chapter 6), social movement studies does also provide us with insights into international terrorism.

Contemporary terrorist movements are said to be marked by their international nature (Adamson, 2005). One of the movements at the forefront of public and academic attention today, Islamic terrorism, has, for example, been described as 'de-territorialized' because terrorists and targets are drawn from across a number of different countries, while the conflicts they respond to are embedded in the nature of global society (Castells, 2004b). Globalization in fact – a process that we considered in the last chapter in relation to social movements – has been cited as the root cause of the strains and grievances that animate Islamic terrorism (Huntington, 1996; Barber, 1995).

Globalization involves the increasing economic, political, and cultural interdependence between countries, such that we can refer to the world as 'one place' or a 'global society' (Cohen and Kennedy, 2013). We analysed the AGM as a response to the dominant mode of globalization that marked the late twentieth and twenty-first centuries: a globalization that spread neoliberalism, capitalism, and an Americanized model of culture across the globe through the mass media and consumerism. Globalization has therefore been associated with the spread of 'Western modernity', namely with tendencies towards rationalization, secularization, and democratization (e.g. the spread of human rights and civil liberties for groups like women). While the AGM is criticizing the Western model as not democratic enough, Islamic terrorism can be understood as a reaction *against* the spread of Western democratization itself. Huntington (1996), for example, explains Islamic terrorism in terms of a 'clash of civilizations' produced by globalization. Religious and cultural differences are magnified and come into conflict as secularism, consumerism, and Western political states become the model of global development. Barber (1995) sums up the clash as one of 'McWorld versus Jihad'.

While in Chapter 6 we identified the AGM as a global social movement fighting for democracy and justice, Islamic terrorism can therefore be seen as its opposite: the 'dark side' of globalization (Bill Clinton, cited in Kellner, 2002, 152). It represents in that respect, the countermovement or 'anti-movement' of the AGM (Touraine, 2002). Michael Wieviorka (2005) therefore calls contemporary post-9/11 terrorism the 'global anti-movement' of the AGM.

Globalization approaches assessed

There are challenges however to the view that globalization is responsible for the rise of Islamic terrorism. Whilst Smelser points to globalization and the rapid pace of social change as a source of grievances for contemporary terrorist movements, he also argues that it is misplaced to interpret post-9/11 terrorism as 'something new...a facet of globalization' because little is actually new about its ideologies, strategies, goals, and tactics (Smelser, 2007, 3). Putting aside the insights we have already gained from social movement theory about strains and grievances not being sufficient as explanations of movement mobilization, there is also some evidence to suggest that globalization in economic and political terms has not been associated with increases in international terrorism. Robison, Crenshaw, and Jenkins, for example, find that foreign direct investment and international trade is associated with decreases in international terrorism, perhaps because they tend to improve economic growth and social welfare, thereby undermining some of the socio-economic conditions that are related to terrorism (Robison et al., 2006, 2022). If any aspect of globalization can be related to Islamic terrorism then it is the cultural aspect (Robison et al., 2006; also see case point).

We know that strains and grievances are not enough to explain the emergence of any social movement, let alone terrorist movements. Social movement theorists who study the AGM also have something to contribute to our understanding of the *mobilization* of international terrorist movements, however. Both the AGM and Islamic terrorism rely, for example, upon 'transnational networks' that have been formed in the course of globalization. Fiona Adamson (2005, 33) argues that the 'mobility of people, capital, goods, and ideas and information across national borders' that is characteristic of globalization, enables terrorist movements to mobilize internationally by creating transnational networks that can be turned to the purposes of political mobilization.

The AGM and contemporary Islamic terrorism are organized therefore through transnational networks. In fact, Castells (2004a) argues that both movements can be conceptualized as global 'network movements' of the information age. Like the AGM, Islamic terrorism relies heavily upon computer-mediated networks and the internet, not only for moving financial resources between countries, but for coordinating global action and communicating their message to a global audience, uncensored by the mass media. Castells (2004a) argues that the similarities between the AGM and Islamic terrorism do not end here. Both in fact can be seen as providing a particular cultural response to neoliberal globalization which asserts the 'power of identity' (cultural, ethnic, and religious) against the logic of the dominant global order (Castells, 2004a).

Case point: Al-Qaeda

Manuel Castells (2004b) traces the current phase of Al-Qaeda back to the establishment of the *World Islamic Front for the Jihad against the Jews and the Crusaders* on 23 February 1998 by Osama Bin Laden and his associates (*Jihad* means 'struggle on behalf of Islam') (Castells, 2004b, 114). Rather than existing within one country, or targeting one country, Al-Qaeda is very much a 'global' movement, with operatives in several countries. While the United States is seen as at the centre of Western power and is therefore a key target for Al-Qaeda, they are by no means the only target. Al-Qaeda attack any 'power that oppresses Muslims' in a bid to create a Muslim world ruled by the Shari'a law (Castells 2004b, 111). For

Castells, the 'success' of Al-Qaeda (in terms of terror operations like the 9/11 attacks on the World Trade Center), has been a result of effective resource mobilization on the one hand (most Al-Qaeda members are well-educated and materially well-off, especially Bin Laden who used his family fortune to fund initial mobilization). On the other hand, it was also the result of successful organization and framing. Al-Qaeda adopted a 'network' form of organization, with few leaders and several terrorist 'cells', which operated with autonomy from the leadership. This decentralized structure was enabled by the simplicity of the mission (to carry out terror on whatever targets you can find, whenever you can, using yourself as the weapon), and the salience of the collective identity underlying the mission (God is on your side). This form of organization was difficult to infiltrate with counterterror activities, because nation states were not adept at dealing with networked forms of resistance. Such resistance has only a few visible targets (like training bases and headquarters). Furthermore, those who carry out the attacks are dead before they can be pressed for any information or give anything up about the organization.

Castells suggests that we should understand Al-Qaeda, and the attraction of it to Islamic fundamentalist youth in the Muslim world, through the lens of neoliberal globalization. The dominant mode of globalization, driven by technological advances, capitalist consumer culture, and essentially, a Western, Americanized culture, has forced many nation states to divorce themselves from the cultural and religious values and identities of groups within their borders in the name of modernization and progress. Globalization is felt therefore as a threat to cultural and religious identity, and, in response, a 'resistance identity against Western cultural domination' is formed (Castells 2004b, 144). These 'resistance identities' find support among fundamentalist terrorist groups, like Al-Qaeda.

- Why has Al-Qaeda been able to successfully mobilize and evade capture?
- How do the religious dimensions of terrorism affect its operation?
- Do you agree with Castells that supporters of Al-Qaeda have developed a 'resistance identity' against Western cultural domination?

Covert social movement networks

So far we have seen that social movement theory can help in explaining both domestic terrorism and contemporary international terrorism. The theories and concepts that movement scholars have devised
to explain largely non-violent cases therefore appear transferable to
violent cases. While we have come across enough examples in the
last two sections to show the merits of this view, here we look at the
limitations. The biggest challenge for movement scholars in transferring their theories and concepts to terrorist cases is not the violence
involved in the activity (as usually supposed), but the *covert* nature of
the activity. Social movement theories and concepts have been created on the basis of social movements who act on the *public* stage;
indeed some conceptualizations of social movements have stressed the
public nature of collective action as an important defining feature.
Can the way in which we study 'public' social movements be so easily
transferred however to 'covert' ones? This is not just a question about
methods (see the methods point), but a question about whether social
movements that mobilize through 'covert' networks really do operate
in the same way as public ones.

Social movements that adopt non-violent repertoires of protest, largely
speaking, operate on the public stage. Indeed, we have seen that it is
imperative that they do so in order to attract publicity for their cause, gain
recruits, exert political pressure, and mobilize resources (see Chapter 3).
When movements adopt violence however as a tactic, then they become
involved in covert activities for two reasons (Crossley et al., 2012):

- The activities they are planning only have an impact if they remain
  secret until executed.
- Employing violent and terrorist tactics means that activists are engaged in illegal, criminal activity (i.e. the act itself, and often other
  criminal activities in order to fund it) and therefore would be subject
  to surveillance and arrest if they did not remain 'underground'.

Whilst we have been attuned in Chapter 5 to the idea that social movement networks might operate in 'submerged' arenas of everyday life
and in that respect be hidden from view until the visible moments of
protest events (Melucci, 1989), we have not so far considered social
movements that operate consciously in covert ways and seek to avoid
detection.

The distinction between public and covert social movements is, of course, not clear cut. Terrorist movements like other social movements, fall somewhere between the two (Crossley et al., 2012). There are groups within the AGM for example who operate covertly by hiding their identities with masks on protest events and limiting public access to their groups and activities (e.g. the anarchist black bloc). Activists within otherwise public social movements may at times participate in protest events and actions that are 'secret' to the general public, or to some fellow activists, especially when they are 'high risk' or involve criminal acts. For example, in their 2008 power station protests, Climate Camp had a 'high risk' group who were going to break in to the power station with wire cutters and this group therefore kept their plans secret from the other Climate Camp activists who signed up for a peaceful demonstration. Although the others knew that there was a high-risk group, the plans of this group remained secret from them (Harries, 2010). Even peaceful social movements have – like terrorist cells –been targets of official surveillance and infiltration by security forces and police who cannot find out enough about their activities otherwise.

Terrorist movements also have some parts of their organization that seek public visibility and operate 'above ground'. Often, terrorist movements are one wing of a wider movement which also includes political parties, for example. This is the case for the IRA, whose political wing has been Sinn Fein. What we are talking about then is a difference in *degree of covertness* rather than whether a social movement is one or the other (Crossley et al., 2012). With this said, it is time to address the question of whether covert social movement networks operate in ways that are similar to or different from public social movement networks.

First, it should be said that this question is very difficult to answer because we do not have much empirical evidence about how covert social movement networks operate in order to carry out a comparison (see methods point). The little evidence that we do have suggests however that while there are some similarities, there may also be important differences. I look at three aspects of covert social movements below in order to unpack these: (a) organization, (b) recruitment, and (c) participation.

(a) *Organization*

The first issue is whether 'covertness' (i.e. operating 'underground' and intending not to be detected, as terrorists most often do when planning their activities) affects the way in which social movements organize. We have come across debates already about the different organizational forms that social movements take (see Chapters 3, 4, and 5). Some movements are formally organized with centralized decision-making structures, and clear leaders. The 'professional' SMOs referred to by McCarthy and Zald (1973), for example, took this form. It was also a form that William Gamson (1990[1975]) associated with social movement success. On the other hand, however, Gerlach and Hine (1970; Gerlach, 1999) noted a very different organizational form that movements can take, which was decentralized and sparse, with no locus of decision-making or leadership. This was the form that we associated with the new social movements (NSMs) (at least in their inception) in Chapter 5, and one camp of the AGM in Chapter 6 (Chesters and Welsh, 2006). So far in the book we have therefore considered the organization of social movements to reflect the extent and success of their resource mobilization (professional SMOs), or their ideological outlook and conscious design (NSMs, AGM), or the technologies on which they depend (AGM).

There is some suggestion, however, that covert social movements may have additional pressures or considerations that affect the structure of their organization. There is some suggestion for example that covert social movement networks must be decentralized (meaning no central hub), and have sparse ties between members (meaning low density). This is the case it is argued because covert networks have, first and foremost, to evade detection. Whilst formal, centralized structures may allow activists to efficiently carry out their activities and mobilize resources (e.g. planning, coordinating, and executing a terrorist attack), there is also a 'trade-off' to be made between 'secrecy and efficiency' (Baker and Faulkner, 1993; Enders and Su, 2007; Klerks, 2001; Krebs, 2002; Lindelauf et al., 2009; Morselli et al., 2007; Rodríguez, 2009).

This trade-off means that covert networks adopt decentralized and sparse network structures which look like a chain, and which are sometimes referred to as 'snake-like', in that each member of the network has few connections to others (so network density is low). This structure is supposed to maximize security in the network because if one node is compromised then the fact that they have few ties to others means that the network itself is not easily compromised. Valdis Krebs (2002), for example, conducted a study of the terrorist networks involved in the 9/11 attacks on the World Trade Center. Krebs maps the network of ties (defined in terms of 'trusted contacts') between the 9/11 hijackers and found that the networks were indeed sparse and snake-like in appearance

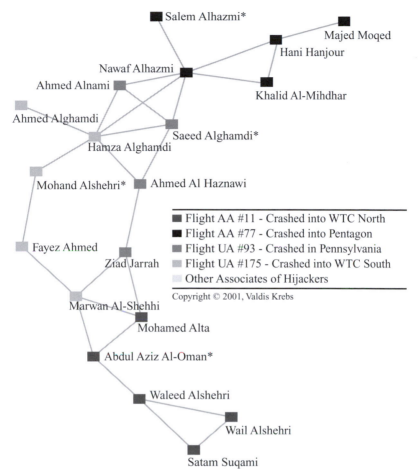

Salem Alhazmi*

Majed Moqed

Hani Hanjour

Nawaf Alhazmi

Ahmed Alnami

Khalid Al-Mihdhar

Ahmed Alghamdi

Saeed Alghamdi*

Hamza Alghamdi

Mohand Alshehri*   Ahmed Al Haznawi

■ Flight AA #11 - Crashed into WTC North
■ Flight AA #77 - Crashed into Pentagon
■ Flight UA #93 - Crashed in Pennsylvania
■ Flight UA #175 - Crashed into WTC South
  Other Associates of Hijackers

Copyright © 2001, Valdis Krebs

Fayez Ahmed

Ziad Jarrah

Marwan Al-Shehhi

Mohamed Alta

Abdul Aziz Al-Oman*

Waleed Alshehri

Wail Alshehri

Satam Suqami

Figure 7.3
Valdis Krebs's network of 9/11 hijackers.
Source: © 2001, Valdis Krebs. Diagram as shown in Krebs (2002), 46.

(Krebs, 2002) (see figure 7.3). This improves network security but also robustness to counterterrorist efforts. If you cut off the head of the snake then it will simply grow another one. In other words, there is always someone else down the chain of command who can take over coordination of the network and its activities should one node be neutralized.

There are arguments against the view that covert social movement networks will take a decentralized and sparse form, however. Lindelauf et al. (2009) argue on the contrary that covertness is best maintained by a centralized network in which a well-connected hub has contact with all the others members (who, in turn, do not have contact with one another). This allows the hub to control and coordinate members through direct communication, minimizing 'go betweens' and improving efficiency and security. Equally, solidarity and emotional commitment is better generated within dense social networks rather than sparse ones in which face-to-face ties with others can generate interpersonal commitments and affective loyalties (Della Porta, 1995).

For these reasons, covert social movement networks may take the form of local, small, dense clusters which are connected to one another by few ties (Coleman, 1990). This kind of structure has been referred to as a 'cell structure' and is associated with Islamic terrorism (Sageman, 2004, 2008). Sageman (2008) refers for example to the 'leaderless resistance' of Islamic terrorism because it involves multiple 'cells' of activists who have sparse connections with one another and who conduct terrorist activities in isolation from the other cells. Sometimes, these cells may only have connections via online or mobile networks, for example, and are unable to compromise each other's security.

While covert social movements do not necessarily adopt unique forms of organization compared to public social movements, there is some evidence to suggest therefore that they balance a different set of concerns compared to public social movements which can give them distinct organizational structures. The cell-like structure associated with contemporary terrorist groups, for example, may reflect the need to generate strong interpersonal commitment while at the same time maintaining secrecy and evading detection (Crossley et al., 2012). Referring to Al-Qaeda cells, Castells states that; 'this is a close-knit circle that becomes a node in a network of close-knit circles around the world' (Castells, 2004b, 138).

(b) *Recruitment*

There is also some evidence to suggest that covert social movements have particular ways of recruiting members, and face particular challenges that public social movements do not. Terrorist movements for example have to be careful about the methods they use to recruit new members. They can hardly sign up new members on protest events, hand out flyers in the streets, or set up a stall in the city centre. 'Social movement scenes' – discussed in Chapter 5 – may be particularly important therefore for covert social movements, who often try to draw new members into covert networks through co-participation in seemingly legitimate and innocuous 'scenes', whether football in the case of far-right movements, or pubs in the case of the IRA (White, 1993).

Approaching new recruits outside movement 'scenes' however depends largely upon pre-existing ties between potential recruits and people already in the movement. We have seen already that pre-existing ties to family and friends who are in a movement is one of the best predictors of involvement, and one of the most effective ways to recruit (Snow et al., 1980). For covert social movements however, pre-existing ties may be the *only* way to recruit considering the demands for secrecy and security. These demands place trust and loyalty at the top of the list of requirements when it comes to recruits, and the people we trust the most tend to be those we already know well.

Erikson (1981) therefore argues that in order to maintain security, covert movements (like secret societies) recruit disproportionately from their pre-existing ties. This is because trust can only be ensured by drawing upon 'strong ties' – in other words, your close family and friends. This is why secret societies tend to grow out of, and recruit, the family and friends of founder members. Pre-existing networks of family and friends are therefore, perhaps, especially important for understanding recruitment to 'underground' militant groups, as Della Porta (1992; 1995) found in her study of German and Italian left-wing militants. Militants were socialized and radicalized within peer groups, for example meeting first in legitimate movement activities and proving their trustworthiness before being recruited by others they already knew into the underground.

(c) *Participation*

We have encountered two contrary explanations of participation in 'public' social movements so far in the book: Blumer's (1951[1946]) theory of how participation is ensured by the construction of emotional commitments between the individual and the group/cause (see Chapter 2); and Olson's (1965) theory of 'selective incentives' offered to the rational activist in order to render the costs of participation personally worthwhile (see Chapter 3). Evidence suggests that in the case of covert social movements, the processes outlined by Blumer may be more accurate.

There are differing views as to whether terrorism can be regarded as a rational choice on the part of the individual (Euben, 2002). Instead, Della Porta (1992, 1995) suggests on the basis of militant biographies that participation is an emotionally driven decision which depends upon the affective commitments and loyalties that exist between members of the underground. Cells were insular groups with strong, affective ties between members which acted like surrogate families (Della Porta, 1992, 266). Within these cells, ties to outsiders were cut so that interpersonal relationships and life experiences became focused solely on the group. The closed nature of the group allowed an unchallenged extremist world view to be sustained. The affective ties to the group effectively kept individuals participating in the underground until the bitter end, even if they wished on some level to exit:

> This kind of involvement with my friends means that, at the end of the
> game, either we are all outside or we are all inside [prison], because
> if some of us are out and some of us are in, I don't give up on my
> friends…This means that if my friends had drowned because of a belief
> that I shared with them, I would decide to drown; well if they are there
> and I can't help them, I prefer to be with them.
>
> (Life History 18, as quoted in Della Porta 1995, 178)

While affective ties and emotional commitment have been associated with social movement participation by Blumer, and in more recent times by those who remind us of the 'passionate' nature of politics (Goodwin et al., 2001), these factors are especially important perhaps in explaining participation in covert social movements, which are difficult to explain in terms of a calculated rational choice because, for example, costs are so high (including the ultimate cost of life when it comes it suicide missions). Whilst suicide missions have been explained in terms of rational action theory (RAT) (Coleman, 1988; Euben, 2002; Pape, 2003), we perhaps gain little in understanding by viewing them as the ultimate realization of individual preferences. Instead, we need a wider appreciation of the emotional and cultural context in which such actions become possibilities in the pursuit of political aims.

Methods point: using protest event analysis/ incident analysis to study terrorism

Studying terrorism brings some obvious challenges to social researchers. Movements which operate underground, try to keep activities and identities secret, are engaged in illegal actions, and are used to countering surveillance attempts as a matter of course, are notoriously difficult to collect accurate data about. We are, of course, not able to go and interview or observe terrorist networks, and so rely upon a range of secondary sources about their activity. Some of these secondary sources do include the archived life histories of ex militants, such as those used by Donatella Della Porta on the Red Brigades and Red Army Faction (1995), and Robert White's oral histories with ex-IRA members (1993). The majority of data on terrorist activity however comes from public sources like the media and police records. This data can be used to build up a picture of terrorist incidents, which can be used for purposes of 'incident analysis'. Incident analysis is similar to a method called protest event analysis (PEA), which has been used to study the occurrence of protest events, primarily drawing upon newspapers (see Earl et al., 2004). PEA involves conducting a survey of protest events, where numbers of events are counted over a period of time, as well as recording details like the number of participants, duration, goals, claims, targets, location, and outcomes. Despite remaining a less conventional method in social movement studies, the 1990s saw PEA developed into a sophisticated quantitative technique for the study of protest within and between countries. The Prodat (protest data) project used PEA to record all protests in Germany 1950–95 (Rucht et al., 1999). Similarly, researchers of terrorism are able to access data from existing international databases that collate information about terrorist incidents from media and government sources and make them available for research. One of the major databases is ITERATE (International Terrorism: Attributes of Terrorist Events) that collates information since 1968 on international terrorist incidents, organizations, tactics, and victims (Mickolus et al., 2003). Colin Beck (2007), for example, uses the Memorial Institute for the Prevention of Terrorism's 'Terrorism Incident Database' (which compiles incidents from news sources) to study eco-terrorism in the United States between 1998 and 2005. The database contained 84 incidents of eco-terrorism in the period (terrorist acts such as arson that were carried out by radical environmentalist groups, like the 'Earth Liberation Front'). Beck argues that incident data can be used for looking at the trends in eco-terrorist activity and geography, but also for estimating the number of radical cells that are part of the movement. Eco-terrorists adopt the 'cell structure' that we have associated with covert social movement networks more generally. If we assume that terrorist incidents are carried out by these cells, then counting the incidents also helps us to estimate the magnitude of the movement (Beck, 2007).

There are problems with using incident data, however, which are shared with PEA more generally. The main concern is the reliability of sources. News sources not only provide uneven coverage of protest events and terrorist incidents, skewed to their editorial agendas, but, as Della Porta argues, when it comes to covert activities, newspapers are not always privy to their existence (Della

Porta 1995, 18). For this reason, police records are important additional sources, although these can suffer from their own inaccuracies and political bias. For example, Crossley et al. (2012) use court data on all suffragette arrests collected by the British Home Office to research how suffragette networks changed between peaceful and violent phases of the campaign. While the court data is the most exhaustive source they have with which to recreate suffragette networks, it has known omissions, and it is limited – like Krebs's (2002) data shown in figure 7.3 – to the operatives involved in the events, and cannot capture the myriad of ties in which they are embedded.

- In what ways can researchers study social movements when they have gone 'underground'?
- What problems could arise in using media sources and police records to build up a picture of the occurrence and nature of terrorist events?
- Can we conduct research on the motivations of groups who employ terrorist tactics if we cannot interview them?

Summary

In this chapter, we have seen that social movement studies has something to offer both the study of domestic and international terrorism:

- Social movement theories regarding political opportunities, the interaction between movements and political authorities, the mobilization process, cultural framing, and global social movements in the information age, can shed light on why social movements may adopt political violence as a tactic of protest.
- As Jeff Goodwin (2006) argues, cultural framing processes are crucial in understanding how *terrorist* tactics in particular become socially constructed as legitimate and appropriate for certain groups at certain times and not for others.

The merits of using social movement theory to study terrorism suggest that the 'blind spot' that has existed in the social movements field as far as terrorist cases are concerned is indeed 'normative' rather than 'analytical' – we have tended to study those movements we like and support (Castells, 2004a), but we *could* use our theories to look at those we do not. What are the main challenges and obstacles that lie ahead if we do?

What I have suggested here is that turning our attention to terrorism has required us to stretch our conceptualization of social movements even further to include 'covert' networks of collective actors, as well as 'public' ones. I have made very tentative moves towards tackling the important question of whether covert social movements operate differently with regards to organization, recruitment and participation (and need to be studied with different methods) compared to public ones. Initial reflections suggest that:

- Some familiar social movement dynamics are in play in covert movements when it comes to network forms of organization, and the important role of interpersonal ties in recruitment processes.
- Additional pressures may exist due to the demands for secrecy that shape the mobilization process of covert movements – and their organizational structure – in particular ways. Cells structures, for example, help to balance the need for close-knit groups and network decentralization.

More evidence is needed however to assess the extent to which covert and public social movement networks operate differently. If we find that they do, then the task for social movement studies in turning its theories and concepts to the study of terrorism may still be rather great. If they do not, then social movement studies should be easily transferred to terrorism studies. We have seen, however, that if a challenge does exist in doing so then it comes from the *covertness*, and not the *violence* employed by terrorists, which is often seen as the feature that makes terrorism something of a 'special case'.

In short, the challenge for social movement studies which is posed by terrorism does not come from trying to explain collective action that involves threats of, or actual, violence (indeed, so many social movements at some point in their history have), but in explaining collective action dynamics *when they go underground*. Stretching our conceptualizations of movements to involve covert as well as public networks in this respect will not only assist the study of terrorism, but also the study of many non-violent and public movements which, at times, involve covert networks and activities which currently get pushed aside in our analysis.

DISCUSSION POINT

- Is 'terrorism' a special case of collective action or can we treat it as tactic used by social movements?
- What factors are important in explaining why social movements turn from peaceful tactics to violence and terrorism?
- Does terrorism confirm social movement theories or challenge them?

FURTHER READING

Donatella Della Porta's (1995) *Social Movements, Political Violence and the State* remains a classic study, and is an interesting read because it draws upon life-histories of German and Italian militants. See also Charles Tilly's (2003) *The Politics of Collective Violence*, and Neil Smelser's (2007) *The Faces of Terrorism* for a post 9/11 consideration. For a good introduction to the way in which social movement theory and concepts could be applied to terrorism, see Colin Beck's (2008) 'The Contribution of Social Movement Theory to the Study of Terrorism', *Sociology Compass*, 2(5): 1565–81. Jeff Goodwin's (2006) 'A Theory of Categorical Terrorism', *Social Forces*, 84(4): 2027–46 is a good discussion of what is particular about terrorist violence that social movement scholars must explain (also, Goodwin, 2004).

From collective behaviour to misbehaviour: redrawing the boundaries of political and cultural resistance

The Ethiopian peasant's fart certainly does not blow the passing lord off his horse, and yet: it is part of the substratum of negativity which, though generally invisible, can flare up in moments of acute social tension … This layer of inarticulate non-subordination, without face, without voice … is the materiality of anti-power, the basis of hope

(John Holloway, 2010b, 159–60)

We began the book with a consideration of 'collective behaviour' (CB), and in this penultimate chapter, we embark upon a consideration of 'misbehaviour'. 'Misbehaviour' literally means not behaving in the way in which you are required to behave. 'Good behaviour' (compliant behaviour) is the basis of the social order. We learnt from Blumer in Chapter 2 that behaviour that subverts the 'cultural pattern' (society's rules, norms, and expectations) rather than conforming to it, is the secret to changing the social order. In this chapter, we employ the concept of 'misbehaviour', taken from organizational studies, to consider not only organized forms of resistance, but 'every impulse to dissent' (Ackroyd and Thompson, 1999, 39).

We have come across a number of indications in the book as to why looking at protest outside social movement organizations (SMOs) could be important. Sometimes, social movements do not engage in direct confrontations with the state, but focus upon symbolic struggles instead (see Chapter 5). This means that, excepting for a few visible moments of public protest, social movement activity can be 'submerged' (Melucci, 1980, 1989), and can involve individuals in constructing cultural alternatives, which, while not divorced from collective efforts at change, can involve them in carrying out collective action 'on their own'.

We continued to detect this 'lifestyle' activism (Haenfler et al., 2012) and attempts to construct alternative cultural values in the alternative globalization movement (AGM) (see Chapter 6), where confrontations with the state not only lost salience in a globalized context, but were also radically critiqued as a social movement strategy. The suggestion instead was that all the small things we *do* in our daily lives can be important to the alter-global/anti-capitalist struggle if only we would *do* differently (Holloway, 2010a [2002], 2010b). Even in the last chapter on terrorism, we were given a useful reminder that not all forms of social movement activity, and not all protest strategies, are about making frequent public 'noise'. Some, quite self-consciously, involve covert activities that operate 'underground', and are all the more successful when they do take the public stage.

In this chapter, we pick up the threads left by previous debates to push our conceptualization of social movements and protest one final step further to look at the surging 'underbelly' of defiance (J. Scott, 1990, 17) that has interested social movement scholars for decades (Piven and Cloward, 1977; Scott, 1985, 1990; Jasper, 1997; Holloway, 2010a [2002], 2010b), but has rarely been given the place it should in our conceptualizations of social movements and protest. By the end of the chapter you should understand why it is important for social movement scholars to look outside SMOs and public protest events. You should be able to appreciate the ways in which individual and non-organized forms of protest relate to collective efforts at social change. You will therefore be able to critically engage with the notion that participation in social movements and visible protest events is the only way in which people in society are engaged in challenging the social order.

The concept of misbehaviour

By turning to organizational studies to borrow concepts for social movement studies, we are hardly trail-blazing. In fact, we are following the first generation of social movement theorists who in the 1960s and 1970s found in organizational studies a rich array of concepts and ideas to help them think about social movements as 'organizations' (Zald, 2005). What is somewhat ironic is that I am now suggesting that turning to concepts in organizational studies can help us to conceptualize social movements and protest *beyond* SMOs.

Stephen Ackroyd and Paul Thompson (1999) introduce the concept of 'misbehaviour' to organizational studies (a field also known as 'organizational behaviour'). They do so for two reasons: first, 'organizational studies' has not given a very accurate picture of what workplaces are really like. They paint a portrait of workers as passive, submissive and compliant in the face of workplace management, when in reality, workers are anything but. Instead, workers frequently engage in 'misbehaviour': while retaining an overall stance of compliance, they are, in fact, finding ways to not do what they are required to do, in the way they are required to do it.

Misbehaviour is therefore a concept that, strictly speaking, can only apply in a context of power inequalities in which there are attempts to direct behaviour as part of maintaining control. In such contexts, 'directions' are given and certain 'responses' are expected. Misbehaviour is about breaking the link between direction and expected response, and can be seen in the context of control as small and often trivial-looking – but nevertheless significant – attempts to assert autonomy (Ackroyd and Thompson 1999, 12).

The kinds of misbehaviour that Ackroyd and Thompson (1999) identify within workplaces include: sabotage, pilfering, joking, sexual misconduct (i.e. forging romantic relations at work rather than professional ones), go-slows, absenteeism, and whistleblowing (also see Jasper, 1997 on whistleblowing, and Roscigno and Hodson, 2004 on individualized worker resistance). Misbehaviour along these lines, they suggest, is the reality of most workplaces. Sabotage in particular has been well-researched in industrial sociology. A famously amusing study of worker sabotage was presented by Laurie Taylor and Paul Walton (1994 [1971]). It involved a worker at a Blackpool rock factory (which makes those sticks of colourful hard candy that you buy at the sea-side and break your teeth on). One worker, in defiance of his employer, substituted the cheery holiday message that normally runs through a stick of rock with one of his own:

> They had to throw away half a mile of Blackpool rock last year, for, instead of the customary motif running through its length, it carried the terse injunction 'Fuck Off'. A worker dismissed by a sweet factory had effectively demonstrated his annoyance by sabotaging the product of his labour.
>
> (Taylor and Walton, 1994 [1971], 321)

Acts of workplace sabotage, among other ways in which workers – short of open defiance – mess around to express their non-compliance to management control, are therefore acts of 'misbehaviour' that show that workers are not passive receptacles of 'direction' from above.

The second reason why Ackroyd and Thompson offer the concept of misbehaviour as important for organizational studies is one that social movement studies should pay particularly close attention to: they note the growing absence of studies about *worker resistance* from academics in the field (Thompson and Ackroyd, 1995; Ackroyd and Thompson, 1999). Trade union membership, as we know from Chapter 5, has declined, and so have incidences of strike action. Studies about the growing power and control of management and the passivity of workers abound.

These studies make a mistake, however, according to Ackroyd and Thompson (1999), in equating worker resistance with only organized collective action, like trade unions. Just because workers are not so active in trade unions, or busy staging strikes, it does not mean that they are compliant. In order to appreciate all the ways in which workers resist control, however, we need to broaden our vision as to different forms that non-compliance can take – not just in terms of 'organized non-compliance' (e.g. strikes), but the non-compliance that is represented by acts of organizational 'misbehaviour' (Thompson and Ackroyd, 1995; Ackroyd and Thompson 1999, 22).

I suggest here that the two reasons that Ackroyd and Thompson have given for why it is important to bring the concept of 'misbehaviour' into organizational studies also stand for social movement studies. We, too, would benefit from adopting a concept of misbehaviour. It could be applied to broaden our vision to the resistance that takes place outside SMOs and public protest events; and it can help us move beyond the rather black-and-white picture we currently have of people as *either* participating in outright, organized, public activism (e.g. in SMOs and public protest events), *or* doing nothing at all. As James Scott states:

> A view of politics focused either on … consent or open rebellion
> represents a far too narrow concept of political life – especially under
> conditions of tyranny or near-tyranny in which much of the world lives.
> (J. Scott, 1990, 20)

In repressive regimes, for example, it can often appear that people are doing nothing at all to resist if we focus purely on public protest events. We often get a rather pessimistic picture of protest, too, when political scientists measure the 'levels' of participation in conventional activities in Western democracies, like voting, writing to MPs, signing petitions, or going on demonstrations. Figure 8.1 shows the percentage of British people who have ever gone on a protest or demonstration in response

Question: About a government action which you thought was unjust and harmful. Have you ever ... Gone on a protest or demonstration?
(0) Never Done
(1) Ever done

Percent answering 'Ever done'

Age group	1983	n	2000	n	2011	n
<25	4.5	222	1.7	241	7.4	241
25–44	2.2	640	11.7	879	7.1	879
45–64	1.6	514	12.6	728	9.6	728
65+	0.6	338	3.6	439	6.1	439

Figure 8.1
Percentage of British people who have ever gone on a protest or demonstration, by age. Source: British Social Attitudes 1983, 2000, 2011. ©CCSR, University of Manchester.

to government action that they perceived as unjust or harmful. You can see from the results that only a minority of the population (less than 10 per cent across all age groups) had ever gone on a demonstration or protest when asked in 2011. You can also see that these levels have stayed consistently low over time, and across different age groups.

What should we take from these statistics? That the 90 per cent who are silent and inactive are happily complying: either successfully coerced or passively duped into a 'false consciousness'? Or are these people sometimes aware of power inequalities, and the control that is exerted over how they must act in society, such that what they show is a superficial 'posturing' of consent while, in private, find ways to defy and subvert it (J. Scott, 1990)? In the next section I will flesh out an answer to this question, and the role I foresee misbehaviour as a concept playing in social movement studies. I do this by looking at misbehaviour and its function in different historical, social, and political contexts. Before we turn to this, however, it is necessary to make three rather important disclaimers about the concept of 'misbehaviour'.

(a) *Misbehaviour is not a 'new' form of 'individualized' protest.*

The first disclaimer is this: the concept of 'misbehaviour' is not meant to suggest that the 'protest' that happens outside SMO and public protest events is *individualized* rather than collective, or that it is something 'new' to the contemporary context. Whilst misbehaviour – not behaving as you are required to do so – is an individual act, it can also be part of a collective strategy for expressing discontent or struggling for social change, and is most analytically interesting and relevant for social movement studies when it is viewed as such (Piven and Cloward, 1977, 5). While some have argued that in contemporary 'post-modern' society efforts at social change themselves must shift from collective to individualized forms, namely from the realm of collective organizations to individualized 'life politics' (Giddens, 1991) or 'subpolitics' (Beck, 1997), this is not the argument being made here. Fewer instances of visible, organized, collective action should not be confused with no *collective* action at all.

Indeed, the point of the concept of 'misbehaviour' is to look at how *collective* challenges can exist, hidden from view, and in different forms. Misbehaviour can, then, be a collective strategy (Ackroyd and Thompson, 1999). Misbehaviour is not by any means condemned to be, or remain, an *individualized* response to power in contemporary society because, for example, we are now supposed to live in an *individualized* world in which collectivist efforts at change are no longer possible (as the post-modernists argue). Misbehaviour, then, is no postmodern treatise on individualized resistance.

(b) *Misbehaviour is related to, but distinct from, Foucauldian 'resistance'.*

This is clear to see in the arguments of the authors of the misbehaviour concept, Stephen Ackroyd and Paul Thompson (1999), and is one of the reasons I suggest it is so attractive. 'Misbehaviour' is a concept preferred to that of 'resistance', offered by Michel Foucault. The French social theorist Michel Foucault (1926–84) is perhaps the obvious starting point for considering political struggles at the level of culture. This is because Foucault can offer us an alternative 'cultural politics' that locates struggles against power in the realms of everyday life, discourse, and identity, rather than state–society interactions (Nash, 2001). Rather than identifying power with the state and political institutions and their interventions into everyday life, Foucault argues that 'power is always already there' (Foucault, 1980, 141).

What this means essentially is that power is already part of the social relations and cultural discourses that construct us as particular types of people in the first place. Our identity is already shaped by power because it has been socially and culturally constructed (Fraser, 1989). While this sounds like we are condemned forever to be the prisoners of power, Foucault also argues that wherever there is power, there is resistance (Foucault, 1982). Attempts to construct and mould our 'subjectivity' (our very sense of who we are) in particular ways are felt as limitations to our choices, autonomy and freedom (Foucault, 1982). 'Resistance' therefore refers to all the small, individual acts of non-compliance that people commit in an effort to refuse the social construction of their identity as a particular kind of identity, which limits who they might otherwise be. If this sounds very Meluccian, then we should note that Melucci does draw upon Foucault, as does Habermas, although both refrain from fully embracing his theory (Melucci, 1999; Habermas, 1987).

Importantly, the social construction of persons does not stop at the level of their psyche and identity, but particular kinds of 'human bodies' are also inscribed by dominant cultural discourses and the normative expectations attached to them. Bodily deportment and appearance, for example, are moulded by power relations. Sandra Lee Bartky (1988) gives a good example of this by looking at how patriarchal power relations shape the very 'bodily activity' of women so as to produce 'gendered bodies' (Bartky, 1988, 62). Women internalize the normative expectations around feminine beauty and shape their bodily practices in relation to them, such as what they wear, how they sit, exercise and diet regimes, make-up and beauty regimes, and so forth.

Foucault (1977) argues therefore that the body is a battlefield for power/resistance. We are socially constructed to be 'docile and useful bodies' in modern society, such that our compliance to forms of control is built into the material fabric of our being and symbolized by it. This is useful for noticing the role played by the 'protesting body' in everyday acts of misbehaviour. Natasha Walter (1998) notes, for example, how practices around applying make-up, which are seen by Bartky (1988) as oppressive in the Western context, can be subversive acts elsewhere, such as when Afghan women apply lipstick in resistance to the Taliban regime.

Acts of body modification have also been analysed as politically significant in this context, representing a desire to withdraw conformity to prevailing social values and reclaim the body as a site of autonomous self-expression. Tattooing and piercing, according to Lauren Langman (2008, 657) can be 'understood as a way of claiming agency to resist domination':

> Body modifications, tattoos, piercings ... have become fashion
> statements indicating a moment of resistance, a rebellion against
> capitalist modernity, the regulation by rational rules and mass produced
> selfhood ... Many of the adherents of such body modification regard
> their embrace of the grotesque as a rejection of the alienation, sterility,
> emptiness and inauthenticity of modernity.
>
> (Langman, 2008, 664)

Attempts to reject ascribed identities and bodies that comply to expected norms can be seen as important kinds of 'resistance', undertaken outside any organized attempts at social change, and by individuals in their everyday lives.

Foucault is useful, then, for thinking about daily resistance undertaken by individuals. Power is everywhere and operates in a myriad of ways; it does not just come 'top down' from the state, but is part of cultural discourses, norms, identities, and bodies (Nash, 2001). Resistance is therefore everywhere, too, and comes in a myriad of forms that are about subverting cultural discourses and norms, ascribed identities and bodies. Although Foucault (1982) has useful insights into cultural resistance, and has been a necessary reference point for other theorists I will come on to discuss (Scott, 1985, 1990; Holloway, 2010a [2002], 2010b), here I consciously employ the concept of 'misbehaviour' *instead* of Foucault's 'resistance'.

'Misbehaviour' was conceived by Stephen Ackroyd and Paul Thompson (1999) as an alternative to Foucault's theory of resistance. An alternative is necessary, they suggest, because Foucault has, by and large and especially in organizational studies, been employed to much better effect to analyse power and domination in modern societies rather than resistance. The idea that 'power is everywhere' may mean, on the one hand, that we can see 'resistance' everywhere too, but it also complicates our idea of the 'subject' – the human being – who *does* the resisting. According to Foucault, power produces this subject in the first place – their identity and material existence are socially constructed by relations of power. The question is: how then are subjects able to rebel? (Habermas 1990; Acroyd and Thompson, 1999).

I suggest here, in line with James Scott (1990), that while individuals may give a public performance of compliance and conformity in their daily lives, and may do all the bodily and discursive 'posturing' necessary to look like they comply to the cultural discourses and normative expectations that maintain power relations, this does not mean that they are *nothing but* the product of power. People are not merely filled up with the 'false consciousness' and delusion that the Frankfurt School theorists thought were keeping the working classes politically docile (Adorno and Horkheimer, 1979 [1944]). Instead, we keep a ceremonial distance from the act we perform, we engage in 'impression management', and beneath that – or 'off-stage' argues James Scott by invoking Erving Goffman's terms – we retain a core of self-autonomy that expresses itself in many small acts of defiance when power is not looking (Scott, 1985, 321). Power may be productive of subjectivity in that subjectivity is socially constructed (Nash, 2001), but we are not merely the effect of power, the puppet dolls of dominant cultural discourses, the empty bodily vessels that are marked with whatever society wishes to inscribe upon us.

There *is* something underneath, a person who does the 'doing', who puts on the performance, and can therefore 'do' this 'doing' differently, as John Holloway argues (2010a [2002], 40–2). In the process, people can subvert or withdraw the performance on which power depends (Scott, 1990; Holloway, 2010a [2002]). This 'doing' subject can, as Holloway argues, be an essential part of dismantling power relations (what he calls 'anti-power') and in that sense can create the kind of transformation of society that Foucault thought was not possible (Holloway, 2010a [2002], 40).

Since the first two disclaimers have been long we had better pause to summarize before moving on: while there are overlaps with some 'postmodern' theories of resistance, the concept of misbehaviour is not one. Unlike Foucault's concept of 'resistance', misbehaviour does not relegate collective struggle to individual resistance that can never transform society. That is why I talk of 'misbehaviour' and not 'resistance' (Ackroyd and Thompson, 1999).

(c) *Misbehaviour is meant to open up 'a can of worms' about political intentionality.*

The third disclaimer surrounds a recurrent problem when looking at 'protest' as acts of non-compliance that take place outside SMOs, and which puts many off undertaking the task: there is a danger that we end up focusing upon the whole range of 'deviance' (and what in other terms might be called 'anti-social' behaviour) to which we cannot impart any *political* motivation whatsoever, and which is better off left to the psychologists, criminologists and so forth (Cloward and Piven, 1979). Indeed, in our enthusiasm for detecting 'every impulse to dissent', we may end up ascribing political intentions to deviants who do not have any. Social deviance may be a wide-ranging and problematic category, but it is not, however, a territory that social movement theorists have no right to enter. As Melucci (1984) pointed out, social movements belong to the same category as other kinds of social deviance in that they are behaviours that the system cannot integrate.

Once in this territory, however, Ackroyd and Thompson (1999, 52) refer to the very real problem of what to do with the 'rebel without a cause'. While what we mean by 'political intentionality' is certainly a 'can of worms' which is opened by this approach, this is, in fact, the point of it. The purpose of looking outside SMOs is to be sensitized to 'every impulse to dissent' (Ackroyd and Thompson, 1999, 39), in order to be able to analyse the relationship that there might be between these acts and the collective strategies used by certain groups to challenge power (including the public, organized, and more obviously political efforts at social change) (Ackroyd and Thompson 1999, 25).

Only by separating out the 'rebels' seemingly 'without a cause', and the rebels with one, can we explore the possibility of a relationship between the two. As James Jasper argues, if our conceptualizations of social movements omit what goes on outside SMOs and says it is beyond our interest then 'this choice renders invisible all the ways that individual acts of protest do or do not feed into more organized movements' (Jasper, 1997, 5).

James Scott (1990) for example has argued that small acts of insubordination committed 'off-stage' (i.e. out of public view) are very much interconnected with the public, organized rebellions that we usually look at in social movement studies. Scott suggests that they form the 'cultural and social infrastructure' of organized protest events and movements, such that he refers to them as 'infrapolitics' (Scott, 1990, 184). John Holloway makes a similar point by arguing, as he puts it, that without looking at all the small, individual acts of non-compliance that take place in daily life we end up concentrating on 'only the smoke rising from the volcano' rather than the layers of sediment beneath it that caused the eruption in the first place (Holloway 2010b, 159). Opening the can of worms so that – clutching them – we fall down the slippery slope of considering all forms of deviance as *potentially* politically significant, is therefore the point.

I suggest however that because the concept of 'misbehaviour' – unlike that of 'resistance' – retains the notion that such deviance can sometimes be a collective strategy used to express collective discontent, and/or employed in collective efforts towards social change, we do keep some analytic purchase and can unpick individual forms of deviance (that arise for other reasons) from the kind of misbehaviour that interests social movement theorists. Piven and Cloward highlight how when they state that 'the problem…is to identify the features of social context which lead people to defy the particular norms they do' (Cloward and Piven, 1979, 651). It is the context, then, through which we determine whether an act is 'misbehaviour', not the act itself (Ackroyd and Thompson, 1999).

This means that there is no universal or definitive list of behaviours that would count as 'misbehaviour'. It wholly depends upon the context in which the behaviour takes place (and of course, the content of the behaviour). While in the next section we will look at examples of misbehaviour that include sabotage, folk tales, grumblings, graffiti, jokes, subversive talk on Facebook, and so forth, this is not to say that these kinds of acts are *always* to be thought of as 'misbehaviour' as if it were some inherent quality of them. Misbehaviour, then, is an analytic category, not an empirical one. Unpicking 'movement' significant deviance from the range of deviance, I admit, is a messy and far from clear-cut process that may take us down mistaken paths. Without engaging in this task, however, we cannot look at the bits of misbehaviour that represent hidden collective strategies and might be politically significant or, indeed, have the potential to be. We will now turn to several examples of misbehaviour in context.

Misbehaviour in context

This section takes seriously the adage – now some three and half decades old – that people can only do what they can do, in the ways that they can do it, and that the times when it is possible for them to succeed in achieving their full objectives are rare (Piven and Cloward, 1977). What this means – and the key argument here – is that the *form* of protest depends upon the political and social circumstances in which people find themselves.

Piven and Cloward (1977) argue, for example, that because poor people often lack the means to launch formally organized political struggles, they have to rely upon individual acts of defiance in which they withdraw their conformity to social order. These acts can nevertheless be viewed as part of a collective effort to achieve social change. Indeed, the 'unorganized' forms of protest that involve individual acts of non-compliance have been referred to by James Scott (1985) as 'weapons of the weak'.

It is true that some social circumstances give people more reason to protest, but it is equally true that some contexts provide more culturally visible means of expressing discontent. In modern Western democracies this means that discontented people often take to the streets with placards, or join SMOs (on- and offline).

In Eastern Europe and the Middle East, where such activities are readily and sometimes violently repressed, it may mean that individuals can only express what they really think in semi-protected spaces within their everyday lives, including perhaps the 'subversive' political talk that takes place via Facebook and Twitter. While Russian and Nigerian youth have in the past been forced to communicate political messages via graffiti in the context of a repressive regime (as I will discuss later in the section), youth today can instead scribble on the walls of their Facebook pages and have their say in tweets, subverting authority with political talk online that they would not be permitted to use in public spaces offline (see debate point).

Debate point: will the revolution be Facebooked?

Do Facebook and Twitter provide new spaces for people to misbehave by engaging in 'subversive political talk' in semi-public virtual spaces? Moreover, can this talk add to a seething 'underbelly' of resistance that can sometimes fall out onto the streets in public protest or be mobilized by SMOs? In considering these questions, let us take the case of the Egyptian revolution of 25 January 2011 (part of the Arab Spring) which overthrew President Mubarak. It has been suggested that Facebook and Twitter boosted an online surge of outrage and dissent which fed into the street demonstrations and the occupation of Tahrir Square (Vargas, 2012). Facebook pages set up by young people in support of the protesters, and publicizing the brutality of the police response to them, helped to raise awareness of the oppression of Egyptian people and point towards the wider corruption of the regime (Ghonim, 2010).

The first point to note is that internet access is not universally available in the Middle East, and that some regimes (like China) have blocked people's access to Facebook and Twitter. In Egypt, about 13.6 million people have got access to the internet (Ghonim, 2010), out of a population of around 82.5 million (World Bank figure, 2011). We need to be careful therefore about overstating the role that social media can play in mobilization because it tends to be a minority of the wealthy and educated in the population who have access to the internet. Armando Salvatore (2013) also challenges the perception that isolated young people in Egypt started the revolution by setting up their own Facebook pages about police brutality towards protesters. Instead, a longer-term view shows that social media had been used by educated and discontened Egytians for some time before the revolution as an alternative sphere of political communication and solidarity-building between different groups. It was a sphere in which they were able to escape the repression of the state authority and the censored media (Iskander, 2011). It was really the long-term networks that had formed between different activist groups through online communication over a period of time that made mobilization at the time of the revolution possible, rather than the impromptu Facebook pages set up by individuals (Salvatore, 2013).

- Have you been converted to a political cause or mobilized for a protest via Facebook?
- Can subversive political talk on Facebook and Twitter *cause* a revolution?
- Do Facebook and Twitter mean that we can all be political activists now, whether we are members of SMOs or not?

Tactics, Blumer (1951[1946]) pointed out, can never be universal, but must always be adapted to the social and cultural context. Using one tactic everywhere is not only bound to fail, but certain styles of protest would surely be inconceivable to people in very different cultural contexts. What I suggest therefore is that in certain contexts, particularly those which are repressive of collective political struggles, misbehaviour might be the only strategy available to people.

The first example of this is already famous in social movement studies. James Scott (1985) studied a small peasant village in Malaysia in 1978–80, which he fictionally named 'Sedaka'. The peasants relied for their livelihood on rice production. Changes imposed to the way in which rice was produced undermined their livelihood and increased poverty in the village. Scott looked at the ways in which peasants resisted the powerful landowners and officials who drove through these adverse changes. As the power differential between the landowners and the peasants was so great, the peasants knew that there was no point in engaging in a public rebellion. Any attempts at organization or public protest would be quashed. The peasants did not even attempt to use such means since they could not win a confrontation with landowners.

Did this mean that the Malaysian peasants merely acquiesced? Scott argues that if we look at protest just in terms of public, organized protest then it would seem that they did. His research however went beyond the 'public performance' of consent and compliance shown by peasants to uncover what he calls 'the hidden transcript' of resistance

(J. Scott, 1985). Peasant resistance revealed itself in covert, anonymous, and everyday acts of defiance that reclaimed some control and autonomy over life and subverted authority but which, at the same time, could not get anyone in trouble.

The 'hidden transcript' was found in subversive folk tales, poems, songs, gossip, rumour, jokes, and grumblings, which contributed to 'steady grinding efforts to hold one's own against overwhelming odds – a spirit and practice that prevents the worst and promises something better' (Scott, 1985, 350). Let us pause to consider jokes as an example of misbehaviour in the 'case point' because, I suggest, there are overlaps here with forms of protest currently used in Western democratic contexts against the power of neoliberal global capitalism (see Chapter 6).

Case point: just joking!

It may strike you as odd to be considering jokes in a book about social movements and protest. There is however a growing literature about humour and social protest, suggesting that it plays a crucial role in several different contexts in framing, collective identity formation, and resource mobilization (Bos and t'Hart, 2008). In terms of misbehaviour, jokes have also been accorded a significant place by Ackroyd and Thompson (1999), who consider joking around at work as one way to subvert authority and create a distance between the direction from above and the expected behavioural response. Indeed, jokes rupture the link between directions and response in contexts of domination and control by providing the last response that those exerting authority expect or desire: laughter. Laughter has a way of puncturing the legitimacy of authority like no other tactic and can therefore be used as a tactic of subversion (Downing, 2001, 107). Studies on the subversive role of humour frequently refer to the work of Mikhail Bakhtin (1984) who considered the function played by carnivals and festival days in medieval Europe (like All Fools' day and the Harvest Festival). Bakhtin argues that festive holidays and carnivals provided moments of pleasure, laughter, and comedy which created an atmosphere in which the usual social structures and power relations were momentarily suspended. Carnivals included clowns and fools, whose mocking of authority, religion, and social superiors provided a space in which to experience a more equal relationship to those who usually ruled over you, providing you with a moment of freedom (J. Scott, 1990, 172–82). It is interesting to note that Herbert Blumer (1951 [1946]) referred to carnival as one of the forms that 'crowds' can take. Carnival crowds play an important expressive function according to Blumer, seen in the dancing and singing which provides an opportunity for unconventional behaviour to be enacted. We see this carnival crowd on public protest events organized by alter-globalization activists in recent years. There are samba bands, dancing, and 'tactical frivolity', for instance (which includes dressing up as fairies and dancing in front of riot police) (Chesters and Welsh, 2006). The alter-global group 'The Insurgent Clandestine Rebel Clown Army' are also illustrative here. They not only embrace humour as a strategy of subversion and protest, but also adopt the characters of the 'fool' and the 'trickster', which James Scott argues have played important subversive roles in folklore history in Malaysia, Thailand, West Africa, India, and North America (J. Scott, 1990, 162). The Rebel Clowns state that they adopt the character of the fool 'because nothing undermines authority like holding it up to ridicule' (www.clownarmy.org/about.html).

- Do you think that jokes can be used to subvert authority in the workplace or in other contexts of life? Can you think of any examples from your own life?
- Why might carnival crowds create moments of freedom?
- Do you think that 'clowning around' is an effective strategy of protest?

In the cases of Malaysian peasants, then, protest had to take the form of misbehaviour – a cultural struggle which involves attempts to subvert authority and directed behaviour – in other words, to *not* say and do (at least in private) what you are required to say and do in public.

Cihan Tugal (2009) argues that similar methods have to be employed in contexts where there is a repressive state authority that tries to control and shape personal identities and everyday practices. In such contexts,

Tugal (2009) argues, cultural struggles that involve not behaving in the way that is directed 'from above' (in this case, the Turkish state), can be even more effective strategies of challenging state power compared to direct confrontation. In Turkey, a secular state is locked in attempts to reshape the daily practices of its Muslim population away from religious authority by undermining prayer times, making difficult the separation of men and women in public spaces, and curbing the authority of mosques and controlling the content of sermons. In response, the Islamist Movement in some parts of Turkey does not directly engage the state in public confrontation, but involves individuals in attempts to wrestle back control over their daily lives and identity by reasserting the centrality of religious creed and practices. Islamism consciously 'avoids noisy protest' (Tugal, 2009, 423) and employs 'silent movement work on everyday practices' instead (Tugal, 2009, 451).

Methods point: ethnography and the 'intentionality' of protest

We have seen that 'misbehaviour' is not inherent in particular kinds of human acts, but can only be determined analytically by relating these acts to the context in which they arise, and by looking at the content of them. It is no surprise therefore, that studying misbehaviour requires, first and foremost, an ethnographic research strategy. Ethnography is a method widely employed by anthropologists seeking to explore the way of life of a particular cultural group. It often requires a long period of participant observation, in which the researcher joins the group and observes their day to day lives, like, for example, the two years that James Scott (1985) spent in the Malaysian peasant village he named 'Sedaka'. In this respect, ethnography is known as an 'insider' technique, which aims to understand the everyday lives of groups *in their own terms*. It looks at the meaning structures that are employed by the group and how they make sense of the world. Ethnographic methods have been seen as particularly valuable for appreciating the complexities of social movement mobilization and participation; taking what is often presented as a straight-forward linear process and – by adopting a 'grassroots' perspective – showing the inherent 'messiness' of the action involved (Plows, 2008). Importantly for studying misbehaviour, ethnography has also been seen as a method that can problematize and challenge how social movement theorists think of 'political intentionality' (Wolford, 2006). We have seen earlier in the chapter that one of the 'can of worms' opened up by the misbehaviour concept is the question of intentionality and the problem of the 'rebel without a cause'. Wendy Wolford's ethnographic study of the Brazilian landless movement, Sem Terra, is particularly instructive here (Wolford, 2006). She interviewed Brazilian plantation workers over a number of years, exploring how their commitment and involvement in the movement changed. Wolford found that her ethnography complicated the dominant way in which social movement studies view participation as a conscious decision-making process (involving either rational or emotional forms of reasoning). Instead, her data suggested that there was little clear, conscious reasoning at all surrounding involvement with the movement. Instead people's relationship to activism lacked an overall coherence, and their actions were often contradictory. Wolford therefore criticizes social movement scholars for perpetrating the idea that 'believing in agency has come to mean believing in intentionality' (Wolford, 2006, 338). While ethnography can, therefore, be a valuable research method for exploring misbehaviour because it looks in detail at the relationship between context, meaning, and everyday behaviour, it may be especially useful when studying 'misbehaviour' because it can consider agency without transferring onto it social-scientific notions of 'political intentionality'.

It can be said, therefore, that people will only protest in the ways available to them within a specific historical, political and social context. Misztal (1992), for example, shows how the Orange Alternative in Poland was forced to rely upon performance art and humour in public spaces, which attempted to subvert the cultural meanings of everyday life, because it was unable to mount an organized political struggle against the state. In repressive regimes historically people have had to find different ways of protesting and asserting their defiance, which are covert and anonymous in nature rather than public.

Another good example of this is graffiti. We think of graffiti as antisocial behaviour, as the vandalism of public space. It some cases it may be. In other contexts, however, graffiti can be an important medium through which to communicate politically subversive messages. Downing (2001) cites several examples of the political use of graffiti, particularly in the context of repressive regimes in which people cannot protest in more overt ways. The first of these comes from Moscow in the 1970s and 1980s, where young Russians wrote the names of their favourite football teams and rock bands in English on the walls of their apartment blocks (Bushnell,

1990). At the time, the Soviet regime had outlawed Western rock music from America and Britain, viewing it as a harmful outside influence that was eroding Russian cultural values and traditions. Downing states:

> the use of English in these graffiti simply but very directly challenged the bureaucrats' stultifying cultural policies … The graffiti neatly and effectively blew off core Soviet propaganda, and invited passers-by to do so, too. The radiant Soviet future – its young people – were blowing the regime a radiant raspberry.
>
> (Downing, 2001, 122)

The second example is from Nigeria in 1991, when Nigerian students – subject to state surveillance and the threat of physical harm if they had spoken out publicly – communicated political opinions through graffiti in university toilets, constructing one of the more unusually sited public spheres of political debate (Nwoye, 1993).

The means of expressing protest, then, varies, and not just across national boundaries but within them as well. The cultural expression of protest differs markedly by class, as the subcultural theorists of the 1960s were adept at showing when they noted the distinctive style of rebellion of working-class youth subcultures (Hebdige, 1979). Working-class youth expressed their resistance to existing social arrangements in the way that they dressed, the values they lived their lives by, and, in the case of the mods and the rockers, the music that they listened to.

In some contexts, therefore, misbehaviour – expressed in gossip, grumbling, jokes, individual acts of defiance, and non-compliance at work and in daily practices, subversive folk tales, poetry and songs, performance art, and graffiti – is all people can do. Sometimes oppositional acts have to be covert, hidden, silent, but the examples provided here should be enough to illustrate that misbehaviour does not have to be seen as an individualized strategy; it can be a collective strategy for expressing discontent, retaining some personal autonomy, and, importantly, for trying to seek social change.

The everyday troublemaker

I have mentioned in the discussion of James Scott's work that, at times, he draws upon the American Sociologist, Erving Goffman (1922–82).

Scott talks for example about the 'public performance' that those in subordinate positions have to put on. This is a public performance of compliance and deference – but, he points out, this cannot be equated with their entire sense of self. This is a useful point to make in reply to both Melucci and Foucault, who sometimes make it sound as if power has got us at the very core, despite out attempts to resist. Instead, people embark upon 'impression management' in social situations; they put on an act (Goffman, 1959). Scott argues that what powerless groups do in private, or 'off-stage' as Goffman puts it, is to engage in defiance and subversion (the 'hidden transcript' that we discussed earlier). In this section, I want to pause to consider how the work of Erving Goffman might also be relevant to the misbehaviour that takes place in *public* places, and is therefore not covert or anonymous.

We have come across one of Goffman's concepts once before: in Chapter 4 when we considered the efforts of social movements to break away from dominant understandings of social situations and instead 'frame' them in terms of injustice (Gamson, 1992). Goffman's work was the origin of 'frame analysis' which, as we saw, has had an important role to play in how we understand the activity that social movements undertake to construct particular cultural meanings of the world (Benford and Snow, 2000). Goffman does however offer a wider tool-kit of concepts that could be useful for opening up the realm of protest. These may be particularly helpful for considering exactly how people manage to misbehave in public as a way of subverting existing social relations. This is because, as Pierre Bourdieu put it, 'Goffman's achievement was that he reintroduced sociology to the infinitely small, to the things which the object-less theoreticians and concept-less observers were incapable of seeing' (Bourdieu, 1983, 112). By engaging with the task of placing the 'infinitely small' acts of daily life under the telescope, Goffman provided a portrait of the everyday troublemaker, who, through misbehaviour in public encounters, could be the 'destroyer of worlds' (Goffman, 1961, 72; Edwards, 2003).

Goffman was interested in the rules of interaction in public encounters. He suggested that social situations have very clear moral codes of conduct attached to them: normative rules that map out how you are expected to behave and how you are not, such that interaction takes on a 'structured' appearance (Goffman, 1967). Our freedom to act is constrained therefore by the rules of the interaction order to which our public performances must conform. Relationships of domination and subordination are symbolically and ritually reproduced in public encounters, through, for example, 'deference patterns' (Goffman, 1967, 65), the struggle to avoid 'stigma' (Goffman, 1967), and 'avoidance rituals' (Goffman, 1969, 11).

These ideas are significant for the study of misbehaviour in public places because they point to the expressive mechanisms that people can employ in social situations to invert the meaning of those situations and their symbolic relationships to others. The everyday troublemaker, for example, is the person who subverts the rules of the interaction order and therefore fails to keep their place within the encounter. Goffman is useful because he tells us how this effect is achieved. People misbehave when they commit 'situational impropriety' (Goffman, 1967), through, for example, their non-compliance to normative rules, their bodily appearance and comportment (Goffman refers to the 'delinquency strut which...communicates an authority challenge', 1969, 191), and their manner and gestures (we can include uses of humour here). Interestingly, because they similarly engage in 'situational impropriety', Goffman draws a parallel between those defined as mentally ill and the members of social movements (perhaps explaining something of the early association between protesters and those 'mad people with mad ideas' we looked at in Chapter 2):

> In the last few years ... situational improprieties of the most flagrant kind have become widely used as a tactic by hippies, the New Left and black militants, and ... they seem too numerous, too able to sustain collective rapport, and too facile at switching into conventional behaviour to be accused of insanity.
>
> (Goffman, 1971, 412)

Situational impropriety is not only used as a tactic by people who misbehave in public outside SMOs, but can also be employed by activists staging public protest events as part of SMOs. Nevertheless, dipping into Goffman's conceptual tool-kit beyond the framing concept helps us to understand how seemingly trivial acts of non-compliant behaviour (through body, dress, comportment, performance) in public situations can have destabilizing effects for the symbolic relationships between dominant and subordinate parties, and why therefore, they might be employed as tactics in politically significant struggles. Misbehaviour does not just take place 'off-stage' in private domains of life (J. Scott, 1990), but the rules of the interaction order in public situations can provide a public stage for non-compliance and the protesting body. It is really in public realms that the everyday troublemaker realizes her potential to be the 'destroyer of worlds' – at least symbolically.

Summary

In times marked by a recurring public discourse about apathy and indifference in Western democratic societies, and by repressive regimes which afford little opportunity to publicly protest at all, it is all the more important to look at what people actually *do* when it comes to the question of protest. In ways sometimes very small, and sometimes very large, ordinary people somewhere are engaged in resisting existing social arrangements, envisioning new ones, and putting their plans into practice. Public commentators, and some sociologists, however, start out with a very particular image of what 'protest' or 'social movements' should look like and, moreover, what a 'successful' movement should achieve. They are very often disappointed therefore with the actual level of interest, participation, commitment, and persistence of 'the people' who must drive them.

In this chapter, I have suggested that social movement studies would benefit from importing another concept from organizational studies, that of 'misbehaviour' (Ackroyd and Thompson, 1999). The reasons for this are threefold:

- 'Misbehaviour' may help us to detect protest in contexts outside Western democratic societies, but also within them.
- It can help us to detect non-organized protest that takes place covertly, as well as in public spaces.
- The emphasis is on looking for what ordinary people actually *do* and not simply to focus upon *either* the hard-core activists *or* the indifferent majority who seemingly acquiesce.

Engaging in this task takes the unwieldy category of 'social deviance' and picks away at it to find moments of political significance. Such a task will always raise challenging questions about political intentionality, about what to do with the 'rebels without a cause' (Ackroyd and Thompson, 1999). Nevertheless, these rebels without a cause might be the *mobilization potential* for rebels who do have a cause, or they might have been inspired by them.

The main argument of this chapter has not been that we need to move from CB to misbehaviour as such, but that we need to explore the relationship between the two:

- the relationship between individual and collective cultural struggle and organized political struggle
- the relationship between hidden/silent protest and public/noisy protest.

Misbehaviour, then, does not mean that protest today merely rests in individualized, multiple, and ultimately futile resistances in everyday life. It means that the acts of non-compliance that exist outside SMOs and public protest events are neither politically insignificant, nor our only hope. To stretch our conceptualization of social movements and protest to include 'misbehaviour' is (to invoke John Holloway's metaphor once again) to pay attention to the volcano before it erupts, as well as fixing our eyes on the smoke that rises.

DISCUSSION POINT

- Do you think that there are circumstances in which acts of body modification (tattoos, piercings), graffiti, sabotage, and jokes can be considered as forms of protest?
- Are acts of protest that take place outside SMOs important to efforts to change society?
- Will social movement studies benefit from looking at 'misbehaviour' or should it be outside our field of interest?

FURTHER READING

The concept of 'misbehaviour' as it is presented in organizational studies comes from Akroyd and Thompson (1999) *Organizational Misbehaviour*. To put this in context of debates in organizational studies, also see Thompson and Ackroyd (1995) 'All Quiet on the Workplace Front? A Critique of Recent Trends in British Industrial Sociology', *Sociology* 29(4): 615–33. James Scott's (1985) *Weapons of the Weak: Everyday Forms of Peasant Resistance*, is already a classic in Social Movement Studies, while his (1990) *Domination and the Arts of Resistance* outlines his theory of the 'hidden transcript'. For a lively and engaging read, see John Holloway's (2010a [2002]) *Change the World without Taking Power: The Meaning of Revolution Today*. On joking and protest in varied historical and national contexts, including alter-globalization, see Dennis Bos and Marjolein t'Hart (2008) (eds.) *Humour and Social Protest*.

9 | Conclusion: the shifting terrain of social movement studies

> Because history doesn't move in straight lines but surges like water, sometimes swirling, sometimes dripping, flowing, flooding – always unknowable, unexpected, uncertain. Because the key to insurgency is brilliant improvisation, not perfect blueprints … Because rebels transform everything – the way they live, create, love, eat, laugh, play, learn, trade, listen, think and most of all the way they rebel.
>
> (The Clandestine Insurgent Rebel Clown Army, www.clownarmy)

The 'unknowable' path of history creates challenges for how we think about and understand social movements. Social movements are, by their very nature, 'unpredictable' phenomena. The essence of collective efforts orientated towards social change is, as Herbert Blumer pointed out, cultural innovation. Although we have seen that innovation in social movements should not be overstated (with lots of borrowing of tactics and ideas from other movements, such that recurring 'repertoires of protest' form), we have also seen that cases of social movements, and the contexts in which they operate, undergo substantial change and alter the very activity, organizational form, and protest tactics of movements themselves. Globalization and the rise of new technological contexts associated with new media, for example, have, for some, altered our very idea of 'what social movements are', the mobilization conditions on which they depend, and the potential that they have for social transformation (Chesters and Welsh, 2006).

In this concluding chapter, we revisit the main debates of the book and spell out the arguments that have been made. We consider the key merits and limitations of the different perspectives we have looked at, and we also revisit the question of how 'new cases and new contexts' have challenged the existing conceptual distinctions drawn around social movements. In the course of this discussion, I also intend to clarify the 'relational' understanding of social movements that has been emerging throughout our critical discussion, and make clear my reasons for supporting it.

The problem with general theories

If anything holds universally true about social movements then it is the assertion from the Rebel Clown Army that 'rebels transform everything, but most of all the way they rebel'. It is not surprising therefore that the field of social movement studies is one of varied and rival conceptualizations. As James Jasper (1997, 8) argues, our ideas about social movements shift when we encounter new cases that challenge and complicate our existing ways of thinking. As a consequence, social movement scholars regularly observe that applying existing concepts to their own cases can feel like chasing shadows of past contentions that never quite fit the emerging contours of today's struggles.

For these reasons, perhaps, we have found in the course of the book that general theories and 'law-like' suppositions about social movements have very often failed to hold sway under the weight of challenge that comes from considering different cases. Alan Scott (1990), for example, suggests that the desire to generate 'general laws' about social movements – rather than engaging with the actual context and particularities of empirical cases – was the critical flaw in Neil Smelser's (1962) structural functionalist approach. Although Smelser's account does provide us with the beginnings of a multi-causal explanation of social movements by identifying a range of factors that movement scholars of different persuasions have subsequently found relevant (Crossley, 2002), his model has nevertheless been wracked by accusations of tautology (i.e. the factors he identifies become self-confirming) (Oberschall, 1968; Currie and Skolnick, 1970; Scott, 1990).

We cannot, therefore, reduce all of the varied and shifting cases of social movements to a six-factor model that can be universally applied to explain them. Instead, as Scott (1990) argues, we need to engage in the details by looking at concrete processes of resource mobilization and strategizing, in other words, the stuff of human action out of which social movements actually emerge. This was the advantage of the alternative that was offered to us by resource mobilization theory (RMT). Even RMT's critic, Alberto Melucci (1980), appreciated that the approach at least looked at the question of 'how' movements mobilize, rather than assuming that they were some kind of automatic response to social conditions, or to our 'beliefs' about them.

The dissatisfaction with building universal models to explain social movements perhaps rears its head again in the 'contentious politics' (CP) approach (McAdam et al., 2001; Tilly and Tarrow, 2006). What collective behaviour (CB) and CP have in common may not be much, but each of the perspectives does take a broader view of collective action, not just concerning themselves with social movements as such, but with other kinds of contentious episodes, from riots to revolutions. While CP does study these episodes in some historical detail, it does so in order to discover the *general mechanisms* (environmental, relational, and cognitive) that are in play and combine – albeit in different ways in different cases – to produce collective contention. Such 'universal-izing' ambitions with regards to general models of explanation (even if unintended), has once again been met with consternation from other scholars (Goodwin and Jasper, 2004b, 2004c; Mees, 2004).

We have, however, found some value in CP, which was brought to bear in our analysis of global social movements (Tarrow, 2006). This value arises from the 'relational thinking' that is embedded in the approach (McAdam et al., 2001). It puts the spotlight on social relationships, for example, and how the mobilization process can be thought of and studied in terms of changing relations between different groups, brought about through processes like diffusion and brokerage. This way of thinking about movement emergence is particularly adept at helping us to understand global 'networked' resistance for example, which involves different actors flexibly combining in different ways, as enabled by new media (Juris, 2004, 2005a; Chesters and Welsh, 2006; Maeckelbergh, 2009).

CP also sees the 'challengers' and 'opponents' that are involved in contentious episodes not as 'pre-existing' social actors, but as actors whose identities are 'made' in the course of contentious interaction itself. This brings home the importance of an insight from new social movement (NSM) theory: social movements *are* the creation of new collective identities, and this work happens in the social relationships and interactions of everyday life (Melucci, 1985; 1996). While critics of CP still highlight a weakness regarding the analysis of cultural factors, it is clear that culture should also be thought of in 'relational' terms – it must be 'seen as part of the action' – as Steinberg (1999, 772) put it – and therefore is embedded within relational mechanisms themselves (McAdam, 2011).

A relational understanding of social movements

I have therefore suggested in the course of the book that while conceptualizations of social movements have been debated, stretched, and challenged, we can also unearth a particular direction in thinking on social movements, which is towards a 'relational' understanding. I have defended the advantages of a relational understanding of social movements in three main ways, which are outlined below.

A relational logic of collective action

First, I have suggested that the 'logic of collective action' must be thought of not primarily as a 'rational' one, but a 'relational' one. We have traced a shift from a rational to a relational logic of collective action by critically engaging with rationalist approaches to social movements such as RMT. I have argued that there is little evidence to suggest that RMT ever uncritically imported the notion of an isolated, individual, rational actor, who makes decisions on their own. This is reflected in Charles Tilly's (1998) statement that:

> Out of all of the things that a rational action model leads you to think
> about what people might be able to do, given some external bundle
> of interests, in fact, they are not even considering doing most of them.
> They don't know how to do most of them, and what they do is strongly
> imbedded in their previous history.
>
> (Tilly, 1998, 204)

It is also clear that in the case of collective action, rational decisions are made in a context of interdependence. This is reflected in game theories of collective action, theories of the critical mass, and the acceptance of the criticism of the 'under-socialized actor' in rational action theory (RAT) (Oberschall, 1973, 1995). This recognition leads us to rethink exactly what 'rationality' means in a context of interdependence. This context is one where people's lives and fates are mutually entwined, where relationships are invested with moral and emotional qualities, and where people are often 'other-orientated' rather than self-interested. As such, the model of 'emotional man' suggested by Helena Flam (1990), is perhaps more appropriate to understanding human decision-making in the case of collective action. Networks matter, for example, not predominantly for the exchange of resources, or for the structural connections to movements that they provide but, as Roger Gould (2003) argues, because they denote the human relationships in which issues are discussed and debated, moral positions are forged, emotional commitments to a cause cemented, and plans of action negotiated. I have suggested therefore that a 'relational logic' of collective action should replace a 'rational' one.

This is not to say that people deciding upon collective action are not rational by the criteria set out by Mancur Olson (1965): they act with a sense of purpose and they go about things in a way that they think will be effective. In the case of collective action, however, human beings mix together rational, normative, and emotional models of action (D. Gould, 2004). 'Rational man' has wrongly been privileged therefore. This is perhaps because, as Craig Calhoun (2001, 48) argues, the new generation of scholars in the 1970s were super-keen to reject the problematic picture of protesters as irrational 'mad hatters' portrayed by CB. Randall Collins (2001, 36–7) was right then when he suggested that the conceptual dualisms in social movement studies – reason/emotion being just one of them – have arisen from the particular intellectual development of the field and are written in to its 'story'.

A relational understanding of the world around a social movement

Alongside arguing for a relational logic of collective action, I have also argued for a relational understanding of the environment in which social movements operate and which provides them with opportunities as well as placing constraints on their action. Political process theories (PPT) of collective action were useful for correcting the over-emphasis upon 'internal' movement factors in RMT, as revealed in the debate between William Gamson and Jack Goldstone. PPT pointed our attention towards the important factor of the 'world around' social movements and how it conditioned their emergence and their success (Tilly, 1978). We saw how PPT has been criticized for being overly 'structuralist' in its approach to social movements, suggesting that social movements depend upon political structures in the external environment being 'favourable' before they can emerge. This understanding does little justice to the creative human action that we have placed at the essence of social movements (Jasper, 1997; Goodwin and Jasper, 2004b).

Rather than understanding the environment in which social movements operate as a static place consisting of immovable structures, I suggested that we understand it in relational terms by employing the concept of 'external relational fields' (Goldstone, 2004; Crossley, 2006). The concept of 'external relational fields' covers the aspects of the external environment that the POS concept had been referring to (Goldstone, 2004, 356), but stresses not structure but interaction. Fields are the symbolic and discursive spaces in which strategic interactions between movements and other players (state, media, corporate, public) take place. This means that rather than being stable, fixed and outside the control of actors (the 'structuralist' understanding), the environment in which movements act is actually shifting all the time (Goodwin and Jasper, 2004b, 12).

It is fair to say that when we probed the 'structuralist' approach in detail, we found much more subtlety to the way in which external structures and creative human action were related, and some big concessions to culturalist and constructionist approaches that argue that the external world does not determine anything about our action because it first has to be perceived and interpreted – a lesson that we should have learned long ago from Herbert Blumer's (1951 [1946]) 'symbolic interactionist' approach to collective behaviour. The main point here was that 'an opportunity not recognized is no opportunity at all' (Gamson and Meyer, 1996, 283), adding considerable weight to the criticism that we found mounting against the conceptual clarity of the 'political opportunity' concept, a concept which keeps on working hard to improve – at times narrowing itself, at other times broadening its vision – but either way, remaining problematic (Goodwin and Jasper, 2004b).

The framing perspective was understood therefore as a necessary complement to the concept of 'political opportunity', enabling scholars to study the way in which the meaning of situations is constructed and communicated in order to assist the mobilization process. By combining the concepts of political opportunity and framing – and placing them alongside RMT's insight about the importance of 'mobilizing structures' and resources – we saw another 'model' of social movements emerge, referred to as the 'political process model' (McAdam et al., 1996). This model is one which largely dominates social movement studies today. We found that this approach was a useful one when turning attention to the case of terrorist movements, and was able to generate insight into the political, organizational, cultural, and cognitive factors that explain political violence and terrorism, although along the way we met challenges regarding the covert nature of some movement activity.

A relational understanding of culture and emotion

The framing concept was itself found wanting, however. The understanding of culture and its relationship to movement mobilization is flawed. To make this case, we looked at theorists who gave us a 'relational' understanding of culture, too. Rather than seeing culture as 'in people's heads' as Polletta (2004) put it (making reference to the way in which culture is reduced to perceptions, meanings, and understandings that individuals hold of the world), culture was instead viewed as part of the very fabric of human relationships. It is, for example, the shared *discourses* (Steinberg, 1999) that shape our understanding of the world, and which, for some, constitute the very stuff of 'structures' as well (Laclau and Mouffe, 1985; Polletta, 2004). This relational understanding of culture also applies to our understanding of emotion: emotions are no more in your heart than culture is in your head. Emotions, like meanings and understandings of the world, are 'intersubjective' – they arise in interaction with others and are shaped and made influential by them.

New cases, new contexts: challenges to existing conceptualizations

Through exploring 'new cases and new contexts' in this book we have found ways to challenge key features of the conceptualization of 'social movements' forwarded by existing approaches. Over the course of the chapters, we have brought four main issues to attention: (1) the necessity of strains, resources and organization; (2) the centrality of the state; (3) the desirability of collective identity; and (4) the distinction between collective, organized protest and unorganized, individual protest. Let us summarize each of these in turn.

(a) *The necessity of strains, resources and organization*

Chapter 2 engaged with the earliest approach to social movements and protest: CB theory. The critical lesson that we took from our engagement with CB was that 'strains' in society are not enough to produce a social movement. Social movements cannot be adequately conceptualized as the 'irrational expression of shared grievances'. CB's critic, RMT, even went as far as suggesting that strains are not necessary *at all* since one of the jobs of a social movement organization (SMO), and movement 'entrepreneurs', is to manufacture and amplify grievances, rather than to mobilize them (McCarthy and Zald, 1977). This much is accepted wisdom in social movement studies. We moved beyond this questioning of strains, however, to pose a question back to RMT: do 'resources' (especially 'tangible' ones) and 'organization' fare any better? Are they not also questionable in terms of their *necessity* for social movements?

The rise of new media, for example, has changed the mobilization environment for social movements significantly, and we saw that the concept of 'resources' needs to change along with it. In Chapter 3, it was suggested that 'virtual resources' are important to social movement mobilization and success, and may well 'level' the playing field between activists and their opponents (Peckham, 1998). With easily accessible ways to communicate and mobilize online, the task of offline resource mobilization by formal organizations may be declining in significance. The work of Jennifer Earl and Katrina Kimport (2011), for instance, suggested that the existence of low-cost, online forms of protest means that we might have to leave those fomally organized SMOs behind in our analysis altogether. Protest online, which is carried out by individuals *outside* SMOs, could be making SMOs less relevant to our picture. Earl and Kimport suggest that we should shift our focus away from SMOs as the unit of analysis, and towards 'protest tactics' instead (something we have done in Chapter 8 by engaging with 'unorganized' protest). If SMOs are declining in significance, then Earl and Kimport (2011, 186) suggest that 'we will have to think of ourselves as scholars of protest rather than scholars of social movements'.

This is the extreme response to the challenge created by new media. In this book we have trod more cautious ground. SMOs have not been seen as synonymous with social movements, but neither have they been seen as irrelevant. In our relational conceptualization of social movements, we have placed SMOs neither at the centre of our picture of 'what social movements are' nor outside it. Instead, 'social movements' are thought of as the networks between SMOs, more informal groups, and individuals. Rather than 'social movement organizations', then, we have thought in terms of 'social movement networks', which became essential when conceptualizing global protest in Chapter 6.

The main point here is that while it has long been acknowledged that 'strains' and 'grievances' should not be central to our understanding of social movements, the same might be said for 'tangible' resources (like offices, money, staff) and formal organization, too. While it is premature to suggest that new media will revoluntionize the form that social movements take, Earl and Kimport (2011) are right to question the way in which the internet changes the costs of mobilization and therefore the contours of the 'collective action problem' that has for so long been at the centre of conceptualizations of social movements (Opp, 2009).

(b) *The centrality of the state*

We saw in Chapter 4 that political process theorists place the nation state at the centre of social movement activity. Social movements were seen to arise in the eighteenth century as the particular vehicles through which citizens made claims on a modern democratic nation state, drawing upon modular repertoires of protest like the street demonstration and petition (Tilly and Tarrow, 2006). The state and its political institutions are therefore viewed as the central targets of social movements, especially for those 'citizenship movements' who forwarded claims for expanded political rights and representation. The state is not only seen as a central *target* of social movement activism, however, but also central to the *opportunities* that social movements have to emerge and be successful. Since social movements are engaging in 'contentious politics' that involve governments in some way in their claims (McAdam et al., 2001), the nature of the political system shapes their chances of being heard. When the state is weakened in its capacity to use repression, for example, then opportunities for social movements to form and succeed may be enhanced.

In Chapter 6, the centrality of the nation state to our understanding of social movements was challenged by the emergence of a 'global society' consisting of 'supranational' economic and political institutions. We saw the central position of the state in networks of power diminish as it became one node in a 'network of global governance' (Castells, 2004a). Political institutions at the international level, alongside economic and financial elites (like multinational corporations) superseded the nation state in decision-making and influence in a global neoliberal economy. Importantly, however, we found that the nation state did not disappear altogether from the environment in which social movements act (Tarrow, 2006). Processes of 'externalization' and 'domestication' mean that grievances, mobilization efforts, and the targets of claims shift between the national and international levels as different opportunities and alliances open up. While the state may be 'de-centred' it has not disappeared, and can equally take on renewed importance as activists bring global concerns to the door of nation states (e.g. climate change). The question for analysis, then, is how national political environments *interact* with, rather than are *superseded* by, global political environments in order to shape social movement activity (Tarrow, 2006).

Nevertheless, neoliberal globalization has also confirmed that social movements can have 'non-state' targets, in particular corporations. Multinational corporations (MNCs) play a powerful role within the global capitalist economy and hence they become targets of collective claims in themselves, as reflected in movements attacking brands (Starr, 2000) and calling for global corporate responsibility (Soule, 2009). The issue of non-state targets was also highlighted in Chapter 5 on the NSMs. NSMs demonstrated that 'citizenship movements' were but one category of social movements (Jasper, 1997). Other social movements do not target the state but actually want autonomy from the state instead. NSMs create cultural alternatives in everyday life that seek to escape from the state, not influence or seize it (Melucci, 1996). This is reflected in Habermas's and Touraine's assertion that NSMs are locked in a battle against increasing state interference and the growing power of technocrats. This argument somewhat exaggerated the relationship between NSMs and the state, which is not as clear cut. Some NSMs did make claims on the state as well (like the women's liberation movement). Nevertheless, it helped us to appreciate different kinds of social movements which are engaged in personal and cultural struggles rather than overtly 'political' ones. This enabled us to understand the significance of 'lifestyle movements' (Haenfler et al., 2012) which seek social change not by targeting the state, but by enacting personal change in everyday life (like the voluntary simplifiers we looked at).

The division between political and cultural movements came into sharp focus in Chapter 6 because the alternative globalization movement (AGM) – rather than fitting neatly into one category or the other – was, in fact, both. Internal divisions in the AGM reflect the differing political and cultural strategies that social movements can employ. One camp targets the state and supranational political institutions with democratic demands, the other rejects the focus on political institutions and seeks instead to enact change from the 'bottom up' through reinventing everyday practices and identities (Pleyers, 2010). While, for some, the state remains a central target in the collective effort to change society, for others, targeting the state is a misplaced strategy. John Holloway (2010a), for example, calls for AGM activists to 'change the world *without* taking power' by concentrating on every-day practices. The question of 'what to do with the state' is not simply a conceptual question therefore, but a practical one that is debated within social movements themselves. We saw in Chapter 8, however, that the relationship that social movements have to the state may not be a matter of choice, but necessity. In authoritarian regimes which do not tolerate public forms of collective claims-making, people have to find ways to resist state power that do not include direct confrontation. We saw this, for example, in Tugal's (2009) work on the Islamist move-ment in Turkey, which engages indirectly with the Turkish state by protecting personal and cultural practices based upon religion.

(c) *The desirability of collective identity*

It has generally been accepted that a 'social movement' is *more* than the network of different actors cooperating together in order to bring about social change (Diani, 1992, 13; Saunders, 2007). This 'something more' is the sense of 'collective identity', which for some defines the very essence of 'what social movements are' (Melucci, 1980). Melucci told us that building a social movement involves constructing a collective identity – a sense of 'we' against 'them' in a struggle over 'this', and not merely mobilizing resources like money, facilities, skills, and leaders. Recognizing the importance of 'collective identity' as a defining feature of social movements was important in helping us to acknowledge that sometimes people can do collective action 'on their own'. Individu-als involved in alternative lifestyles, for example, can be seen as part of broader collective efforts at change to the extent that they share a collective identity which draws their individual efforts into a wider 'movement'.

The importance of collective identity was challenged, however, in Chapter 6 when we considered the nature of global social movements. The AGM, for example, is marked by a lack of unity, reflected in dis-agreements over issues as basic as what to name the movement. Rather than a social movement in the conventional sense, the AGM appears as a network of other social movements (a 'movement of movements', as Mertes (2004) put it), which held together only to the extent that it refrained from constructing a sense of 'we' against 'them' in a struggle over 'this'. One reason for this is practical – such varied groups as socialists, feminists, anarchists, farmers, urban youth, and so on have such differing interpretations of the key issues that achieving a united sense of 'we' is unlikely. The other reason, however, is ideological. In a movement like the AGM that stands for direct forms of democracy, the network structure of the movement brings advantages. 'Rhizome' networks for example – which are polycentric (many-headed) and so complex that no one can control them – allow different groups to retain their autonomous identities and frames of meaning while connecting together for mutual benefit (Chesters and Welsh, 2006).

While some see the AGM as qualifying as a 'social movement' to the extent that its diverse network is able to pin a 'collective identity' on 'resistance to neoliberalism' (Pleyers, 2010), others see the possibility of the AGM sustaining itself as a 'social movement' to the extent that it refrains from imposing a sense of collective identity. Global social movements like the AGM therefore raise two sorts of challenge to conceptualizations of social movements. First, is a collective identity a realistically *achieveable* feature of global social movements, which involve connections between diverse groups, lack common frames of reference, and communicate more often than not online? Secondly, is collective identity even a *desirable* feature of a social movement, or are more democratic forms of collective action enabled by unleashing the 'will of the many' who retain autonomy to think of themselves, the opposition, and the stakes in their own terms?

(d) *The distinction between organized, collective protest, and unorganized, individual protest*

We have seen in the course of the book that protest is not 'synonymous' with social movements (Crossley, 2002). While protest does often accompany social movements, we have come across social movements that do not organize protest events at all, like McCarthy and Zald's (1973) 'professional social movements'. These social movements act much more like formal business organizations that create glossy campaigns 'on behalf' of aggrieved populations, rather than coordinating protest events. Where there is a social movement, then, there is not always protest.

We have also seen that the opposite is true, and is important to consider: *where there is protest there is not always a social movement.* In

Chapter 8 we saw that individuals can engage in 'protest' without being involved in a public event organized by a social movement. People can protest in their everyday lives, and without having a membership card for an SMO. By making this claim I have not argued that protest is necessarily *individualized* in terms of its efforts towards social change, or that this is characteristic of a 'post-modern' or 'high modern' society more broadly (as others like Ulrich Beck, 1997 and Anthony Giddens, 1991 have argued). My statement should be qualified therefore: where there is protest there is not always a social movement *organization*.

Capturing the kind of protest that takes place outside SMOs has required us to stretch our conceptualization of 'protest' too. Social movement studies has predominantly conceived of 'protest' as 'noise': the disruption that can be created through a protest event that, for example, marches through the streets with a loud-speaker. While protest as collective 'noise' is important, we also need to conceive of protest as an act that can be 'silent' and covert (in either private or public realms of life), and sometimes has to be (Tugal, 2009), an act that can be 'hidden' in individual transgressions, and is sometimes all the more effective for being so (Cloward and Piven, 1979).

We have seen that there is a need to think of protest both in terms of social movements and outside them, complicating the collective and individual dimensions of social movement activism. In doing this, we have drawn upon some classic reference points in social movement studies, like the work of Frances Fox Piven and Richard Cloward (1977, 1979), James Scott (1985, 1990), and more recently, John Holloway (2010a [2002], 2010b). They have helped us, alongside Ackroyd and Thompson's (1999) work in organizational studies, to look at 'misbehaviour', those individual acts of non-compliance, and the ways in which they provide potential for social movement mobilization. We have seen therefore that protests are what social movements organize and employ, but they can also be those unorganized bits of action outside social movements that intersect with social movements in interesting ways.

Closing thought

Challenging the conceptual distinction made between individual and collective efforts towards change has therefore been a key contribution of this book. I have suggested that this is essential conceptual work to do in the field, but it has also opened up a question about the relationship that ordinary individuals – like you – have to social movements and protest. We often get the impression that there are two groups in society when it comes to protest: the hard-core activists who do it and the rest of the apathetic majority who don't. This is just one more dualism in social movement studies that cannot be maintained.

I have argued that very often individuals find ways to 'misbehave', and while political intentions cannot be unproblematically overlaid onto such actions, the context in which they take place should be able to tell us whether there is potential for acts of everyday non-compliance to become organized, public, efforts at social change. We might not all sign petitions, go on protest marches, or devote our lives to a cause; but we do all have the ability to react to social and political injustice (the basic human reaction that John Holloway calls the 'scream of refusal') (Holloway, 2010a, 1). Will you scream?

Bibliography

Ackroyd, S. and Thompson, P. (1999) *Organizational Misbehaviour*. London: Sage.

Adamson, F. (2005) 'Globalisation, Transnational Political Mobilisation, and Networks of Violence'. *Cambridge Review of International Affairs* 18(1): 31–49.

Adorno, T. and Horkheimer, M. (1979) *Dialectic of Enlightenment*. London: Verso. First published 1944.

Aelst, P. van and Walgrave, S. (2002) 'New Media, New Movements? The Role of the Internet in Shaping the "Anti-Globalisation" Movement'. *Information, Communication and Society* 5(4): 465–93.

Aguirre, B. E., Quarantelli, E. L., and Mendoza, J. L. (1988) 'The Collective Behaviour of Fads: The Characteristics, Effects, and Career of Streaking'. *American Sociological Review* 53(4): 569–84.

Allsop, J., Jones, K., and Baggott, R. (2004) 'Health Consumer Groups in the UK: A New Social Movement?'. *Sociology of Health and Illness* 26(6): 737–56.

Almeida, P. D. (2009) 'Opportunity, Organizations, and Threat-Induced Contention: Protest Waves in Authoritarian Settings' in D. McAdam and D. Snow (eds.) *Readings on Social Movements: Origins, Dynamics and Outcomes*. Oxford University Press. 2nd edn.

Aminzade, R., Goldstone, J. A., McAdam, D., Perry, E. J., Sewell, W. H., Tarrow, S., and Tilly, C. (eds.) (2001) *Silence and Voice in the Study of Contentious Politics*. Cambridge University Press.

Aveni, A. (1977) 'The Not So Lonely Crowd: Friendship Groups in Collective Behavior'. *Sociometry* 40(1): 96–9.

Bagguley, P. (1992) 'Social Change, the Middle Class, and the Emergence of New Social Movements: A Critical Analysis'. *The Sociological Review* 40(1): 26–48.

Baker, W. and Faulkner, R. (1993) 'The Social Organisation of Conspiracy: Illegal Networks in the Heavy Electric Equipment Industry'. *American Sociological Review* 58(6): 837–60.

Bakhtin, M. (1984) *Rabelais and His World*. Bloomington, IN: Indiana University Press.

Barber, B. (1995) *Jihad versus McWorld: How Globalism and Tribalism Are Reshaping the World*. New York: Times Books.

Barker, C., Cox, L., Krinsky, J, and Nilsen, A. (eds.) (2013) *Marxism and Social Movements*. Historical Materialism Book Series. Vol. 46. Brill. Forthcoming.

Barker, C. and Dale, G. (1998) 'Protest Waves in Western Europe: A Critique of New Social Movement Theory'. *Critical Sociology* 24: 65–104.

Bartky, S. L. (1988) 'Foucault, Femininity, and the Modernization of Patriarchal Power' in I. Diamond and and L. Quinby (eds.) *Feminism and Foucault: Reflections on Resistance*. Boston: Northeastern University Press.

Bayard de Volo, L. (2000) 'Global and Local Framing of Maternal Identity: Obligation and the Mothers of Matagalpa Nicaragua' in J. A. Guidry, M. D. Kennedy, and M. N. Zald (eds.) *Globalization and Social Movements: Culture, Power and the Transnational Public Sphere.* University of Michigan Press.

Bearman, C. (2005) 'An Examination of Suffragette Violence'. *English Historical Review* 120(486): 365–79.

(2007) 'Confronting the Suffragette Mythology'. *BBC History Magazine* February.

Beck, C. (2007) 'On the Radical Cusp: Ecoterrorism in the United States, 1998–2005'. *Mobilization* 12(2): 161–76.

(2008) 'The Contribution of Social Movement Theory to Understanding Terrorism'. *Sociology Compass* 2(5):1565–81.

Beck, U. (1997) *The Reinvention of Politics: Rethinking Modernity in the Global Social Order.* Cambridge: Polity.

Bell, D. (1976) *The Coming of Post-Industrial Society: A Venture in Social Forecasting.* New York: Basic Books.

Benford, R. (1993a) '"You Could Be the Hundredth Monkey": Collective Action Frames and Vocabularies of Motive within the Nuclear Disarmament Movement'. *The Sociological Quarterly* 34(2):195–2 16.

(1993b) 'Frame Disputes within the Nuclear Disarmament Movement'. *Social Forces* 71(3): 677–701.

(1997) 'An Insider's Critique of the Social Movement Framing Perspective'. *Sociological Inquiry* 67(4): 409–30.

Benford, R. and Hunt, S. (1992) 'Dramaturgy and Social Movements: The Social Construction and Communication of Power'. *Sociological Inquiry* 62:36–55.

Benford, R. and Snow, D. (2000) 'Framing Processes and Social Movements'. *Annual Review of Sociology* 26: 611–39.

Bennett, W. L. (2003) 'Communicating Global Activism: Strengths and Vulnerabilities of Networked Politics'. *Information, Communication and Society* 6(2): 143–68.

Beynon, H. (1973) *Working for Ford.* London: Allen Lane.

Blumer, H. (1951) 'Social Movements' in A. McClung Lee (ed.) *Principles of Sociology.* New York: Barnes & Noble. 2nd edn. First published 1946.

(1971) 'Social Problems as Collective Behaviour'. *Social Problems* 18: 298–306.

Bonacich, P. (1987) 'Power and Centrality: A Family of Measures'. *American Journal of Sociology* 95(5): 1170–82.

Borgatti, S., Everett, M., and Freeman, L. (2002) *Ucinet for Windows: Software for Social Network Analysis.* Harvard, MA: Analytic Technologies.

Bos, D. and t'Hart, M. (2008) (eds.) *Humour and Social Protest.* Cambridge University Press.

Bourdieu, P. (1983) 'Erving Goffman, Discoverer of the Infinitely Small'. *Theory, Culture and Society* 2: 112–13.

Braverman, H. (1974) *Labor and Monopoly Capital: The Degradation of Work in the Twentieth Century.* New York: Monthly Review Press.

Brown, P., Zavestoski, S., McCormick, S., Mayer, B., Morello-Frosch, R., and Gasior Altman, R. (2004) 'Embodied Health Movements: New Approaches to Social Movements in Health'. *Sociology of Health and Illness* 26(1): 50–80.

Brownlie, N. (2012) 'Trade Union Membership 2011'. Department for Business, Innovation and Skills, www.bis.gov.uk/policies/employment-matters/research/trade-union-stats.

Buechler, S. (1995) 'New Social Movement Theories'. *The Sociological Quarterly* 36(3): 441–64.

(2004) 'The Strange Career of Strain and Breakdown Theories' in D. Snow, S. Soule, and K. Hanspeter (eds.) *The Blackwell Companion to Social Movements*. Oxford: Blackwell.

Bushnell, J. (1990) *Moscow Graffiti: Language and Subculture*. Boston: Unwin Hyman.

Calhoun, C. (1995) 'New Social Movements of the Early Nineteenth Century' in M. Traugott (ed.) *Repertoires and Cycles of Collective Action*. Durham, NC: Duke University Press.

(2001) 'Putting Emotions in their Place' in J. Goodwin, J. Jasper, and F. Polletta (eds.) *Passionate Politics: Emotions and Social Movements*. University of Chicago Press.

Callinicos, A. (2003) *An Anti-Capitalist Manifesto*. Cambridge: Polity Press.

Carducci, V. (2006) 'Culture Jamming: A Sociological Perspective'. *Journal of Consumer Culture* 6(1): 116–38.

Carey, S. C. (2006) 'The Dynamic Relationship between Protest and Repression'. *Political Research Quarterly* 59(1): 1–11.

Carty, V. (2002) 'Technology and Counter-Hegemonic Movements: The Case of Nike Corporation'. *Social Movement Studies: Journal of Social, Cultural and Political Protest* 1(2):129–46.

Castells, M. (2004a) *The Power of Identity, II: The Information Age: Economy, Society and Culture*. Oxford: Blackwell. 2nd edn. First published 1997.

(2004b) 'Al-Qaeda, 9/11 and Beyond: Global Terror in the Name of God' in *Power of Identity*. 3 vols. Vol. II. 2nd edn.

(2007) 'Communication, Power and Counter-Power in the Network Society'. *International Journal of Communication* 1: 238–66.

(2009) *Communication Power*. Oxford University Press.

(2012) 'The Crisis Always Rings Twice'. Public Lecture, 8 October 2012, LSE.

Castells, M., Fernandez-Ardevol, M., Qiu, J. L., and Sey, A. (2006). *Mobile Communication and Society: A Global Perspective*. Cambridge, MA: MIT Press.

Cherrier, H. (2007) 'Ethical Consumption Practices: Co-production of Self-Expression and Social Recognition'. *Journal of Consumer Behaviour* 6: 321–35.

Chesters, G. and Welsh, I. (2006) *Complexity and Social Movements: Multitudes at the Edge of Chaos*. Oxford: Routledge.

(2011) *Social Movements: Key Concepts*. London: Routledge.

Clark, P. B. and Wilson, J. Q. (1961) 'Incentive Systems: A Theory of Organizations'. *Administrative Science Quarterly* 6(2): 129–66.

Cloward, R. and Piven, F. F. (1979) 'Hidden Protest: The Channeling of Female Innovation and Resistance'. *Signs* 4(4): 651–69.

Cohen, J. L. (1985) 'Strategy or Identity: New Theoretical Paradigms and Contemporary Social Movements'. *Social Research* 52(4): 663–761.

(1995) 'Critical Social Theory and Feminist Critiques: The Debate with Jürgen Habermas' in J. Meehan (ed.) *Feminists Read Habermas: Gendering the Subject of Discourse.* London: Routledge.

Cohen, R. and Kennedy, P. (2013) *Global Sociology.* New York University Press.

Coleman, J. (1988) 'Free Riders and Zealots: The Role of Social Networks'. *Sociological Theory* 6(1): 52–7.

(1990) *The Foundations of Social Theory.* Cambridge, MA: Harvard University Press.

Collins, R. (2001) 'Social Movements and the Focus of Emotional Attention' in J. Goodwin, J. Jasper, and F. Polletta (eds.) *Passionate Politics: Emotions and Social Movements.* University of Chicago Press.

Couch, C. (1968) 'Collective Behaviour: An Examination of Some Stereotypes'. *Social Problems* 15(3): 310–22.

Cox, L. and Nilsen, A. (2005) '"At the Heart of Society Burns the Fire of Social Movements": What Would a Marxist Theory of Social Movements Look Like?' in Proceedings Tenth International Conference on Alternative Futures and Popular Protest. http://eprints.nuim.ie/460/.

Crenshaw, M. (1990) 'The Logic of Terrorism: Terrorist Behaviour as a Product of Strategic Choice in W. Reich (ed.) *Origins of Terrorism: Psychologies, Ideologies, Theologies, States of Mind.* Cambridge University Press.

(1995) 'Thoughts on Relating Terrorism to Historical Contexts' in M. Crenshaw (ed.) *Terrorism in Context.* Pennsylvania State University Press.

(2000) 'The Psychology of Terrorism: An Agenda for the Twentieth Century'. *Political Psychology* 21(2): 405–20.

Crossley, N. (2002) *Making Sense of Social Movements.* Buckingham: Open University Press.

(2003) 'Even Newer Social Movements? Anti-Corporate Protests, Capitalist Crises and the Rationalisation of Society'. *Organization* 10(2): 287–305.

(2005) 'The Field of Psychiatric Contention'. *Social Science and Medicine* 62(3): 552–63.

(2006) *Contesting Psychiatry.* London: Routledge.

Crossley, N., Edwards, G., Harries, E., and Stevenson, R. (2012) 'Covert Social Movement Networks and the Secrecy–Efficiency Trade-Off: The Case of UK Suffragettes (1906–1914)'. *Social Networks* 34(4): 634–44.

Currie, E. and Skolnick, J. H. (1970) 'A Critical Note on Conceptions of Collective Behaviour'. *The Annals of the American Academy of Political and Social Science* 391(1): 34–45.

Curtis, R. L. and Zurcher, L. A. (1973) 'Stable Resources of Protest Movements: The Multi-Organizational Field'. *Social Forces* 52(1): 53–61.

Dahlberg, L. (2005) 'The Corporate Colonization of Online Attention and the Marginalization of Critical Communication?'. *Journal of Communication Inquiry* 29(2): 160–80.

Deleuze, G. and Guattari, F. (1987) *A Thousand Plateaus: Capitalism and Schizophrenia.* The University of Minnesota Press.

Della Porta, D. (1992) 'Political Socialization in Left-Wing Underground Organizations: Biographies of Italian and German Militants' in D. Della Porta (ed.) *Social Movements and Violence: Participation in Underground Organizations.* Greenwich, CT: JAI Press.

    (1995) *Social Movements, Political Violence and the State.* Cambridge/New York: Cambridge University Press.

    (2005) 'Making the Polis: Social Forums and Democracy in the Global Justice Movement'. *Mobilization* 10(1): 73–94.

    (2008) 'Research on Social Movements and Political Violence'. *Qualitative Sociology* 31(3): 221–30.

Della Porta, D. (ed.) (2007) *The Global Justice Movement: Cross-National and Transnational Perspectives.* Boulder/London: Paradigm Publishers.

Della Porta, D. and Diani, M. (1999) *Social Movements: An Introduction.* 1st edn.

    (2006) *Social Movements: An Introduction.* Oxford: Blackwell. 2nd edn. First published 1999.

Della Porta, D. and Reiter, H. (eds.) (1998) *Policing Protest: The Control of Mass Demonstrations in Western Democracies.* Minneapolis/London: University of Minnesota Press.

Della Porta, D. and Tarrow, S. (eds.) (2005) *Transnational Protest and Global Activism.* Lanham: Rowman & Littlefield.

Diani, M. (1990) 'The Network Structure of the Italian Ecology Movement'. *Social Science Information* 29: 5–31.

    (1992) 'The Concept of Social Movement'. *Sociological Review* 40: 1–25.

    (1995) *Green Networks: A Structural Analysis of the Italian Environmental Movement.* Edinburgh University Press.

    (2000) 'Social Movement Networks Virtual and Real'. *Information, Communication & Society* 3(3): 386–401.

Diani, M. and McAdam, D. (2003) *Social Movements and Networks.* Oxford/New York: Oxford University Press.

Donk, W. van de, Loader, B. D., and Rucht, D. (2004) *Cyberprotest: New Media, Citizens and Social Movements.* London: Routledge.

Downing, D. H. (2001) *Radical Media: Rebellious Communication and Social Movements.* London: Sage.

Dubet, F. and Wieviorka, M. (1996) 'Touraine and the Method of Sociological Intervention' in J. Clark and M. Diani (eds.) *Alain Touraine.* London: The Falmer Press.

Dyke, N. van and Soule, S. (2002) 'Structural Social Change and the Mobilizing Effect of Threat: Explaining Levels of Patriot and Militia Organizing in the United States'. *Social Problems* 49(4): 497–520.

Dyke, N. van, Soule, S. A., and Taylor, V. A. (2004) 'The Targets of Social Movements: Beyond a Focus on the State'. *Research in Social Movements, Conflicts and Change* 25(1): 27–51.

Earl, J. and Kimport, K. (2011) *Digitally Enabled Social Change: Activism in the Internet Age.* Cambridge, MA: MIT Press.

Earl, J., Martin, A., McCarthy, J. D., and Soule, S. A. (2004) 'The Use of Newspaper Data in the Study of Collective Action'. *Annual Review of Sociology* 30: 65–80.

Eder, C. (1993) *The New Politics of Class: Social Movements and Cultural Dynamics in Advanced Societies.* London: Sage.

Edwards, G. (2003) 'Bourdieu, Goffman and Structuralist Constructivism: The Missing Links in Social Movement Theory?'. Sociology Working Papers 31. University of Manchester: Sociology.

(2004) 'Habermas and Social Movements: What's "New"?' in N. Crossley and J. M. Roberts (eds.) *After Habermas: New Perspectives on the Public Sphere.* Oxford: Blackwell/The Sociological Review.

(2007) 'Habermas, Activism and Acquiescence: Reactions to Colonization in UK Trade Unions'. *Social Movement Studies* 6(2): 111–30.

(2008) 'The Lifeworld as a Resource for Social Movement Participation and the Consequences of its Colonization'. *Sociology* 42(2): 299–316.

(2009) 'Habermas and Social Movement Theory'. *Sociology Compass* 3(3): 381–93.

(2010) 'Mixed Method Approaches to Social Network Analysis'. NCRM Discussion Paper, no. 842, http://eprints.ncrm.ac.uk/842/.

(2011) 'Jurgen Habermas: Politics and Morality in Health and Medicine' in G. Scambler (eds.) *Contemporary Theorists for Medical Sociology.* London: Routledge.

(2014) 'Infectious Innovations? The Diffusion of Tactical Innovation in Social Movement Networks, the case of Suffragette Militancy'. *Social Movement Studies* 13(1).

Edwards, G. and Crossley, N. (2009) 'Measures and Meanings: Exploring the Ego-Net of Helen Kirkpatrick Watts, Militant Suffragette'. *Methodological Innovations Online* 4: 37–61.

Eisinger, P. (1973) 'The Conditions of Protest Behavior in American Cities'. *American Political Science Review* 67: 11–28.

Elster, J. (1989) *Nuts and Bolts for the Social Sciences.* Cambridge University Press.

Enders, W. and Su, X. (2007) 'Rational Terrorists and Optimal Network Structure'. *The Journal of Conflict Resolution* 51(1): 33–57.

Epstein, S. (1996) *Impure Science: AIDS, Activism and the Politics of Knowledge.* Berkeley: University of California Press.

Erikson, B. H. (1981) 'Secret Societies and Social Structure'. *Social Forces* 60(1): 188–210.

Escobar, A. (2004) 'Other Worlds are (Already) Possible: Self-Organisation, Complexity, and Post-Capitalist Culture' in J. Sen, A. Anand, A. Escobar, and P. Waterman (eds.) *World Social Forum: Challenging Empires.* Viveka Foundation: New Delhi.

Estellés, I. S. (2011) 'The Political-Opportunity Structure of the Spanish Anti-War movement (2002–4) and its Impact'. *The Sociological Review* 58(s2): 246–69.

Euben, R. (2002) 'Killing (for) Politics: Jihad, Martyrdom and Political Action'. *Political Theory* 30(1): 4–35.

Evans, S. M. and Boyte, H. C. (1992) *Free Spaces: The Sources of Democratic Change in America.* University of Chicago Press.

Eyerman, R. and Jamison, A. (1991) *Social Movements: A Cognitive Approach.* Cambridge: Polity Press.

Fantasia, R. (1989) *Cultures of Solidarity: Consciousness, Action, and Contemporary American Workers.* University of California Press.

Ferree, M. M. (1992) 'The Political Context of Rationality: Rational Choice Theory and Resource Mobilization' in A. Morris and C. McClurg Mueller (eds.) *Frontiers in Social Movement Theory.* New Haven: Yale University Press.

Ferree, M. M. and Merill, D. A. (2000) 'Hot Movements, Cold Cognition: Thinking about Social Movements in Gendered Frames'. *Contemporary Sociology* 29(3):454–62.

Finkel, S., Muller, E., and Opp, K. D. (1989) 'Personal Influence, Collective Rationality, and Mass Political Action'. *American Political Science Review* 83(3): 885–903.

Fisher, W. F. and Ponniah, T. (2003) *Another World is Possible.* London: Zed Books.

Flacks, R. (2004) 'Knowledge for What? Thoughts on the State of Social Movement Studies' in J. Goodwin and J. Jasper (eds.) *Rethinking Social Movements: Structure, Meaning and Emotion.* Lanham/Oxford: Rowman & Littlefield.

Flam, H. (1990) 'Emotional "Man", I: The Emotional "Man" and the Problem of Collective Action'. *International Sociology* 5: 39–56.

Foucault, M. (1977) *Discipline and Punish: The Birth of the Prison.* New York: Vintage.

(1980) *Power/Knowledge: Selected Interviews and Other Writings, 1972–77,* with G. Gordan (ed.). Sussex: Harvester Press.

(1982) 'The Subject and Power'. *Critical Inquiry* 8(4): 777–95.

Fraser, N. (1989) 'Foucault on Modern Power: Empirical Insights and Normative Confusions' in *Unruly Practices: Power, Discourse and Gender in Contemporary Social Theory.* Cambridge: Polity.

Fraser, N. and Honneth, A. (2003) *Redistribution or Recognition? A Political-Philosphical Exchange.* London/New York: Verso.

Freeman, J. (1973) 'The Origins of the Women's Liberation Movement'. *American Journal of Sociology* 4: 792–811.

(1979) 'Resource Mobilization and Strategy: A Model for Analyzing Social Movement Organization Actions' in Mayer N. Zald and John D. McCarthy (eds.) *The Dynamics of Social Movements.* Cambridge: Winthrop Publishers.

Frey, R. S., Dietz, T., and Kalof, L. (1992) 'Characteristics of Successful American Protest Groups: Another Look at Gamson's Strategy of Social Protest'. *American Journal of Sociology* 98(2): 368–87.

Gallie, W. B. (1956) 'Essentially Contested Concepts'. *Meeting of the Aristotelian Society* at 21, Bedford Square, London, W.C.1, on 12 March 1956, at 7.30 p.m.

Gamson, W. (1980) 'Understanding the Careers of Challenging Groups: A Commentary on Goldstone'. *American Journal of Sociology* 85(5): 1043–60.

(1990) *The Strategy of Social Protest*. Belmont, CA: Wadsworth. 2nd edn. First published 1975.

(1992) *Talking Politics*. Cambridge University Press.

Gamson, W. A. and Meyer, D. (1996) 'Framing political opportunity' in D. McAdam, J. McCarthy and M. Zald (ed.) *Comparative Perspectives on Social Movements*. Cambridge University Press.

Gentry, C. (2004) 'The Relationship Between New Social Movement Theory and Terrorism Studies: The Role of Leadership, Membership, Ideology and Gender'. *Terrorism and Political Violence* 16(2): 274–93.

George, S. (1988) *A Fate Worse than Debt: A Radical Analysis of the Debt Crisis*. London: Penguin Books.

Gerlach, L. P. (1999) 'The Structure of Social Movements: Environmental Activism and its Opponents' in J. Freeman and V. Johnson (eds.) *Waves of Protest*. Lanham, MA: Rowman and Littlefield.

Gerlach, L. P. and Hine, V. H. (1970) *People, Power and Change*. Indianapolis: Bobbs-Merrill.

Ghonim, W. (2010) *Revolution 2.0. The Power of the People is Greater than the People in Power: A Memoir*. Boston: Houghton Mifflin Harcourt.

Giddens, A. (1991) *Modernity and Self-Identity: Self and Society in the Late Modern Age*. Stanford University Press.

Gillan, K. (2006) 'Another Ideology? Novelty and Familiarity in the Belief Structures of Social Forum Participants'. Political Studies Association 57th Annual Conference 17.

(2009) 'The UK Anti-War Movement Online: Uses and Limitations of Internet Technologies for Contemporary Activism'. *Information, Communication & Society* 12(1): 25–43.

Gillan, K., Pickerill, J., and Webster, F. (2008) *Anti-War Activism: New Media and Protest in the Information Age*. Basingstoke: Palgrave Macmillan.

Gitlin, T. (1980) *The Whole World is Watching: Mass Media in the Making and Unmaking of the New Left*. Berkeley, CA: University of California Press.

(2012) 'Occupy's Predicament'. BJS Annual Lecture, 18 October, 2012, LSE.

Giugni, M. (2011) 'Institutional Opportunities, Discursive Opportunities, and the Political Participation of Migrants' in L. Morales and M. Giugni (eds.) *Social Capital, Political Participation, and Migration in Europe*. Basingstoke: Palgrave McMillan.

Giugni, M., Bandler, M., and Eggert, N. (2006) 'The Global Justice Movement: How Far Does the Classic Social Movement Agenda Go in Explaining

Transnational Contention?'. United Nations Research Institute for Social Development, Civil Society and Social Movements. Programme Paper 24, June 2006.

Givan, R. K., Soule, S. A., and Roberts, K. M. (eds.) (2010) *The Diffusion of Social Movements: Actors, Mechanisms, and Political Effects.* Cambridge University Press.

Goffman, E. (1959) *The Presentation of Self in Everyday Life.* Harmondsworth: Penguin.

(1961) *Encounters: Two Studies in the Sociology of Interaction.* London: Allen Lane/The Penguin Press.

(1963) 'Social Interaction and Social Structure – The Neglected Situation' in C. Lemert and A. Branaman (eds.) (1997) *The Goffman Reader.* Oxford: Blackwell.

(1967) *Interaction Ritual: Essays in Face to Face Behavior.* New York: Anchor Books.

(1969) *Where the Action Is: Three Essays.* London: Allen Lane/The Penguin Press.

(1971) *Relations in Public: Microstudies of the Public Order.* London: Penguin.

(1974) *Frame Analysis.* Cambridge, MA: Harvard University Press.

Goldstone, J. (1980) 'The Weakness of Organization: A New Look at Gamson's *The Strategy of Social Protest'. American Journal of Sociology* 85(5): 1017–42.

(2004) 'More Social Movements or Fewer? Beyond Political Opportunity Structures to Relational Fields'. *Theory and Society* 33(3): 333–65.

Goldstone, J. and Tilly, C. (2001) 'Threat (and Opportunity): Popular Action and State Response in the Dynamics of Collective Action' in R. Aminzade, J. A. Goldstone, D. McAdam, E. J. Perry, W. H. Sewell, S. Tarrow, and C. Tilly (eds.) *Silence and Voice in the Study of Contentious Politics.* Cambridge University Press.

Goodwin, J. (2004) 'What Must We Explain to Explain Terrorism' (a review essay on Jessica Stern, *Terror in the Name of God: Why Religious Militants Kill*). *Social Movement Studies* 3(2): 259–65.

(2006) 'A Theory of Categorical Terrorism'. *Social Forces* 84(4): 2027–46.

Goodwin, J. and Jasper, J. (2004a) *Rethinking Social Movements: Structure, Meaning and Emotion.* Lanham/Oxford: Rowman & Littlefield.

(2004b) 'Caught in a Winding, Snarling Vine: The Structural Bias of Political Process Theory' in J. Goodwin and J. Jasper (eds.) *Rethinking Social Movements: Structure, Meaning and Emotion.* Lanham/Oxford: Rowman & Littlefield.

(2004c) 'Trouble in Paradigms' in J. Goodwin and J. Jasper (eds.) *Rethinking Social Movements: Structure, Meaning and Emotion.* Lanham/Oxford: Rowman & Littlefield.

Goodwin, J., Jasper, J., and Polletta, F. (eds.) (2001) *Passionate Politics: Emotions and Social Movements.* University of Chicago Press.

Gould, D. (2004) 'Passionate Political Processes: Bringing Emotions Back into the Study of Social Movements' in J. Goodwin and J. Jasper (eds.) *Rethinking*

Social Movements: Structure, Meaning and Emotion. Lanham/Oxford: Rowman & Littlefield.

(2009) *Moving Politics: Emotion and ACT UP's Fight against AIDS.* University of Chicago Press.

Gould, R. (1991) 'Multiple Networks and Mobilization in the Paris Commune 1871'. *American Sociological Review* 56: 716–29.

(2003) 'Why Do Networks Matter? Rationalist and Structuralist Interpretations' in M. Diani and D. McAdam (2003) *Social Movements and Networks.* Oxford/New York: Oxford University Press.

Graeber, D. (2002) 'The New Anarchists'. *New Left Review* 13.

Granovetter, M. (1973) 'The Strength of Weak Ties'. *American Journal of Sociology* 78: 1360–80.

Guardian datablog (2010) 'How Trade Union Membership Has Grown – and Shrunk'. www.guardian.co.uk/news/datablog/2010/apr/30/union-membership-data.

Gurr, T. (1968) 'A Causal Model of Civil Strife: A Comparative Analysis Using New Indices'. *American Political Science Review* 62(4): 1104–24.

(1970) *Why Men Rebel.* Princeton University Press.

Gusfield, J. (1962) 'Mass Society and Extremist Politics'. *American Sociological Review* 27: 19–30.

Habermas, J. (1976) *Legitimation Crisis.* London: Heinemann.

(1981) 'New Social Movements'. *Telos* 49: 33–7.

(1986) in P. Dews (ed.) *Autonomy and Solidarity: Interviews with Jürgen Habermas.* London: Verso.

(1987) *The Theory of Communicative Action.* 2 vols. Vol. II. Cambridge: Polity Press.

(1989) *The Structural Transformation of the Public Sphere.* Cambridge: Polity. First published in German in 1962.

(1990) *The Philosophical Discourse of Modernity.* Cambridge: Polity.

Haenfler, R., Johnson, B., and Jones, E. (2012) 'Lifestyle Movements: Exploring the Intersection of Lifestyle and Social Movements'. *Social Movement Studies* 11(1): 1–20.

Hanisch, C. (1970) 'The Personal Is Political' in S. Firestone and A. Koedt (eds.) *Notes from the Second Year – Women's Liberation: Major Writings of the Radical Feminists.* New York: Women's Liberation Movement.

Hara, N. and Estrada, Z. (2005) 'Analyzing the Mobilization of Grassroots Activities via the Internet: A Case Study'. *Journal of Information Science* 31(6): 503–14.

Harries, E. (2010) 'The Social Networks of Climate Camp Activists'. Unpublished MSc thesis, University of Manchester.

Hart, S. (1996) 'The Cultural Dimension of Social Movements: A Theoretical Assessment and Literature Review'. *Sociology of Religion* 57: 87–100.

Harvey, D. (2012) *Rebel Cities: From the Right to the City to the Urban Revolution.* London: Verso.

Hebdige, D. (1979) *Subculture: The Meaning of Style.* London: Routledge.

Hedström, P. (1994) 'Contagious Collectivities: On the Spatial Diffusion of Swedish Trade Unions, 1890–1940'. *American Journal of Sociology* 99: 1157–79.

Hertz, N. (2001) *The Silent Takeover: Global Capitalism and the Death of Democracy.* New York: HarperBusiness.

Hirschman, A. (1982) *Shifting Involvements: Private Interests and Public Action.* Princeton University Press.

  (1991) *The Rhetoric of Reaction.* Cambridge, MA: Harvard University Press.

Hobsbawm, E. (1952) 'The Machine Breakers'. *Past and Present* 1(1): 57–70.

Hoffman, B. (2006) *Inside Terrorism.* New York: Columbia University Press.

Hollis, M. (1994) *The Philosophy of Social Science.* Cambridge University Press.

Holloway, J. (2010a) *Change the World Without Taking Power: The Meaning of Revolution Today.* London: Pluto Press. First published 2002.

  (2010b) *Crack Capitalism.* London: Pluto Press.

Honneth, A. (1995) *The Struggle for Recognition: The Moral Grammar of Social Conflicts.* Cambridge: Polity.

Honneth, A., Knodler-Bunte, E.. and Widmann, A. (1981) 'The Dialectics of Rationalization: An Interview with Jürgen Habermas'. *Telos* 49: 5–31.

Hubbard, G. and Miller, D. (2005) *Arguments against G8.* London: Pluto.

Huntington, S. (1996) *The Clash of Civilizations and the Remaking of the World Order.* New York: Simon & Schuster.

Ibrahim, J. (2009) 'Understanding the Alternative Globalisation Movement'. *Sociology Compass* 3(3): 394–416.

  (2011) 'Political Distinction in the British Anti-Capitalist Movement'. *Sociology* 45(2): 318–34.

  (2013) 'The Struggle for Symbolic Dominance in the British Anti-Capitalist Movement'. *Social Movement Studies* 12(1): 63–80.

Inglehart, R. (1977) *The Silent Revolution: Changing Values and Political Styles among Western Publics.* Princeton University Press.

Iskander, E. (2011) 'Connecting the National and the Virtual. Can Facebook Activism Remain Relevant after Egypt's January 25 Uprising?'. *International Journal of Communication* 5: 1225–37.

Jackson, R. Murphy, E., and Poynting, S. (2009) (eds.) *Contemporary State Terrorism: Theory and Practice.* London: Routledge.

Jasper, J. (1997) *The Art of Moral Protest: Culture, Biography, and Creativity in Social Movements.* Chicago and London: University of Chicago Press.

Jasper, J. and Poulsen, J. (1995) 'Recruiting Strangers and Friends: Moral Shocks and Social Networks in Animal Rights and Anti-Nuclear Protests'. *Social Problems* 42: 493–512.

Jenkins, J. C. (1983) 'Resource Mobilization Theory and the Study of Social Movements'. *Annual Review of Sociology* 9:527–53.

Jenkins, J. C. and Perrow, C. (1977) 'Insurgency of the Powerless: The Farm
    Worker Movements 1946-1972'. *American Sociological Review* 42: 249-
    68.
Johnston, H. (1991) *Tales of Nationalism: Catalonia, 1939-1979*. New Brunswick,
    NJ: Rutgers University Press.
Johnston, H. and Klandermans, B. (1995) (eds.) *Social Movements and Culture.*
    Minneapolis/London: University of Minnesota Press/UCL Press.
Johnston, H. and Noakes, J. A. (2005) *Frames of Protest: Social Movements and
    the Framing Perspective.* Boston: Rowman and Littlefield.
Jordan, T. and Taylor, P. (2004) *Hactivism and Cyberwars: Rebels with a Cause?*
    London: Routledge.
Josselin, D. (2007) 'From Transnational Protest to Domestic Political
    Opportunities: Insights from the Debt Cancellation Campaign'. *Social
    Movement Studies* 6(1):21-38.
Juergensmeyer, M. (2003) *Terror in the Mind of God: The Global Rise of Religious
    Violence.* University of California Press. 3rd edn.
Jung, J. K. (2010) 'Disentangling Protest Cycles: An Event History Analysis of
    New Social Movements in Western Europe'. *Mobilization* 15(1): 25-44.
Juris, J. S. (2004) 'Networked Social Movements: Global Movements for
    Global Justice' in M. Castells (ed.) *The Network Society: a Cross-Cultural
    Perspective.* Cheltenham: Edward Elgar.
    (2005a) 'The New Digital Media and Activist Networking in the Anti-Corporate
    Globalization Movement'. *ANNALS, AAPSS* 597: 189-208.
    (2005b) 'Violence Performed and Imagined: The Black Bloc and the Mass Media
    in Genoa'. *Critique of Anthropology* 25(4): 413-32.
    (2005c) 'Social Forums and their Margins: Networking Logics and the Cultural
    Politics of Autonomous Space'. *Ephemera* 5(2): 253-72.
Kahn, R. and Kellner, D. (2004), 'New Media and Internet Activism: From the
    Battle of Seattle to Blogging'. *New Media and Society* 6(1): 87-95.
Kanigel, R. (2005) *The One Best Way: Frederick Winslow Taylor and the Enigma
    of Efficiency.* Cambridge, MA/London: MIT Press. First published 1997.
Keck, M. and Sikkink, K. (1998) *Activists Beyond Borders: Advocacy Networks in
    International Politics.* Ithaca: Cornell University Press.
Kelleher, D. (1994) 'Self-Help Groups and their Relationship to Medicine' in J.
    Gabe, D. Kelleher, and G. Williams (eds.) *Challenging Medicine.* London:
    Routledge.
    (2001) 'New Social Movements in the Health Domain' in G. Scambler (ed.)
    Habermas, Critical Theory and Health. London: Routledge.
Kellner, D. (2002) 'September 11, Social Theory and Democratic Politics'. *Theory,
    Culture & Society* 19(4): 147-59.
Keraghel, C. and Sen, J. (2004) 'Explorations in Open Space: The World Social
    Forum and Cultures Of Politics'. *International Journal of Social Science*
    56(4): 483-493.
Kingsnorth, P. (2004) *One No, Many Yeses.* London: Free Press.

Kitschelt, H. (1986) 'Political Opportunity Structures and Political Protest: Anti-Nuclear Movements in Four Democracies'. *British Journal of Political Science* 16: 57–85.

Kitts, J. (2000) 'Mobilizing in Black Boxes: Social Networks and SMO Participation'. *Mobilization* 5: 241–57.

Klandermans, B. (1984) 'Mobilization and Participation: Social-Psychological Expansions of Resource Mobilization Theory'. *American Sociological Review* 49: 583–600.

Klein, N. (2000) *No Logo*. London: Flamingo/ Harper Collins.

  (2007) *The Shock Doctrine: The Rise of Disaster Capitalism*. London: Allen.

Klerks, P. (2001) 'The Network Paradigm Applied to Criminal Organisations: Theoretical Nitpicking or a Relevant Doctrine for Investigators? Recent Developments in the Netherlands'. *Connections* 24(3): 53–65.

Koopmans, R. (1997) 'Dynamics of Repression and Mobilization: The German Extreme Right in the 1990s'. *Mobilization* 2: 149–65.

  (2004) 'Political Opportunity Structure: Some Splitting to Balance the Lumping' in J. Goodwin and J. Jasper (eds.) *Rethinking Social Movements: Structure, Meaning and Emotion*. Lanham/Oxford: Rowman & Littlefield.

Koopmans, R. and Olzak, S. (2004) 'Discursive Opportunities and the Evolution of Right Wing Violence in Germany'. *American Journal Sociology* 110(1): 198–230.

Kornhauser, W. (1959) *The Politics of Mass Society*. Glencoe: Free Press.

Krebs, V. (2002) 'Mapping Networks of Terrorist Cells'. *Connections* 24(3): 43–52.

Kriesi, H (1995) 'The Political Opportunity Structure of New Social Movements: Its Impact on their Mobilization' in J. C. Jenkins and B. Klandermans (eds.) *The Politics of Social Protest*. Minneapolis/London: University of Minnesota Press/UCL Press.

Kriesi, H., Koopmans, R., Duyvendak, J. W., and Giugni, M. (1992) 'New Social Movements and Political Opportunities in Western Europe'. *European Journal of Political Research* 22: 219–44.

  (1995) *New Social Movements in Western Europe: A Comparative Analysis*. Minneapolis/London: University of Minnesota /UCL Press.

Krueger, A. B. and Malecková, J. (2003) 'Education, Poverty and Terrorism: Is there a Causal Connection?'. *Journal of Economic Perspectives* 17(4): 119–44.

Kurzman, C. (2004) 'The Poststructuralist Consensus in Social Movement Theory' in J. Goodwin and J. Jasper (eds.) *Rethinking Social Movements: Structure, Meaning and Emotion*. Lanham/Oxford: Rowman & Littlefield.

Laclau, E. and Mouffe, C. (1985) *Hegemony and Socialist Strategy: Towards a Radical Democratic Politics*. London: Verso.

Laer, J. van and Aelst, P. van (2010) 'Internet and Social Movement Action Repertoires: Opportunities and Limitations'. *Information, Communication & Society* 13(8): 1146–71.

Lang, K. and Lang, G. (1961) *Collective Dynamics*. New York: Thomas and
    Cromwell.
    (1970) 'Collective Behavior Theory and the Escalated Riots of the Sixties' in T.
    Shibutani (ed.) *Human Nature and Collective Behavior: Papers in Honor of
    Herbert Blumer*. Englewood Cliffs, NJ: Prentice Hall.
Langman, L. (2008) 'Punk, Porn and Resistance: Carnivalization and the Body in
    Popular Culture'. *Current Sociology* 56(4): 657–77.
Laqueur, W. (1999) *The New Terrorism: Fanaticism and the Arms of Mass
    Destruction*. Oxford University Press.
    (2001) *A History of Terrorism*. New Brunswick/New Jersey: Transaction
    Publishers. First published 1977, Little Brown & Co.
Lash, S. and Urry, J. (1987) *The End of Organized Capitalism*. Cambridge: Polity.
    (1994) *Economies of Signs and Space*. London: Sage.
Leach, D. K. and Haunss, S. (2009) 'Social Movements and Scenes' in H. Johnston
    (ed.) *Culture, Social Movements, and Protest*. London: Ashgate.
Le Bon, G. (2009) *The Crowd: A Study of the Popular Mind*. The Floating Press.
    First published 1896.
Lee, A. K. McClung (ed.) (1951) *Principles of Sociology*. New York: Barnes and
    Noble. 2nd edn. First published 1946.
Leites, N. and Wolf, C. (1970) *Rebellion and Authority: An Analytic Essay on
    Insurgent Conflicts*. Chicago: Markham Publishing Co.
Levidow, L. (2004) 'Making Another World Possible? The European Social Forum'.
    Radical Philosophy 128: 6–11.
Lindelauf, R., Borm, P., and Hamers, H. (2009) 'The Influence of Secrecy on the
    Communication Structure of Covert Networks'. *Social Networks* 31: 126–37.
McAdam, D. (1982) *Political Process and the Development of Black Insurgency,
    1930–1970*. Chicago: Chicago University Press.
    (1986) 'Recruitment to High-Risk Activism: The Case of Freedom Summer'.
    American Journal of Sociology 92: 64–90.
    (1988) *Freedom Summer*. New York/Oxford: Oxford University Press.
    (1995) '"Initiator" and "Spinoff" Movements: Diffusion Processes in Protest
    Cycles' in M. Traugott (ed.) *Repertoires and Cycles of Collective Action*.
    Durham, NC: Duke University Press.
    (1996) 'The Framing Function of Movement Tactics: Strategic Dramaturgy in
    the American Civil Rights Movement' in D. McAdam, J. D. McCarthy, and
    M. N. Zald (eds.) *Comparative Perspectives on Social Movements: Political
    Opportunities, Mobilizing Structures, and Cultural Framing*. Cambridge/
    New York: Cambridge University Press.
    (2003) 'Beyond Structural Analysis: Toward a More Dynamic Understanding of
    Social Movements' in M. Diani and D. McAdam (2003) *Social Movements
    and Networks*. Oxford/New York: Oxford University Press.
    (2004) 'Revisiting the U.S. Civil Rights Movement: Towards a More Synthetic
    Understanding of the Origins of Contention' in J. Goodwin and J. Jasper
    (eds.) *Rethinking Social Movements: Structure, Meaning and Emotion*.
    Lanham/Oxford: Rowman & Littlefield.

McAdam, D., McCarthy, J. D., and Zald, M. N. (eds.) (1996) *Comparative Perspectives on Social Movements: Political Opportunities, Mobilizing Structures, and Cultural Framing.* Cambridge/New York: Cambridge University Press.

McAdam, D. and Paulsen, R. (1993) 'Specifying the Relationship between Social Ties and Activism'. *American Journal of Sociology* 99: 640–67.

McAdam, D. and Rucht, D. (1993) 'The Cross-National Diffusion of Movement Ideas'. *The Annals of the AAPSS* 528: 56–74.

McAdam, D. and Tarrow, S. (2011) 'Introduction: Dynamics of Contention Ten Years On'. *Mobilization* 16(1): 1–10.

　(2012) 'Social Movements, Elections and Contentious Politics: Building Conceptual Bridges', in J. van Stekelenburg, C. M. Roggeband, and B. Klandermans (eds.) *The Changing Dynamics of Contention.* Minneapolis: University of Minnesota Press.

McAdam, D., Tarrow, S., and Tilly, C. (2001) *Dynamics of Contention.* New York: Cambridge University Press.

McAfee, K. and Wood, M. (1969) 'Bread and Roses'. *Leviathan*, June 1969.

McCarthy, J. D. (1994) 'Activists, Authorities, and Media Framing of Drunk Driving' in E. Larana, H. Johnston, and J. R. Gusfield (eds.) *New Social Movements: From Ideology to Identity.* Philadelphia: Temple University Press.

McCarthy, J. D., Smith, J. and Zald, M. N. (1996) in 'Media Discourse, Movement Publicity, and the Generation of Collective Action Frames: Theoretical and Empirical Exercises in Meaning Construction' in D. McAdam, J. D. McCarthy, and M. N. Zald (eds.) *Comparative Perspectives on Social Movements: Political Opportunities, Mobilizing Structures, and Cultural Framing.* Cambridge/New York: Cambridge University Press.

McCarthy, J. D. and Zald, M. N. (1973) *The Trend of Social Movements in America: Professionalization and Resource Mobilization.* Morristown: General Learning Press.

　(1977) Resource Mobilization Theory and Social Movements: A Partial Theory'. *American Journal of Sociology* 82: 1212–41.

　(2002) 'The Enduring Vitality of the Resource Mobilization Theory of Social Movements' in J. H. Turner (ed). *Handbook of Sociological Theory.* New York: Kluwer Academic/Plenum Publishers.

McCormick, S. (2006) 'The Brazilian Anti-Dam Movement: Knowledge Contestation as Communicative Action'. *Organization and Environment* 19(3): 321–46.

MacLeod, S. (2006) 'Civil Disobedience and Political Agitation: The Art Museum as a Site of Protest in the Early Twentieth Century'. *Museum and Society* 5(1): 44–57.

McPhail, C. (1991) *The Myth of the Madding Crowd.* New York: Aldine de Gruyter.
　(2006) 'The Crowd and Collective Behavior: Bringing Symbolic Interaction Back In'. *Symbolic Interaction* 29(4): 433–63.

Maeckelbergh, M. E. (2009) *The Will of the Many: How the Alter Globalization Movement Is Changing the Face of Democracy.* London: Pluto Press.

Marcus, S. (2010) *Girls to the Front: The True Story of the Riot Grrrl Revolution.* New York: HarperCollins.

Marwell, G. and Oliver, P (1988) 'The Paradox of Group Size in Collective Action: A Theory of the Critical Mass II'. *American Sociological Review,* 53(1): 1–8.

(1993) *The Critical Mass in Collective Action: A Micro-Social Theory.* Cambridge/New York: Cambridge University Press.

Marx, K. and Engels, F. (1967) *The Communist Manifesto.* Harmondsworth: Penguin/Pelican. First published 1848.

Mayo, M. (2008) 'Globalization and Gender: New Threats, New Strategies', in V. Ruggiero and N. Montagna (eds.) *Social Movements: A Reader.* London: Routledge.

Mead, G. H. (1934) *Mind, Self, and Society.* Chicago University Press.

Mees, L. (2004) 'Politics, Economy, or Culture? The Rise and Development of Basque Nationalism in the Light of Social Movement Theory'. *Theory and Society* 33(3/4): 311–31.

Melucci, A. (1980) 'The New Social Movements: A Theoretical Approach'. *Social Science Information* 19(2): 199–226.

(1984) 'An End to Social Movements? Introductory Paper to the Sessions on 'New Movements and Change in Organizational Forms'. *Social Science Information* 23(4/5): 819–35.

(1985) 'The Symbolic Challenge of Contemporary Movements'. *Social Research* 54(4): 789–816.

(1988) 'New Perspectives on Social Movements: An Interview with Alberto Melucci' in (1989) *Nomads of the Present.* London: Hutchinson Radius.

(1989) *Nomads of the Present.* London: Hutchinson Radius.

(1996) *Challenging Codes.* Cambridge/New York: Cambridge University Press.

(1999) 'An Interview with Alberto Melucci', conducted by Y. Yamanouchi and S. Yazawa at Hitosubashi University, Tokyo, September 1994. *Arena Journal,* 22 March 1999.

Mertes, T. (2004) *A Movement of Movements: Is Another World Really Possible?* London: Verso.

Merton, R. (1961) 'Social Problems and Sociological Theory' in R. Merton and R. Nisbet (eds.) *Contemporary Social Problems: An Introduction to the Sociology of Deviant Behavior and Social Disorganization.* Harcourt, Brace & World.

Meyer, D. (2004a) 'Protest and Political Opportunities'. *Annual Review of Sociology* 30: 125–45.

(2004b) 'Tending the Vineyard: Cultivating Political Process Research' in J. Goodwin and J. Jasper (eds.) *Rethinking Social Movements: Structure, Meaning and Emotions.* Lanham: Rowman & Littlefield.

Meyer, D. and Staggenborg, S. (1996) 'Movements, Countermovements and the Structure of Political Opportunities'. *American Journal of Sociology* 101(1): 628–60.

Meyer, D. and Tarrow, S. (eds.) (1998) *The Social Movement Society*. Lanham: Rowman & Littlefield.

Meyer, D. and Whittier, N. (1994) 'Social Movement Spillover'. *Social Problems* 41: 277–98.

Michels, R. (1915) *Political Parties: A Sociological Study of the Oligarchical Tendencies of Modern Democracy*. Glencoe: Free Press.

Mickolus, E., Sandler, T., Murdock, J. M., and Flemming, P. A. (2003) *International Terrorism: Attributes of Terrorist Events (ITERATE)*. Vineyard Software.

Minkoff, D. (1995) *Organizing for Equality: The Evolution of Women's and Racial-Ethnic Organizations in America*. New Brunswick: Rutgers University Press.

Mische, A. (2003) 'Cross-Talk in Movements: Reconceiving the Culture-Network Link' in M. Diani and D. McAdam (eds.) *Social Movements and Networks*. Oxford/New York: Oxford University Press.

(2008) *Partisan Publics: Communication and Contention across Brazilian Youth Activist Networks*. Princeton University Press.

Misztal, B. (1992) 'One Movement, Two Interpretations: The Orange Alternative Movement in Poland'. *British Journal of Sociology* 43(1): 55–79.

Monbiot, G. (2003). *The Age of Consent: A Manifesto for a New World Order*. London: Flamingo.

Morris, A. (1984) *The Origins of the Civil Rights Movement: Black Communities Organizing for Change*. New York: Free Press.

(2000) 'Reflections on Social Movement Theory: Criticisms and Proposals'. *Contemporary Sociology* 29(3): 445–54.

Morselli, C., Giuere, C., and Petit, K. (2007) 'The Efficiency/Security Trade-Off in Criminal Networks'. *Social Networks* 29: 149–53.

Mueller, C. (1994) 'Conflict Networks and the Origins of Women's Liberation' in E. Larana, H. Johnston, and J. R. Gusfield (eds.) *New Social Movements: From Ideology to Identity*. Philadelphia: Temple University Press.

Nash, K. (2001) 'The "Cultural Turn" in Social Theory: Towards a Theory of Cultural Politics'. *Sociology* 35(1): 77–92.

Nilsen, A. (2007) 'History Does Nothing: Notes towards a Marxist Theory of Social Movements'. *Sosiologisk Årbok* 1–2: 1–30.

(2009) 'The Authors and the Actors of their Own Drama: Towards a Marxist Theory of Social Movements'. *Capital and Class* 33(3): 109–39.

Notes from Nowhere (2003) *We Are Everywhere: The Irresistible Rise of Global Anti-Capitalism*. London: Verso.

Nunes, R. (2005) 'Networks, Open Spaces, Horizontality: Instantiations'. *Ephemera* 5(2): 297–318.

Nwoye, O. G. (1993) 'Social issues on walls: Graffiti in university lavatories'. *Discourse and Society*, 4: 419–42.

Oberschall, A. (1968) 'The Los Angeles Riot of August, 1965'. *Social Problems* 15(3): 322–41.

(1973) *Social Conflict and Social Movements*. Englewood Cliffs, NY: Prentice-Hall.

(1995) *Social Movements: Ideologies, Interests, and Identities*. New Brunswick, NJ/London: Transaction.

(2004) 'Explaining Terrorism: The Contribution of Collective Action Theory'. *Sociological Theory* 22(1): 26–37.

Offe, C. (1985) 'New Social Movements: Changing Boundaries of the Political'. *Social Research* 52: 817–68.

Oliver, M. (1990) *The Politics of Disablement*. Basingstoke: Macmillan.

Oliver, P. (1984) '"If You Don't Do It, Nobody Else Will": Active and Token Contributors to Local Collective Action'. *American Sociological Review* 49: 601–10.

Oliver, P. and Johnston, H. (2000) 'What a Good Idea! Ideology and Frames in Social Movement Research'. *Mobilization* 5: 37–54.

Olson, M. (1965) *The Logic of Collective Action*. Cambridge, MA: Harvard University Press.

Opp, K. D. (2009) *Theories of Political Protest and Social Movements*. London: Routledge.

O'Shea, S. (2013) *A Social Network Analysis of the Ladyfest Feminist Music and Cultural Movement in the UK*. Unpublished PhD thesis, CCSR, University of Manchester.

Pape, R. A. (2003) 'The Strategic Logic of Suicide Terrorism'. *American Political Science Review* 3, 20–32.

Parkin, F. (1968) *Middle Class Radicalism*. New York: Praeger.

Parsons, T. (1970) *The Social System*. Glencoe, IL: Free Press.

Passy, F. (2003) 'Social Networks Matter: But How?' in M. Diani and D. McAdam (eds.) *Social Movements and Networks*. Oxford/New York: Oxford University Press.

Peckham, M. (1998) 'New Dimensions of Movement/Countermovement Interaction: The Case of Scientology and its Internet Critics'. *The Canadian Journal of Sociology* 23(4): 317–47.

Pichardo, N. (1997) 'New Social Movements: A Critical Review'. *Annual Review of Sociology* 23: 411–30.

Pickard, V. W. (2006) 'United Yet Autonomous: Indymedia and the Struggle to Sustain a Radical Democratic Network'. *Media, Culture & Society* 28(3): 315–36.

Pickerill, J. (2003). *Cyberprotest: Environmental Activism Online*. Manchester University Press.

(2007) '"Autonomy Online": Indymedia and Practices of Alter-Globalisation'. *Environment and Planning* 39: 2668–84.

Pinard, M. (1968) 'Mass Society and Political Movements: A New Formulation'. *American Journal of Sociology* 73: 682–90.

Piven, F. Fox. and Cloward, R. (1977) *Poor People's Movements*. New York: Pantheon.

(1992) 'Normalizing Collective Protest' in A. Morris and C. McClurg Mueller (eds.) *Frontiers in Social Movement Theory*. New Haven: Yale University Press.

Platt, G. M. (2004) 'Unifying Social Movement Theories'. *Qualitative Sociology* 27(1): 107–16.

Pleyers, G. (2010) *Alter-Globalization: Becoming Actors in the Global Age.*
Cambridge: Polity.

Plows, A. (2008) 'Social Movements and Ethnographic Methodologies: An
Analysis Using Case Study Examples'. *Sociology Compass* 2(5): 1523–38.

Polletta, F. (1998) '"It Was Like a Fever": Narrative and Identity in Social Protest'.
Social Problems 45: 137–59.

(1999) 'Free Spaces in Collective Action'. *Theory and Society* 28: 1–38.

(2004) 'Culture Is Not Just in Your Head' in J. Goodwin and J. Jasper (eds.)
Rethinking Social Movements: Structure, Meaning and Emotions. Lanham:
Rowman & Littlefield.

Polletta, F. and Jasper, J. (2001) 'Collective Identity and Social Movement'.
Annual Review of Sociology 27: 283–305.

Purvis, J. (2007) 'Radical Fighters in a Just Cause'. *BBC History Magazine*
February.

Reid, H. G. (1979) 'A Review of Alain Touraine's *The Self Production of Society*'.
Human Studies 2(1): 91–4.

Rheingold, H. (2002) *Smart Mobs: The Next Social Revolution.* New York: Perseus.

Robison, K., Crenshaw, E., and Jenkins, J. (2006) 'Ideologies of Violence: The
Social Origins of Islamist and Leftist Transnational Terrorism'. *Social Forces*
84(4): 2027–46.

Rodríguez, J. (2009) 'Weakness and Strengths of Terrorist Networks: The Madrid
March 11 Attacks'. Paper presented at the annual meeting of the American
Sociological Association. www.allacademic.com/meta/p243052_index.html.

Rootes, C. (1995) 'A New Class? The Higher Educated and the New Politics' in L.
Maheu (ed.) *Social Movements and Social Classes: The Future of Collective
Action.* London: Sage.

(1999) 'Political Opportunity Structures: Promises, Problems and Prospects'. *La
Lettre de la maison Française d'Oxford* 10: 75–97. www.kent.ac.uk/sspssr/
staff/academic/rootes/pos.pdf.

Roscigno, V. J. and Danaher, W. F. (2001) 'Media and Mobilization: The Case of
Radio and the Southern Textile Worker Insurgency, 1929–1934'. *American
Sociological Review* 66(1): 21–48.

Roscigno, V. J. and Hodson, R. (2004) 'The Organizational and Social Foundations
of Worker Resistance'. *American Sociological Review* 69(1): 14–39.

Rose, F. (1997) 'Toward a Class-Cultural Theory of Social Movements:
Reinterpreting New Social Movements'. *Sociological Forum* 12(2): 461–94.

Rosenthal, N., Fingrudt, M., Ethier, M., Karant, R., and McDonald, D. (1985)
'Social Movements and Network Analysis: A Case-Study of Nineteenth
Century Women's Reform in New York State'. *American Journal of
Sociology* 90: 1022–54.

Routledge, P., Cumbers, A., and Nativel, C. (2007) 'Grassrooting Network
Imaginaries: Relationality, Power and Mutual Solidarity in Global Justice
Networks'. *Environment and Planning* 39: 2572–92.

(2008) 'The Entangled Geographies of Global Justice Networks'. *Progress in
Human Geography* 32: 183–201.

Rowbotham, S. (1997) *A Century of Women: The History of Women in Britain and the US*. London: Viking Penguin.

Rucht, D., Koopmans, R., and Neidhardt, F. (1999) *Acts of Dissent: New Developments in the Study of Protest*. Lanham: Rowman and Littlefield.

Rule, J. B. (1988) *Theories of Civil Violence*. University of California Press.

Ryan, C. (1991) *Prime Time Activism: Media Strategies for Grassroots Organizing*. Boston: South End Press.

Sageman, M. (2004) *Understanding Terror Networks*. Philadelphia: University of Pennsylvania Press.

(2008) *Leaderless Jihad: Terror Networks in the Twenty-First Century*. Philadelphia: Pennsylvania University Press.

Salter, L. (2003) 'New Social Movements and the Internet: A Habermasian Analysis' in M. Ayers and M. McCaughey (eds.) *Cyberactivism: Critical Practices and Theories of Online Activism*. New York: Routledge.

(2005) 'Juridification and Colonization Processes in the Development of the World Wide Web'. *New Media and Society* 7(3): 291–309.

Salvatore, A. (2013) 'New Media, the "Arab Spring", and the Metamorphosis of the Public Sphere: Beyond Western Assumptions on Collective Agency and Democratic Politics'. *Constellations* 20(2): 1–12.

Sasson-Levy, O. and Rapoport, T. (2003) 'Body, Gender and Knowledge in Protest Movements'. *Gender and Society* 17(3): 379–403.

Saunders, C. (2007) 'Using Social Network Analysis to Explore Social Movements: A Relational Approach'. *Social Movement Studies* 6(3): 227–43.

Scambler, G. (1987) 'Habermas and the Power of Medical Expertise' in G. Scambler (ed.) *Sociological Theory and Medical Sociology*, London: Tavistock Publications.

Scambler, G. and Kelleher, D. (2006) 'New Social and Health Movements: Issues of Representation and Change'. *Critical Public Health* 16(3): 219–31.

Schurman, R. and Munro, W. A. (2010). *Fighting for the Future of Food: Activists Versus Agribusiness in the Struggle Over Biotechnology*. University of Minnesota Press.

Scott, A. (1990) *Ideology and the New Social Movements*. Unwin Hyman Ltd. Reprinted 1995, London and New York: Routledge.

Scott, J. (1985) *Weapons of the Weak: Everyday Forms of Peasant Resistance*. New Haven and London: Yale University Press.

(1990) *Domination and the Arts of Resistance: Hidden Transcripts*. New Haven and London: Yale University Press.

Scott, J. (2000) *Social Network Analysis: A Handbook*. London: Sage. 2nd edn.

Shorter, E. and Tilly, C. (1974) *Strikes in France, 1830–1968*. Cambridge University Press.

Sklair, L. (1998) 'Social Movements and Global Capitalism' in F. Jameson and M. Miyoshi (eds.) *The Cultures of Globalization*. Durham: Duke University Press.

Smelser, N. (1962) *Theory of Collective Behaviour*. New York: Free Press.

(2007) *The Faces of Terrorism: Social and Psychological Dimensions*. Princeton and Oxford: Princeton University Press.

Smith, J. (2001) 'Globalizing Resistance: The Battle of Seattle and the Future of Social Movements'. *Mobilization* 6: 1–19.

Smith, J. and Johnston, H. (2002) (eds.) *Globalization and Resistance: Transnational Dimensions of Social Movements*. Lanham: Rowman & Littlefield.

Snow, D. A. and Benford, R. D. (1992) 'Master Frames and Cycles of Protest' in A. D. Moms and C. McClurg Mueller (eds.) *Frontiers in Social Movement Theory*. New Haven, CT: Yale University Press.

Snow, D. A., Zurcher, L. A., and Ekland-Olson, S. (1980) 'Social Networks and Social Movements: A Microstructural Approach to Differential Recruitment'. *American Sociological Review* 45(5): 787–801.

(1986) 'Frame Alignment Processes, Micromobilization, and Movement Participation'. *American Sociological Review* 51(4): 464–81.

Snyder, D. and Tilly, C. (1972) 'Hardship and Collective Violence in France, 1830–1960'. *American Sociological Review* 37: 520–32.

Somers, M. (1994) 'The Narrative Constitution of Identity: A Relational and Network Approach'. *Theory and Society* 23: 605–49.

Soule, S. (1997) 'The Student Divestment Movement in the United States and Tactical Diffusion: The Shantytown Protest'. *Social Forces* 75: 855–83.

(2009) *Contention and Corporate Social Responsibility*. Cambridge University Press.

Staggenborg, S. (1988) 'The Consequences of Professionalization and Formalization in the Pro-Choice Movement'. *American Sociological Review* 53: 585–606.

(1991) *The Pro-Choice Movement: Organization and Activism in the Abortion Conflict*. New York: Oxford University Press.

Starr, A. (2000) *Naming the Enemy: Anti-Corporate Movements Confront Globalization*. London: Zed.

Steinberg, M. (1999) 'The Talk and Back Talk of Collective Action: A Dialogic Analysis of Repertoires of Discourse among Nineteenth Century English Cotton Spinners'. *American Journal of Sociology* 105: 736–80.

Stevenson, R. and Crossley (2014) 'Covert Social Movement Networks in Context: Exploring Change in the Inner Circle of the Provisional Irish Republican Army'. *Social Movement Studies* 13(1).

Stiglitz, J. (2003) *Globalization and Its Discontents* (new edn). Penguin Books Ltd.

(2006) *Making Globalization Work*. Allen Lane.

Swidler, A. (1986) 'Culture in Action: Symbols and Strategies'. *American Sociological Review* 51: 273–86.

Tarrow, S. (1998) *Power in Movement*. New York/Cambridge: Cambridge University Press. First published 1994.

(2004) 'Paradigm Warriors: Regress and Progress in the Study of Contentious Politics' in J. Goodwin and J. Jasper (eds.) *Rethinking Social Movements: Structure, Meaning and Emotion*. Lanham/Oxford: Rowman & Littlefield.

(2006) *The New Transnational Contention*. New York/Cambridge: Cambridge University Press. First published 2005.

Tarrow, S. and Tilly, C. (2009) 'Contentious Politics and Social Movements' in S. Stokes and C. Boix (eds.) *The Oxford Handbook of Comparative Politics*. Oxford: Oxford University Press.

Taylor, L. and Walton, P. (1994) 'Industrial Sabotage' in H. Clark, J. Chandler, and J. Barry (eds.) *Organisation and Identities: Text and Readings in Organisational Behaviour*. London: Chapman & Hall/Thomson.

Taylor, V. (1989) 'Social Movement Continuity: The Women's Movement in Abeyance'. *American Sociological Review* 54: 761–75.

Taylor, V. and Whittier, N. (1992) 'Collective Identity in Social Movement Communities: Lesbian Feminist Mobilization' in A. Morris and C. McClurg Mueller (eds.) *Frontiers in Social Movement Theory*. New Haven: Yale University Press.

   (1995) 'Analytical Approaches to Social Movement Culture: The Culture of the Women's Movement' in H. Johnston and B. Klandermans (eds.) *Social Movements and Culture*. Minneapolis/London: University of Minnesota Press/UCL Press.

The Yes Men (2004) *The Yes Men: The True Story of the End of the World Trade Organization*. New York: Disinformation Company Limited.

Thomas, W. I. and Thomas, D. S. 'The Methodology of Behavior Study' in W. I. Thomas (1928) *The Child in America: Behavior Problems and Programs*. New York: Alfred A. Knopf.

Thompson, E. P. (1991) *The Making of the English Working Class*. Toronto: Penguin. First published 1963.

Thompson, P. and Ackroyd, S. (1995) 'All Quiet on the Workplace Front? A Critique of Recent Trends in British Industrial Sociology'. *Sociology* 29(4): 615–33.

Tilly, C. (1978) *From Mobilization to Revolution*. Reading, MA: Addison-Wesley.

   (1995) *Popular Contention in Great Britain, 1758–1834*. Cambridge, MA: Harvard University Press.

   (1998) 'A Conversation with Charles Tilly: Urban History and Urban Sociology', Bruce M. Stave. *Journal of Urban History* 24: 184–225.

   (2003) *The Politics of Collective Violence*. Cambridge University Press.

   (2004) 'Wise Quacks' in J. Goodwin and J. Jasper (eds.) *Rethinking Social Movements: Structure, Meaning and Emotion*. Lanham/Oxford: Rowman & Littlefield.

   (2006) *Regimes and Repertoires*. University of Chicago Press.

Tilly, C. and Tarrow, S. (2006) *Contentious Politics*. Boulder, CO: Paradigm Publishers.

Tilly, C., Tilly, L., and Tilly, R. (1975) *The Rebellious Century 1830–1930*. Cambridge, MA: Harvard University Press.

Tormey, S. (2005) 'From Utopian Worlds to Utopian Spaces: Reflections on the Contemporary Radical Imaginary and the Social Forum Process'. *Ephemera: Theory and Organisation in Politics* 5(2): 394–408.

Touraine, A. (1971) *The Post-Industrial Society: Tomorrow's Social History: Classes, Conflicts and Culture in the Programmed Society*. New York: Random House.

(1977) *The Self-Production of Society.* Chicago University Press.

(1981) *The Voice and the Eye: An Analysis of Social Movements.* Cambridge University Press.

(1983) *Anti-Nuclear Protest: The Opposition to Nuclear Energy in France.* Cambridge University Press.

(1988) *Return of the Actor: Social Theory in Postindustrial Society.* Minneapolis: University of Minnesota Press.

(1992) 'Beyond Social Movements?'. *Theory, Culture & Society* 9(1): 125–45.

(2002) 'The Importance of Social Movements'. *Social Movement Studies* 1(1): 89–95.

(2007) *A New Paradigm for Understanding Today's World.* Cambridge: Polity.

Tucker, K. (1991) 'How New Are the New Social Movements?'. *Theory, Culture & Society* 8(2): 75–98.

Tugal, C. (2009) 'Transforming Everyday Life: Islamism and Social Movement Theory'. *Theory and Society* 38(5): 423–58.

Turner, R. and Killian, L. (1987) *Collective Behaviour.* Englewood Cliffs: Prentice-Hall.

Vargas, J. A. (2012) 'Spring Awakening: How an Egyptian Revolution Started on Facebook'. *New York Times Sunday Book Review.* 17 February. www. NYTimes.com.

Veldman, M. (1994) *Fantasy, the Bomb, and the Greening of Britain: Romantic Protest 1945–80.* Cambridge University Press.

Wagner, P. (2001) 'A Bird in Hand: Rational Choice – the Default Mode of Social Theorizing' in M. Archer and J. Tritter (eds.) *Rational Choice Theory: Resisting Colonization.* London: Routledge.

Walter, N. (1998) *The New Feminism.* London:Virago.

Walton, J. and Seddon, D. (1994) *Free Markets and Food Riots.* Oxford: Blackwell.

Wasserman, S. and Faust, K. (1994) *Social Network Analysis.* Cambridge/New York: Cambridge University Press.

Waters, M. (1995) *Globalization.* London: Routledge.

White, H. (1992) *Identity and Control: A Structural Theory of Social Action.* Princeton University Press.

White, R. (1989) 'From Peaceful Protest to Guerilla War: Micromobilization of the Provisional Irish Republican Army'. *The American Journal of Sociology* 94(6): 1277–302

(1993) *Provisional Irish Republicans: An Oral and Interpretative History.* Westport, CT: Greenwood Press.

Whittaker, D. (2003) *The Terrorism Reader.* London: Routledge. 2nd edn.

Whittier, N. (1995) *Feminist Generations: The Persistence of the Radical Women's Movement.* Philadelphia: Temple University Press.

Wieviorka, M. (2005) 'After New Social Movements'. *Social Movement Studies* 4(1): 1–19.

Wiktorowicz, Q. (ed.) (2004) *Islamic Activism: A Social Movement Theory Approach,* Bloomington, IN: Indiana University Press.

Wills, J. and Simms, M. (2004) 'Building Reciprocal Community Unionism in the UK'. *Capital and Class* 28(1): 59–84.

Wilson, J. Q. (1973) *Political Organizations*. New York: Basic Books.

Wolford, W. (2006) 'The Difference Ethnography Can Make: Understanding Social Mobilization and Development in the Brazilian Northeast. *Qualitative Sociology* 29(3): 335–52.

Wood, L. (2012) *Direct Action, Deliberation, and Diffusion: Collective Action after the WTO Protests in Seattle*. Cambridge University Press.

Yates, L. (2013) 'Everyday Politics, Social Practices and Movement Networks: Daily Life in Barcelona's Social Centres'. Forthcoming.

Young, M. (2001) 'A Revolution of the Soul: Transformative Experiences and Immediate Abolition' in J. Goodwin, J. Jasper, and F. Polletta (eds.) *Passionate Politics: Emotions and Social Movements*. University of Chicago Press.

Zald, M. N. (2005) 'The Strange Career of an Idea and its Resurrection: Social Movements in Organizations'. *Journal of Management Inquiry* 14(2): 157–66.

Zald, M. N. and Ash, R. (1966) 'Social Movement Organizations: Growth, Decay and Change'. *Social Forces* 44: 327–40.

Index